GOSPEL STUDIES SERIES

Your Study of

Jeremiah

Made Easier

GOSPEL STUDIES SERIES

Your Study of

Jeremiah

Made Easier

David J. Ridges

Springville, Utah

ISBN 13: 978-1-59955-400-6

Published by CFI, an imprint of Cedar Fort, Inc.
2373 W. 700 S., Springville, UT, 84663
Distributed by Cedar Fort, Inc., www.cedarfort.com

LIBRARY OF CONGRESS CATALOGING-IN-PUBLICATION DATA

Ridges, David J.
Jeremiah made easier / David J. Ridges.
p. cm.
ISBN 978-1-59955-400-6
1. Bible. O.T. Jeremiah--Commentaries. 2. Church of Jesus Christ of Latter-day Saints--Doctrines.
I. Title.

BS1525.53.R53 2010
224'.2077--dc22

2009051864

Cover design by Tanya Quinlan
Cover design © 2009 by Lyle Mortimer
Edited by Heather Holm

Printed in Canada

10 9 8 7 6 5 4 3 2 1

Printed on acid-free paper

Books
by David J. Ridges

The Gospel Studies Series:

- *Isaiah Made Easier, Second Edition*
- *The New Testament Made Easier, Part 1 (Second Edition)*
- *The New Testament Made Easier, Part 2 (Second Edition)*
- *Your Study of The Book of Mormon Made Easier, Part 1*
- *Your Study of The Book of Mormon Made Easier, Part 2*
- *Your Study of The Book of Mormon Made Easier, Part 3*
- *Your Study of The Doctrine and Covenants Made Easier, Part 1*
- *Your Study of The Doctrine and Covenants Made Easier, Part 2*
- *Your Study of The Doctrine and Covenants Made Easier, Part 3*
- *The Old Testament Made Easier—Selections from the Old Testament, Part 1*
- *The Old Testament Made Easier—Selections from the Old Testament, Part 2*
- *The Old Testament Made Easier—Selections from the Old Testament, Part 3*
- *Your Study of the Pearl of Great Price Made Easier*
- *Your Study of Jeremiah Made Easier (Coming May 2010)*

Additional titles by David J. Ridges:

- *Our Savior, Jesus Christ: His Life and Mission to Cleanse and Heal*
- *Mormon Beliefs and Doctrines Made Easier*
- *The Proclamation on the Family: The Word of the Lord on More Than 30 Current Issues*
- *65 Signs of the Times and the Second Coming*
- *Doctrinal Details of the Plan of Salvation: From Premortality to Exaltation*

Watch for these titles to also become available through
Cedar Fort as e-books and on CD.

THE GOSPEL STUDIES SERIES

Welcome to this volume of the Gospel Studies Series, which will take you through every verse of Jeremiah, with brief notes and commentary within and between verses designed to keep you in the scripture while providing instruction and help along the way.

As with other study guides in the Gospel Studies Series dealing with the LDS scriptures, this work is intended to be a user-friendly, introductory study of Jeremiah, as well as a refresher course for more advanced students of the scriptures. It is also designed and formatted to be a quick-reference resource that will enable readers to easily look up a particular verse or set of verses and gain additional understanding regarding them. It is hoped by the author that readers will write in the margins of their own scriptures some of the notes given in this study guide in order to assist them as they read and study Jeremiah in the future.

—David J. Ridges

CONTENTS

FOREWORD

The book of Jeremiah is a rich treasure from the Lord. Many who gain a basic understanding of his writings are surprised at how applicable his teachings are to conditions in our world today. This great prophet of God describes political, social, and military circumstances in his own day that accurately parallel circumstances in our day. He also prescribes solutions to problems and pending destruction that likewise apply in our day. Not surprisingly, many miss much in Jeremiah because of difficulty understanding his language and use of symbolism that reflects the "manner of prophesying among the Jews" (2 Nephi 25:1).

The format used in this book is designed to help you enjoy reading and studying Jeremiah. It helps you gain instant understanding of his writings and messages at a basic level. The approach in this study guide is intentionally simple and somewhat conversational. It keeps you right in the scriptures themselves, with brief notes of explanation in italics within brackets right in the verses as well as short notes between verses as needed.

—David J. Ridges

THE BOOK OF THE PROPHET
JEREMIAH

General Background

Jeremiah is a well-known prophet in the Old Testament. There are at least sixty-two prophecies given in his writings. The book of Jeremiah has almost twenty-two thousand words, making it somewhat longer than Isaiah, and making it the second longest book in the Old Testament (only Psalms is longer). Just so you know, if you were to count the pages of Jeremiah and Isaiah in our LDS Bible, in English, you would come up with more pages for Isaiah than for Jeremiah. That is because there is more space taken up for footnotes in Isaiah. In a page count in a King James Bible without footnotes, Jeremiah is several pages longer than Isaiah.

The book of Jeremiah can be divided roughly into the following sections:

Chapters 1–25

Prophecies about Judah and Jerusalem

Chapters 26–35

Prophecies about the restoration of Israel and Judah

Chapters 36–45

History and life story of Jeremiah

Chapters 46–51

Prophecies against foreign nations

Chapter 52

Basically an appendix giving some details of the Babylonian captivity of Jerusalem and wicked King Zedekiah's downfall, including the carrying of the Jews into Babylon

Jeremiah was born into a priestly family in the Levite town of Anathoth (see Jeremiah 1:1 and Bible Dictionary under "Jeremiah"), which was located about three miles northeast of Jerusalem and is known today as Anata. According to the Bible Dictionary in our LDS English edition of the Bible, he served as a prophet in Jerusalem for over forty years, from about 626 B.C. to 586 B.C. After the fall of Jerusalem to Babylonian captivity in about 587 B.C., a group of Jews who escaped into Egypt took Jeremiah with them (Jeremiah 43:5–7), and, according to tradition, later stoned him to death.

Jeremiah was a contemporary of Lehi and several other prophets who preached during the same time period when the wickedness of the people in and around Jerusalem was setting the stage for the Babylonian captivity of Jerusalem, in about 587 B.C., when the Jews were carried captive to Babylon. Babylon was a very large city located about fifty miles south of modern-day Bagdad, Iraq. It was nearly six hundred miles directly east of Jerusalem, across the desert, and was about nine hundred miles away from Jerusalem by land travel routes. As you will perhaps recall, Lehi and his family fled Jerusalem in 600 B.C., as directed by the Lord, and journeyed to the promised land of America.

In 1 Nephi 1:4, Nephi mentions "many prophets" who prophesied at the time Lehi, his father, was prophesying and preaching. You might wish to go to the Chronology in your Bible Dictionary (in the back of your LDS Bible) and note several of these prophets in the "Internal History" column, beginning with 642 B.C. You will see Nahum (with a ?), Jeremiah, Zephaniah, Obadiah (with a ?), and Habakkuk, as well as Daniel and Ezekiel who prophesied while in Babylonian captivity.

Jeremiah was one of the few ancient prophets who prophesied destruction for the people and then saw the fulfillment of his prophecies during his own lifetime. In a way, he was a lot like Mormon, in the Book of Mormon, who was called by the Lord to work with a people for whom there was little hope, because of their extreme wickedness (see Mormon 2:15, 19; 3:12; 5:2).

Jeremiah ministered as a prophet during the reign of the last five kings of Judah, which kingdom came to an end in 587 B.C. with the final wave of the Babylonian captivity. Remember that the kingdom of Israel (the northern ten tribes) had previously been carried away into captivity by the Assyrians about 722 B.C., and had thus become the "lost ten tribes." The two remaining tribes, Judah and part of Benjamin, were known collectively as "Judah," with headquarters in Jerusalem.

Three of these last kings of Judah are mentioned in Jeremiah 1:2–3. A more detailed study of Biblical history shows that there were actually five kings who reigned during Jeremiah's ministry, but two of them ruled for only three months apiece. They were Jehoahaz, who reigned for three months before being exiled to Egypt in 609 B.C., and Jehoiachin, who ruled three months before he was exiled to Babylon in 598 B.C.

Of these kings, all but King Josiah were wicked, and led their people deeper into depravity and toward destruction. The last, King Zedekiah, is probably most familiar to members of the Church because Nephi mentions him as being the king in Jerusalem when Lehi began preaching (see 1 Nephi 1:4). Zedekiah was twenty-one years old at the time he began ruling as king (see 2 Kings 24:18), and reigned for eleven years before his captivity. One of his sons, Mulek, somehow escaped captivity and was brought by the Lord to America (see Helaman 6:10; 8:21). We know his descendants in the Book of Mormon as Mulekites.

We will provide a quote used in the *Old Testament Student Manual: 1 Kings–Malachi*, for the Church's institutes of religion (page 235) that describes the conditions under which Jeremiah served as a prophet:

"With the exception of Josiah, all of the kings of Judah during Jeremiah's ministry were unworthy men under whom the country suffered severely. Even during the reign of an earlier king, the wicked Manasseh, the Baal cult was restored among the Jews, and there was introduced the worship of the heavenly planets in accordance with the dictates of the Assyro-Babylonian religion. Jeremiah therefore found idolatry, hill-worship, and heathen religious practices rampant among his people. Heathen idols stood in the temple (Jeremiah 32:34), children were sacrificed to Baal-Moloch (7:31; 19:5; 32:35), and Baal was especially invoked as the usual heathen deity. The worship of the 'queen of Heaven' ought also to be mentioned (7:18; 44:19). The corruption of the nation's religious worship was, of course, accompanied by all manner of immorality and unrighteousness, against which the prophet had continually to testify. The poor were forgotten. Jeremiah was surrounded on all sides by almost total apostasy. But professional prophets there were aplenty. Says Dr. H. L. Willett:

'He was surrounded by plenty of prophets, but they were the smooth, easy-going, popular, professional preachers whose words awakened no conscience, and who assured the people that the nation was safe in the protecting care of God. This was a true message in Isaiah's day, but that time was long since past, and Jerusalem was destined for captivity. Thus Jeremiah was doomed to preach an unwelcome message, while the false prophets persuaded the people that he was unpatriotic, uninspired, and pessimistic (14:13, 14).' " (Sidney B. Sperry, *The Voice of Israel's Prophets*, p. 153.)

As you study Jeremiah's writings, you will see much symbolism and imagery (as is the case with studying Isaiah). For example, we will look ahead at three verses that describe the people of Judah during Jeremiah's time as hardened clay, no longer moldable by the Lord. This image basically sums up the description of Judah given by Brother Sperry in the above quote. We will use **bold**, as usual, to point things out to you.

Jeremiah 19:1, 10–11

1 THUS saith the LORD, Go and get a potter's **earthen bottle** [*a hardened clay jar, no longer moldable; symbolic of the people of Judah who are no longer willing to be molded and shaped by the hands of the Lord*], and *take* of the ancients of the people, and of the ancients of the priests;

10 Then shalt thou **break the bottle** [*symbolic of the fact that Judah will soon be "broken" by the Babylonian captivity—see verse 11, next*] in the sight of the men that go with thee,

11 And shalt say unto them, **Thus saith the LORD of hosts; Even so will I break this people** [*the kingdom of Judah*] **and this city** [*Jerusalem*], **as** *one* **breaketh a potter's vessel** [*a clay jar*], **that cannot be made whole again**: and they shall bury *them* in Tophet [*a location south of Jerusalem where human sacrifices were offered*], till *there be* no place to bury.

During King Zedekiah's wicked rule, Jeremiah spent much time in prison. The king kept him in a dismal dungeon with deep mud, bringing him out of the dungeon from time to time to see if he had anything new to say or had changed his mind about the things he had prophesied concerning the Kingdom of Judah. We read especially about these most difficult conditions for this humble prophet in Jeremiah, chapters 38–39.

Jeremiah was probably a relatively young man when he began his ministry (in approximately 628–626 B.C., depending on which historical sources used), preaching and prophesying about the rampant evils of society among the people of Judah. We read about his call in chapter 1. One of the major doctrines taught in this chapter is that of premortal life. Few, if any, Christian denominations teach that we lived before we were born on earth, even though it is so clearly taught in Jeremiah 1:5.

We will now proceed with chapter 1.

JEREMIAH 1

1 **THE words of Jeremiah** the son of Hilkiah, of the priests that *were* in Anathoth [*a town about three miles northeast of Jerusalem*] in the land of Benjamin [*the area given to the tribe of Benjamin when the twelve tribes of Israel arrived in the land of Canaan*]:

Next, in verse 2, Jeremiah, without additional explanation, humbly and simply tells us that he was called by the Lord to be a prophet in the thirteenth year of the reign of Josiah, king of Judah, which, according to most sources, would be approximately 627 B.C. (about twenty-seven years before Lehi and his family left Jerusalem).

Jeremiah's Call

2 **To whom the word of the LORD came** in the days of Josiah the son of Amon king of Judah, in the thirteenth year of his reign.

Next, in verse 3, Jeremiah states, in effect, that he continued to receive and deliver the word of the Lord to the people of Judah, as a prophet, for over forty years, until Jerusalem was taken captive by Babylon at the end of King Zedekiah's reign.

3 **It** [*the word of the Lord to Jeremiah*] **came also in the days of Jehoiakim** the son of Josiah king of Judah, **unto the end of the eleventh year of Zedekiah** the son of Josiah king of Judah, unto the carrying away of Jerusalem captive in the fifth month.

Few if any other Christian churches teach the doctrine of premortality as a vital part of the plan of salvation. Perhaps you have been surprised or even amazed that they do not teach it, since Jeremiah teaches it clearly here in verses 4–5.

Doctrine
We lived in premortality before we were born into mortality.

4 **Then the word of the LORD came unto me, saying,**

5 **Before I** [*the Lord*] **formed thee in the belly** [*before you were conceived and grew in your mother's womb; in other words, in the premortal life*] **I knew thee**; and **before thou camest forth out of the womb** I sanctified thee, *and* **I ordained thee a prophet unto the nations** [*Before Jeremiah was born, he was foreordained to be a prophet*].

Doctrine
In addition to the doctrine of premortality in verse 5, we also see the doctrine of foreordination.

Verse 5, above, tells us that Jeremiah was "ordained," in other words, "foreordained" to be a prophet on earth, while he was yet in his premortal existence. He was no doubt one of the "noble and great ones" spoken of in Abraham 3:22–23.

Being foreordained does not imply loss of agency, nor does it mean "predestined." Rather, it means that we were set apart or ordained in our premortal lives to accomplish certain tasks in the work of the Lord here on earth. Joseph Smith explained this. He taught:

"Every man who has a calling to minister to the inhabitants of the world was ordained to that very purpose in the Grand Council of heaven before this world was. I suppose I was ordained to this very office in that Grand Council" (*Teachings of the Prophet Joseph Smith*, page 365).

Foreordination is very similar in concept to patriarchal blessings. Direction is given and potential to do good and fulfill specific work in the Lord's plan is revealed, yet agency is preserved.

Jeremiah was overwhelmed by this call from the Lord, as has been the case with countless others throughout the ages who have been called to fulfill the Lord's will in unexpected ways. This would include Moses (see Exodus 3:11), Isaiah (see Isaiah 6:5), Enoch (Moses 6:31), and Mary (Luke 1:34). You have very likely experienced similar feelings. We see Jeremiah's reaction to the call in verse 6, next, and the Lord's response to his concerns, in verses 7–9.

6 Then said I, **Ah, Lord GOD! behold, I cannot speak** [*perhaps*

meaning "I am speechless." Could also mean "I am not old enough to be taken seriously by the people"]: **for I *am* a child.**

7 ¶ **But the LORD said** unto me, **Say not, I *am* a child: for thou shalt go to all that I shall send thee, and whatsoever I command thee thou shalt speak.**

8 **Be not afraid** of their faces: **for I *am* with thee** to deliver thee, saith the LORD.

Next, the Lord (the premortal Jesus Christ, who is the God of the Old Testament—see for example Ether 3:6 and 14) gives Jeremiah the gift of speaking the mind and will of God clearly.

9 Then **the LORD put forth his hand, and touched my mouth**. And the LORD said unto me, Behold, **I have put my words in thy mouth**.

This scene with Jeremiah is very similar to the scene with Enoch at the time he was called to preach the gospel. We will take a moment to read two verses about Enoch's call from the book of Moses:

Moses 6:31–32
31 And **when Enoch had heard these words** [*his call from the Lord*], **he** bowed himself to the earth, before the Lord, and **spake** before the Lord, saying: Why is it that I have found favor in thy sight, and **am but a lad**, and all the people hate me; for **I am**

slow of speech; wherefore [*why*] am I thy servant?

32 **And the Lord said** unto Enoch: Go forth and do as I have commanded thee, and no man shall pierce thee. **Open thy mouth, and it shall be filled, and I will give thee utterance,** for all flesh is in my hands, and I will do as seemeth me good.

Next, the Savior describes the scope of Jeremiah's mission for him.

10 See, **I have this day set thee over the nations and over the kingdoms, to root out** [*to expose and destroy evil*], and to **pull down,** and to **destroy,** and to **throw down** [*to destroy wickedness and the wicked—see Jeremiah 12:17 and 18:7*], to **build** [*righteousness*], and to **plant** [*including planting the seeds of the gospel in peoples' lives*].

Next, the Lord shows Jeremiah two visions, one described in verses 11–12, and the other in verses 13–16.

Vision

11 ¶ Moreover **the word of the LORD came unto me, saying,** Jeremiah, **what seest thou?** And I said, **I see a rod of an almond tree** [*the first tree to blossom in the spring in the Jerusalem area of Jeremiah's day*].

12 Then said the LORD unto me, Thou hast well seen: for **I will hasten my word to perform it** [*perhaps meaning that the Lord will fulfill Jeremiah's prophecies about coming destruction of Judah sooner than expected*].

Vision

13 And **the word of the LORD came unto me the second time,** saying, **What seest thou?** And I said, **I see a seething pot** [*a boiling cauldron*]; **and the face thereof is toward the north** [*the invading Babylonian armies will come from Babylon (about six hundred miles across the desert directly east of Jerusalem). But their route will be the trade route which will bring them northwest up over the Arabian Desert and then west and then south, down to Jerusalem; therefore, the "seething pot" would likely symbolize the conquering enemy armies of Babylon who will come from the north as they swoop down on the wicked people of Judah*].

14 Then the LORD said unto me, **Out of the north an evil** [*probably referring to the Babylonian armies, which will come upon the people of Judah in about forty years*] **shall break forth upon all the inhabitants of the land.**

15 For, lo, **I will call all the families of the kingdoms of the north** [*most likely the Babylonians*], saith the LORD; and **they shall come,** and they **shall set every one his throne at the entering of the gates** [*symbolic of conquering a city*] of Jerusalem, and against all the walls

thereof round about, and against all the cities of Judah.

16 And **I will utter my judgments** [*the punishments of God*] **against them** [*the people of Judah*] touching all their wickedness, **who have forsaken me**, and have **burned incense unto other gods** [*who have turned to idol worship*], and **worshipped the works of their own hands** [*idols, which they have made with their own hands*].

Verses 17–19, next, appear to be a repetition of the Lord's instructions to Jeremiah in verses 7–8, above, with a bit more detail as to how the Lord will enable him to accomplish his mission, if he exercises faith.

17 ¶ Thou therefore **gird up thy loins** [*prepare for action*], and **arise**, and **speak unto them** [*the inhabitants of the kingdom of Judah*] **all that I command thee: be not dismayed at their faces**, lest I confound thee before them [*if you falter in faith, you will not be blessed to succeed*]. 18 For, behold, **I have made thee this day a defenced city**, and **an iron pillar**, and **brasen walls** [*in other words, the Lord will defend Jeremiah*] against the whole land, against the kings of Judah, against the princes [*leaders*] thereof, against the priests thereof, and against the people of the land.

Next, in verse 19, the Savior prophesies that Jeremiah will face much opposition during his ministry.

19 And **they shall fight against thee; but they shall not prevail** [*win*] **against thee; for I** *am* **with thee**, saith the LORD, to deliver thee.

One of the important messages for us in verse 19, above, is that, with the Lord on our side, our enemies cannot ultimately triumph over us spiritually. Such was the case with Jeremiah. Although he was subjected to much physical misery during mortality, his enemies did not win against him spiritually. And that is everything, as we view things from the perspective of the eternal truths given in the plan of salvation.

JEREMIAH 2

Background
In this chapter, Jeremiah basically says that the Lord loves His people and that they once had a loyal, tender relationship with Him. But now they have deserted Him and are worshiping false gods. The prophet rebukes the people, describing their apostasy in some detail.

1 MOREOVER **the word of the LORD came to me** [*Jeremiah*]**, saying,**

Next, in verses 2–3, Jeremiah speaks for the Lord, reminding the people of the Lord's love for them and of good times in the past when the Israelites kept the commandments and were close to Him.

2 Go and cry in the ears of Jerusalem [*the people of Judah*], saying, Thus saith the LORD; **I remember thee, the kindness of thy youth** [*the love and tenderness of the earlier days of our relationship*]**, the love of thine espousals** [*when you made covenants of loyalty to Me*]**, when thou wentest after me in the wilderness** [*when you followed Me in the wilderness, a cloud by day and a pillar of fire by night*]**, in a land** *that* **was** **not sown** [*in the unplanted wilderness, when I provided manna for you*].

3 **Israel** *was* **holiness unto the LORD**, *and* **the firstfruits of his increase** [*you belonged to Me and were dedicated to being My covenant people*]: **all that devour him shall offend; evil shall come upon them, saith the LORD** [*it was said at that time that any enemies who came upon Israel were held guilty by the Lord and disaster came upon them*].

The implication in verse 3, above, is that the Lord protected covenant Israel in times past, but now, because of their wickedness, He will allow their enemies (Babylon) to come upon them. In other words, disastrous punishments will no longer come upon Judah's enemies, rather, they will be allowed to conquer and humble Judah, because of wickedness among her people.

Perhaps you've noticed that we keep using the terms "Israel," "Judah," "Israelites," and other terms somewhat interchangeably. This can be a bit confusing. Let's have a brief review:

"Israel" is a general term for the twelve tribes of Israel. These twelve tribes were descendants of the twelve sons of Jacob (son of Isaac and grandson of Abraham), whose name was later changed to "Israel." The Lord made a covenant with Abraham (see Abraham 2:9–11). Part of the covenant was that he and his descendants, through Isaac, were to carry the gospel and the blessings of the priesthood to all the world. Thus, the descendants of Abraham, through Isaac and Jacob, are often referred to as "the covenant people of the Lord." They are also referred to as "Israel." Likewise, they are "Israelites," and were also called "the children of Israel," especially when Moses was leading them in the wilderness.

"Judah" was one specific group of Israelites, headquartered in Jerusalem. When Joshua led the children of Israel across the Jordan River and into the promised land (the land of Canaan), he divided the land up among the twelve tribes. Eventually, these twelve tribes broke up and formed two nations, one consisting of ten tribes and the other consisting of two tribes. The ten tribes, with Ephraim as the dominant tribe, became known as the "Northern Kingdom" and retained the name, "Israel." The other two tribes, with Judah as the dominant tribe, became known as the "Southern Kingdom," or "Judah," and were headquartered in Jerusalem.

In about 722 B.C., the Assyrians conquered the northern ten tribes, headquartered in Samaria, and carried most of them away into captivity. They became the "lost ten tribes of Israel."

The two remaining tribes, Judah and Benjamin, known collectively as "Judah," remained. Jeremiah was sent to warn them and preach to them. He continued to preach and prophesy to Judah until the Babylonians conquered them in about 587 B.C.

Remember that the people of Judah are from the "house of Jacob," in other words they are descendants of Jacob (Israel), and, therefore, are Israelites. Thus, in verse 4, next, Jeremiah addresses them as the "house of Jacob." In verse 5 the Lord will ask these wicked people what wickedness they have found in Him that has caused them to leave Him.

Details of Israel's apostasy
(Verses 4–13)

4 **Hear ye the word of the LORD, O house of Jacob** [*Israel*], and all the families of the **house of Israel**:

5 ¶ Thus saith the LORD, **What iniquity have your fathers** [*ancestors*] **found in me** [*the Lord*], **that**

they are gone far from me [*that has given them a reason to have left Me, apostatized*], and **have walked after vanity** [*things that have no value— see verse 11*], and **are become vain** [*have lost their value as a covenant people of the* Lord]?

One of the causes of apostasy is not remembering past blessings from the Lord. This is pointed out in verses 6–8, next.

6 **Neither said they, Where** *is* **the LORD that brought us up out of the land of Egypt**, that **led us through the wilderness**, through a land of **deserts** and of **pits**, through a land of **drought**, and of the **shadow of death**, through a land [*the deserts of Sinai*] that no man passed through, and **where no man dwelt**?

7 And **I brought you into a plentiful country** [*Canaan, the promised land*], **to eat the fruit thereof and the goodness thereof**; but when ye entered, **ye defiled my land** [*polluted the promised land with wickedness*], and **made mine heritage an abomination** [*you polluted your inheritance given to you by Me*].

8 **The priests said not, Where** *is* **the LORD?** [*In other words, were not faithful to God.*] and **they that handle the law knew me not** [*your priests and leaders led you astray*]: **the pastors also transgressed against me**, and **the prophets prophesied by Baal** [*you accepted and followed false religious leaders*

and prophets who led you to worship Baal, a major false religion of the day], and **walked after** *things that* do not profit.

The word "plead," in verse 9, next, means "to bring charges against" as in a formal court of law. In other words, sadly, Israel is guilty of leaving God and turning instead to false gods and the abominable practices associated with their worship. The Lord, operating under the law of justice, is, in effect, formally charging wicked Judah with apostasy.

9 ¶ Wherefore [*this is the reason*] **I will yet plead with you** [*bring charges against you*], saith the LORD, **and with your children's children will I plead**.

10 For pass over the isles of Chittim [*Cyprus and beyond*], and see; and send unto Kedar [*in the Arabian Desert*], and consider diligently, and **see if there be such a thing** [*look far and wide and see if you can find such a thing as people changing gods*].

11 **Hath a nation changed** *their* **gods,** which *are* yet no gods [*can you find a nation who has changed their false gods, who have no power at all*]? **but my people** [*Israel*] **have changed their glory** [*have exchanged the glory and blessings of their God, who does have power*] **for** *that which* **doth not profit**.

12 **Be astonished,** O ye heavens, **at** **this,** and **be horribly afraid,** be ye very desolate, saith the LORD.

13 For **my people have committed two evils;** they have **forsaken me** [*Jehovah, Jesus Christ*] the fountain of living waters [*the source of the true gospel—see John 4:10 and 14*], *and* hewed them out cisterns, broken cisterns, that can hold no water [*and have replaced Me with leaky containers (false gods) that are incapable of holding "living water," in other words, that cannot save*].

Next, in verse 14, the Lord asks why Israel is being so foolish. What could possibly lead the covenant people to abandon their True God and worship powerless false gods? What reasons could they have?

14 ¶ *Is* **Israel a servant?** *is* he **a homeborn** *slave* [*does he not stand a chance of "promotion" to exaltation*]? **why is he spoiled** [*why has Israel become easy prey for their enemies*]?

Perhaps you have noticed that ancient prophets among the Israelites often spoke of the future as if it had already taken place. This is part of the "manner of prophesying among the Jews" (2 Nephi 25:1) spoken of by Nephi which is difficult for many modern students of the scriptures to grasp. We see examples of this in the next verses as the Lord speaks of coming destruction upon Israel because of wickedness, as if it had already taken place.

15 **The young lions** [*symbolic of terrible destruction*] **roared upon him** [*Israel*], *and* yelled, and **they made his land waste: his cities are burned without inhabitant**.

16 Also **the children of Noph** [*the men of Memphis, an ancient city in Egypt not far south of modern Cairo*] **and Tahapanes** [*in Egypt*] **have broken the crown of thy head** [*have cracked your skull*].

17 **Hast thou not procured this unto thyself** [*did you not ask for this*], **in that thou hast forsaken the LORD** thy God, when he led thee by the way [*in spite of the fact that He led you in safety in times past*]?

Next, in verse 18, the Lord refers to the fact that Israel has adopted the wicked practices common in the world, symbolized by Egypt and Babylon. In other words, they have sunk to the level of spiritual depravity that existed in that day in these nations.

Have you noticed that Egypt and especially Babylon are often used elsewhere in the scriptures to symbolize worldly wickedness?

18 And now **what hast thou to do in the way of Egypt, to drink the waters of Sihor** [*the Nile River; in other words, can the Nile (symbolic of Egypt) provide you with "living water—verse 13*]? **or what hast thou to do in the way of Assyria,**
to drink the waters of the river [*why have you turned to the spiritually lifeless waters of idolatrous Babylon*]?

Major Message (verse 19)
We are often punished "by" our sins as well as "for" them.

19 **Thine own wickedness shall correct** [*punish*] **thee, and thy backslidings shall reprove thee**: know therefore and see that *it is* **an evil** *thing* **and bitter, that thou hast forsaken** [*abandoned*] **the LORD thy God**, and that **my fear** [*respect, reverence, awe before God*] *is* **not in thee**, saith the Lord GOD of hosts.

A scathing rebuke of Judah
(Verses 20–37)

20 ¶ For **of old time** [*in days gone by*] **I** [*the Lord*] **have broken thy yoke,** *and* **burst thy bands** [*I set you free from the bondage of Egypt (symbolic of being set free from the bondage of sin)*]; **and thou saidst, I will not transgress; when upon every high hill and under every green tree thou wanderest, playing the harlot** [*you promised to keep the commandments while at the same time you were engaging in worshiping false gods*].

"Under every green tree, in verse 20, above, has reference to sexual immorality engaged in with temple prostitutes used in the worship of idols of the day, especially in Baal worship. The phrase "playing the harlot" refers to "spiritual adultery" in the sense that the people, who had made covenants of loyalty to God, were "stepping out on Him" as they worshiped false gods.

21 Yet **I had planted thee a noble vine, wholly a right seed** [*I gave you the best possible start, as My covenant people with the true gospel*]: **how then art thou turned into the degenerate plant of a strange vine unto me** [*how could you possibly leave Me and become an apostate people, producing bitter fruit*]?

In verse 22, next, the word, "nitre," means lye, carbonate of soda—see footnote 22b in your LDS Bible. It was a strong cleansing agent used in ancient times. The point is that the people of Judah cannot continue in wickedness and hope to still be clean.

22 For **though thou wash thee with nitre, and take thee much soap,** *yet* **thine iniquity** [*wickedness*] **is marked before me**, saith the Lord GOD.

23 **How canst thou say** [*claim*], **I am not polluted**, I have not gone after Baalim [*I have not worshiped Baal*]? **see thy way in the valley** [*look back at your tracks*], know what thou hast done: *thou art* a swift dromedary traversing her ways;

We will quote from the *Old Testament Student Manual: 1 Kings—*

Malachi for the explanation of the "dromedary" (camel) in verse 23, above, and the wild ass in verse 24, next.

"The imagery indicates that as a camel or a wild ass in heat runs back and forth during the mating season, so did Israel run after false gods" (*Old Testament Student Manual*, page 236).

24 A wild ass used to the wilderness, *that* snuffeth up the wind at her pleasure; in her occasion [*when she is in heat*] who can turn her away? all they that seek her will not weary themselves; in her month they shall find her.

The JST (Joseph Smith Translation of the Bible) of verse 24, above, changes the position of "not," implying that the wicked wear themselves out in evil pursuits, but do not ultimately find satisfaction.

JST Jeremiah 2:24
24 A wild ass used to the wilderness, *that* snuffeth up the wind at her pleasure; in her who can turn her away? all they that seek her will weary themselves; in her month they shall **not** find her.

The imagery in verse 25, next, is that of people so anxious to get on with the sinful life of worshiping false gods that they won't even take time to put on shoes or get a drink of water to slake their thirst before they run out of their houses to pursue idolatry.

25 **Withhold thy foot from being unshod** [*at least take time to put on your shoes*], **and thy throat from thirst** [*at least get a drink*]: **but thou saidst, There is no hope** [*I am hopeless*]: **no; for I have loved strangers** [*I am an idol worshiper*], **and after them will I go** [*and that is what I want to keep doing*].

We see from verse 26, next, that Judah is corrupt, through and through.

26 **As the thief is ashamed** [*put to shame, disgraced*] **when he is found** [*caught*], **so is the house of Israel ashamed; they, their kings,** their **princes,** and their **priests,** and their **prophets** [*their false prophets*],

In verses 27–28, Jeremiah points out how ridiculous idol worship is.

27 **Saying to a stock** [*a piece of wood which they have carved into an idol*], **Thou** *art* **my father;** and **to a stone** [*an idol*], **Thou hast brought me forth** [*you are my creator*]: **for they** [*Judah*] **have turned** *their* **back unto me** [*have rejected the Lord*], **and not** *their* **face: but in the time of their trouble they will say, Arise, and save us** [*Israel has a track record of turning to the Lord only in times of trouble*].

28 But **where** *are* **thy gods that thou hast made** thee? **let them** arise, if they can **save thee in the time of thy trouble:** for *according to* the number of thy cities are thy gods [*you have as many idols, false gods, as you have cities*], O Judah.

It was common practice for each city to have its own god, represented by a specific idol. And when one city prevailed over another, it was thought that their god was more powerful than the losing city's god.

The Lord goes on in verse 29 to ask, in effect, what complaint Judah has against Him which caused the people to turn to other gods.

29 **Wherefore** [*why*] **will ye plead** [*quarrel, argue—see footnote 29a in your LDS Bible*] **with me? ye all** have transgressed against me, saith the LORD.

Next, in verse 30, the Lord tells Judah that it has not done a bit of good for Him to punish Israelites, such as the northern ten tribes, who are gone now. Judah has not repented at all.

30 **In vain have I smitten your** [*Israel's*] **children; they received no correction:** your own sword hath devoured your prophets [*you have destroyed the prophets I have sent to correct you*], like a destroying lion.

31 ¶ O generation, see ye the word of the LORD. **Have I been a wilderness unto Israel** [*have I not blessed Israel abundantly*]? a land of darkness? **wherefore say my**

people, **We are lords; we will come no more unto thee** [*why do My people arrogantly say that they will no longer consider Me to be their God*]?

32 **Can a maid forget her ornaments,** *or* **a bride her attire** [*her wedding gown, her finest clothing; in other words, have you ever known a bride to forget to prepare for her wedding; symbolic of covenant Israel keeping covenants in preparation to meet the Groom (the Savior)*]? **yet my people have forgotten me days without number** [*they have a long track record of forgetting Me*].

33 **Why trimmest thou thy way to seek love** [*why do you demonstrate such skill in pursuing false gods*]? **Therefore** [*because of your skill in evil ways*] **hast thou also taught the wicked ones thy ways** [*even the most wicked can learn more evil from you*].

34 Also **in thy skirts is found the blood of the souls of the poor innocents** [*your guilt against the righteous is obvious, is written all over you*]: I have not found it by secret search, but upon all these.

Verse 35, next, is very applicable today. The wicked claim that what they are doing is not against God's will. Therefore, they are innocent, and thus God's punishments will not come upon them.

In the second half of the verse, the Lord says that He will indeed bring them to accountability and punishment for their wickedness.

35 Yet **thou** [*Judah*] **sayest, Because I am innocent, surely his anger shall turn from me**. Behold, I [*the Lord*] will plead with thee [*will bring charges against you*], because thou sayest, I have not sinned.

36 **Why gaddest thou about so much to change thy way** [*why do you go back and forth so much, constantly changing your loyalties*]? **thou also shalt be ashamed of Egypt** [*Egypt will provide no protection for you*], **as thou wast ashamed of Assyria** [*just as Assyria was no protection for your brethren of the Northern Kingdom, when they tried to make alliances with them for protection*].

37 Yea, **thou shalt go forth from him, and thine hands upon thine head** [*you will be enslaved*]: for **the LORD hath rejected thy confidences** [*your trust in other gods*], **and thou shalt not prosper in them**.

JEREMIAH 3

Background
In this chapter, Jeremiah uses the imagery of a wife being unfaithful to her husband and divorcing him to represent Judah's apostasy from the Lord. In other words, the wife is symbolic of Judah (and Israel in general), and the husband is symbolic of the Lord. The phrase

"played the harlot" (in verse 1) is a phrase that means "committed adultery." In this case, it is used to mean "spiritual adultery," in other words, breaking covenants made with the Lord through personal and national wickedness. Actual physical sexual immorality is a major player in the spiritual adultery committed by Israel and Judah against the Lord.

In spite of the extreme wickedness of the people in Jeremiah's day, you will see an invitation to repent and return to God in several verses within the chapter, thus reminding us of the tender love of the Savior and His desire to have sinners return to Him and thus to His Father. It is also a reminder of the power of the Atonement to cleanse and heal.

In this chapter, you will also see a prophecy that Israel will be gathered again in the last days, some one at a time, and sometimes just a few members of a family at a time. They will be brought into the latter-day Zion through the restored gospel of Jesus Christ.

Watch now as Jeremiah points out the wickedness of Judah and the open invitation, still in place, for them to repent.

1 **THEY say, If a man put away his wife** [*it is said that if a man divorces his wife (implying that she has been unfaithful to him)*],

and she go from [*leave*] **him, and become another man's** [*symbolic in this case of worshiping idols*], **shall he return unto her again** [*do you think he would ever take her back (answer: No, according to the law of Moses—see Deuteronomy 24:3–4)*]? **shall not that land be greatly polluted** [*wouldn't that ruin that nation*]? **but thou** [*Judah specifically, Israel in general*] **hast played the harlot with many lovers** [*you have worshiped many false gods; you have broken covenants made with God*]; **yet return again to me**, saith the LORD [*please return, it is not too late*].

Next, in verse 2, Jeremiah invites the people of wicked Judah to look all around them to see obvious evidence of their apostasy. The "high places" are the mountains and groves of trees on them where idolatry typically takes place, including literal adultery with temple prostitutes as a part of idol worship, especially Baal worship.

2 **Lift up thine eyes unto the high places, and see where thou hast not been lien with** [*see if you can find any places where idol worship and associated adultery has not taken place; symbolically, look all around you and see if you can find any people of Judah who have not been involved in idolatry*]. **In the ways hast thou sat for them** [*you have waited by the side of the road for idols to worship just like a harlot waits along*]

the path for potential lovers], as the Arabian in the wilderness [*as is the common practice*]; and **thou hast polluted the land** [*the promised land*] with thy whoredoms [*unfaithfulness to God*] and with thy wickedness.

We will quote from the Bible Dictionary (in the back of your LDS Bible) for a general statement on the subject of sexual immorality commonly associated with idol worship. We will use **bold** for emphasis:

Bible Dictionary: Idol

"Among the nations of Canaan and W. Syria Baal was the sun god or source of life, and Ashtoreth was the corresponding female deity. In addition each nation had its own peculiar god to whom it ascribed its prosperity and misfortunes (see *Chemosh; Molech*). The idolatry into which the Israelites so often fell consisted either in making images that stood for Jehovah, such as the calves of Jeroboam (1 Kgs. 12:28); or in worshipping, in addition to Jehovah, one of the gods of the heathen nations around them (1 Kgs. 11:7, 33; 2 Kgs. 21:3–6; 23:10; Jer. 7:31; Ezek. 20:26–49), **such idolatry** being some form of nature worship, which **encouraged as a rule immoral practices**."

Next, in verse 3, the Lord tells the people that their wickedness is the cause of drought in their land. Then, He points out that the people of Judah are not even ashamed of their wickedness.

3 **Therefore** [*because you have "played the harlot"*] **the showers have been withholden**, and there hath been no latter rain [*the spring rains have been withheld by the Lord*]; and **thou hadst a whore's forehead** [*you advertised your wickedness like a prostitute marks her forehead (a cultural practice of that day) to attract lovers*], **thou refusedst to be ashamed** [*and you weren't even embarrassed at your public display of wickedness*].

4 **Wilt thou not from this time cry unto me, My father, thou** *art* **the guide of my youth** [*won't you please return to Me and seek guidance from Me as in times past*]?

Next, the people ask, in effect, how long the Lord will be angry with them. Jeremiah then points out their shallowness and hypocrisy, noting that even while they are asking the question about the Lord's anger, they continue in their evil ways.

5 **Will he** [*the Lord*] **reserve** [*keep*] **his anger for ever? will he keep** *it* **to the end?** Behold, thou [*Judah*] hast spoken [*asked the above questions*] **and done evil things as thou couldest** [*the people ask how long the Lord will be angry with them but they keep right on being wicked*].

Next, Jeremiah tells the people what the Lord had called his attention to previously during the reign of King Josiah. Jehovah had used Israel (the ten tribes who were carried away captive by the Assyrians about one hundred years ago, in 722 B.C.) as an example of what happens to covenant people who get completely caught up in wickedness. Judah should look at what happened to Israel, wake up and repent.

6 ¶ **The LORD said also unto me** in the days of Josiah the king, **Hast thou seen** *that* **which backsliding Israel hath done?** she is gone up upon every high mountain and under every green tree, and there hath played the harlot [*apostate Israel was deeply involved with idol worship before their destruction by the Assyrians*].

The Lord points out that in spite of Israel's wickedness, He had still invited them to repent. But they refused.

7 **And I said after she** [*Israel—the northern ten tribes*] **had done all these** *things,* **Turn thou unto me. But she returned not**. And her treacherous sister Judah saw *it*.

In verses 8–11, next, the Lord continues to point out that the people of Judah have not learned a lesson from what happened to their fellow Israelites, the northern ten tribes (referred to as "Israel" in this context).

8 **And I** [*the Lord*] **saw, when for all the causes whereby backsliding**

Israel committed adultery [*broke her covenants with Me*] **I had put her away, and given her a bill of divorce** [*I rejected her and let her be carried away into Assyrian captivity*]; **yet her treacherous sister Judah feared not, but went and played the harlot also** [*Judah did not learn from what happened to Israel, rather, continued breaking covenants*].

As has been previously stated, the word, "adultery," as used in verse 8, above, often means "apostasy." We will quote from the Bible Dictionary on this subject (**bold** added for emphasis):

Bible Dictionary: Adultery
While adultery is usually spoken of in the individual sense, **it is sometimes used to illustrate the apostasy of a nation or a whole people from the ways of the Lord**, such as Israel forsaking her God and going after strange gods and strange practices (Ex. 20:14; Jer. 3:7–10; Matt. 5:27–32; Luke 18:11; D&C 43:24–25).

9 **And it came to pass through the lightness of her whoredom** [*she did not consider her disloyalty to God to be a serious matter*], that she defiled the land, and **committed adultery with stones and with stocks** [*she committed spiritual adultery by worshiping idols of rock and wood*].

10 And **yet for all this** [*in view of all this evidence*] her treacher-

ous sister **Judah hath not turned unto me** with her whole heart, but feignedly [*merely pretended*], saith the LORD.

11 And the LORD said unto me [*Jeremiah*], The **backsliding Israel hath justified herself more than treacherous Judah** [*even apostate Israel was not as wicked as Judah has become*].

Unless we realize that verses 12–18, next, are a prophecy about the future, we can become confused. As we read verse 12, we might think, "Wait a minute. Israel is gone. The Assyrians took the people away over one hundred years ago. How can Jeremiah talk to them?" But when we understand that it is a prophecy about the future gathering of Israel (see heading to this chapter in your Bible), it makes sense. And we realize that we are watching a major portion of the fulfillment of this prophecy in our day.

12 ¶ Go and **proclaim these words toward the north** [*address this message to Israel*]**, and say,** Return, thou backsliding Israel, saith the LORD; *and* I will not cause mine anger to fall upon you: for I *am* **merciful, saith the LORD,** *and* I will not keep *anger* for ever.

In verses 13–14, next, the Lord explains in the simplest terms how Israel will someday be enabled to return to Him.

13 Only **acknowledge thine iniquity, that thou hast transgressed against the LORD thy God**, and hast scattered thy ways to the strangers [*you have joined the ways of the world, participated in their evil ways*] under every green tree [*a reference to the immoral practices associated with ancient idol worship*], and ye have not obeyed my voice [*the problem*], saith the LORD.

14 **Turn, O backsliding children, saith the LORD**; for I am married unto you [*I am your God; you can be My covenant people again*]: and **I will take you** [*gather you*] **one of a city, and two of a family, and I will bring you to Zion:**

In times past, wicked priests and false prophets led Israel astray. Verse 15, next, prophesies that in conjunction with the gathering of Israel in the last days, we will once again have righteous leaders whose hearts are in tune with God. They will nourish us with correct doctrine.

15 And **I will give you pastors** [*leaders*] **according to mine heart** [*whose hearts are in harmony with the Lord's heart*], which **shall feed you with knowledge and understanding**.

Verse 16, next, appears to be saying that, in the last days when the gospel is restored and Israel is being gathered, the focus will no longer be on the law of

Moses, with the ark of the covenant, etc. Rather the emphasis will be on the restored gospel of Jesus Christ.

16 And it shall come to pass, **when ye be multiplied and increased in the land, in those days** [*when Israel is gathered in the last days*], saith the LORD, **they shall say no more, The ark of the covenant** of the LORD: neither shall it come to mind: neither shall they remember it; **neither shall they visit** *it;* neither shall *that* be done any more [*the people will no longer live by the law of Moses*].

Verse 17, next, appears to refer to the Millennium, when the Savior will be "KING OF KINGS AND LORD OF LORDS" (Revelation 19:16) as He rules and reigns on earth during the Millennium. During the one thousand years of peace, there will be two headquarters of the Church on earth, one in Zion (Independence, Jackson County, Missouri) and one in Old Jerusalem. We will say a bit more about this and give a reference for it, after verse 17.

17 **At that time** [*during the Millennium*] **they shall call Jerusalem the throne of the LORD** [*Jerusalem will be a headquarters for the Savior during the Millennium*]; and all the nations [*people from all nations*] shall be gathered unto it, to the name of the LORD, to Jerusalem: **neither shall they walk any more after the**

imagination of their evil heart [*the people will not be wicked*].

Joseph Fielding Smith (who became the tenth president of the Church) taught about the two cities that would become headquarters of the kingdom of God during the Millennium. He said:

"ZION AND JERUSALEM: TWO WORLD CAPITALS. When Joseph Smith translated the Book of Mormon, he learned that America is the land of Zion which was given to Joseph and his children and that on this land the City Zion, or New Jerusalem, is to be built. He also learned that Jerusalem in Palestine is to be rebuilt and become a holy city. **These two cities, one in the land of Zion and one in Palestine, are to become capitals for the kingdom of God during the millennium"** (*Doctrines of Salvation*, vol. 3, page 71).

Verse 18, next, contains an additional prophecy. As you perhaps recall, after settling in the Holy Land, the twelve tribes of Israel eventually broke up into two nations, Israel (ten tribes) and Judah (two tribes). This happened after King Solomon's death. There was much hatred and animosity between the two nations. Verse 18 foretells the day when Judah and Israel will once again be united in peace and harmony.

18 In those days **the house of Judah shall walk with the house of Israel,**

and they shall come together out of the land of the north to the land that I have given for an inheritance unto your fathers.

Verse 19, next, gives a simple answer as to how Israel and Judah can someday live in peace and be the Lord's covenant people.

19 But I said, How shall I put thee among the children, and give thee a pleasant land, a goodly heritage of the hosts of nations? and I said, **Thou shalt call me, My father; and shalt not turn away from me** [*they will accept the gospel of Jesus Christ and remain faithful to Him*].

Verses 20–22, next, review once again what got these people into such a mess and the invitation to repent is given yet again.

20 ¶ Surely *as* **a wife treacherously departeth from her husband, so have ye dealt treacherously with me, O house of Israel**, saith the LORD.

21 A voice was heard upon the high places, weeping *and* supplications of **the children of Israel**: for they **have perverted their way,** *and* **they have forgotten the LORD their God**.

22 **Return, ye backsliding children,** *and* **I will heal** your backslidings. Behold, we come unto thee; for thou *art* the LORD our God.

The last half of verse 22, above, and verses 23–25, next, may be understood to be Israel's reply to the Lord, in the last days, as they repent and return to Him, affirming that He is the only one who can provide salvation.

23 **Truly in vain** *is salvation hoped for* **from the hills** [*salvation is not available through the worship of false gods*], *and from* the multitude of mountains: **truly in the LORD our God** *is* **the salvation of Israel**.

24 **For shame hath devoured the labour of our fathers from our youth** [*we have long since apostatized from the foundations laid by our ancestors*]; their flocks and their herds, their sons and their daughters.

25 We lie down in our shame, and our confusion covereth us: for **we have sinned against the LORD our God, we and our fathers, from our youth even unto this day, and have not obeyed the voice of the LORD** our God.

JEREMIAH 4

Background
In Helaman in the Book of Mormon we are informed that Jeremiah prophesied of the destruction of Jerusalem. We read:

Helaman 8:20
20 And behold, also Zenock, and also Ezias, and also Isaiah, and Jeremiah, (**Jeremiah** being that

same prophet who **testified of the destruction of Jerusalem**) and now we know that Jerusalem was destroyed according to the words of Jeremiah. O then why not the Son of God come, according to his prophecy?

We read one of Jeremiah's many prophecies of Jerusalem's coming destruction, starting with verse 7 here in chapter 4 and going through chapter 5, verse 13. But first, beginning with verse 1, we read another invitation to repent. You will see that the first requirement for returning to God is a desire to repent.

1 **IF thou wilt** [*if you have a desire to*] **return**, O Israel, saith the LORD, **return unto me** [*just do it*]: and **if thou wilt put away thine abominations out of my sight** [*if you will stop being wicked; this is the next step*], then shalt thou not remove [*then you will remain My covenant people*].

The next step, as given in verse 2, is for the people to sincerely and seriously commit to Jehovah as their God.

2 And **thou shalt swear** [*pledge, commit*], The LORD liveth, in truth, in judgment, and in righteousness; and the nations shall bless themselves in him, and in him shall they glory.

Did you notice the phrase in verse 2, above, which says, in effect, that we are doing ourselves a tremendous favor when

we are loyal to the Lord? It is "the nations shall bless themselves in him."

Verses 3 and 4, next, appear to be an invitation to the men of Judah, with headquarters in Jerusalem, to repent and become clean. The Lord uses considerable symbolism to get the message across.

3 ¶ For thus saith the LORD to the men of Judah and Jerusalem, **Break up your fallow** [*unplowed*] **ground** [*perhaps meaning you have yet another chance to become productive as the Lord's covenant people*], and **sow** [*plant*] **not among thorns** [*don't try to mix the gospel and wickedness together in your lives*].

4 **Circumcise yourselves to the LORD** [*dedicate yourselves to the Lord*], and **take away the foreskins of your heart** [*dedicate your hearts to the Lord*], ye men of Judah and inhabitants of Jerusalem: **lest my fury come forth like fire**, and burn that none can quench *it*, [*otherwise, the punishments of the Lord will come upon you and none will stop them*] because of the evil of your doings.

5 Declare ye in Judah, and publish in Jerusalem [*spread the word throughout the people of Judah*]; and say, Blow ye the trumpet in the land: cry, gather together, and say, Assemble yourselves, and let us go into the defenced [*fortified*] cities [*in other words, spread the word that we must gather to the Lord for*

protection against the enemies].

6 Set up the standard [*sound the alarm, raise the flag, signaling to gather*] toward Zion [*symbolic of returning to the Lord*]: retire, stay not [*don't hesitate*]: for I will bring evil from the north [*the Babylonians are coming*], and a great destruction.

Next, Jeremiah uses fearsome images to warn the people of Judah of the destruction that is coming if they don't repent.

7 **The lion** [*the King of Babylon and his armies; symbolic of Satan and his evil hosts*] **is come up from his thicket** [*has come out of hiding*], and the destroyer of the Gentiles [*the Babylonian armies have destroyed many Gentile cities*] is on his way; he is gone forth from his place to make thy land desolate; *and* thy cities shall be laid waste, without an inhabitant.

8 For this [*because of this*] **gird you with sackcloth** [*clothe yourselves with course, uncomfortable cloth to symbolize that you are going into mourning*], **lament and howl**: for the fierce anger of the LORD is not turned back from us [*we are still in trouble with the Lord, (because, as a nation, they have not repented)*].

9 And **it shall come to pass at that day** [*when the punishments and destructions come*], saith the LORD, *that* the heart [*courage*] **of the king shall perish, and the heart of the princes** [*the leaders of the land will lose courage*]; and the priests shall be astonished [*the false priests will be horrified*], and the prophets shall wonder [*the false prophets will be appalled*].

Verse 10, next, is a problem as it stands. Surely, Jeremiah would not say such a thing to the Lord. Either something is missing or the translation is wrong. Let's read the verse and then look at an alternate translation.

10 Then said I, Ah, Lord GOD! surely thou hast greatly deceived this people and Jerusalem, saying, Ye shall have peace; whereas the sword reacheth unto the soul.

The Martin Luther translation of the German Bible may provide some help for us regarding verse 10, above. It has Jeremiah saying, in effect, "Lord, thou has allowed these people and Jerusalem to be led far astray, because their false prophets and priests said to them that they would have peace [*in spite of their wickedness*], whereas in reality the sword is about to destroy their souls."

Verses 11–20, next, carry on the prophetic theme of coming destruction.

11 At that time [*when destruction comes to Judah and Jerusalem*] shall it be said to this people and to Jerusalem, **A dry wind** [*symbolic of destruction*] of the high places in

the wilderness **toward the daughter of my people** [*Jerusalem*], not to fan, nor to cleanse [*not a pleasant, cleansing breeze*],

12 *Even* **a full wind** [*a very devastating destruction*] from those *places* shall come unto me: now also will I give sentence against them.

13 Behold, he shall come up as clouds, and his chariots *shall be* **as a whirlwind**: his horses are swifter than eagles. Woe unto us! for we are spoiled.

14 O Jerusalem, **wash thine heart from wickedness** [*repent and be baptized*], that thou mayest be saved. **How long shall thy vain thoughts lodge within thee** [*how long will your wicked and foolish thinking stay with you*]?

Joseph Fielding Smith indicated that verse 14, above, is a reference to baptism. Speaking of the fact that the Jews were not surprised by the baptisms performed by John the Baptist, because it was a common Old Testament ordinance, he said:

"John stood forth in the spirit of the prophets of old to preach his baptism of repentance symbolized by cleansing with water. (See Jer. 4:14; Ezek. 36:25; Zech. 13:1.)" (*Answers to Gospel Questions*, vol. 2, page 68)

It is helpful for understanding verse 15, next, to know that the land of Dan was the farthest

north among the inheritances of the twelve tribes when they arrived in the promised land.

15 For a voice declareth from Dan [*the news of destruction is coming from the north*], and publisheth affliction from mount Ephraim.

16 **Make ye mention to the nations** [*spread the news*]; behold, publish against Jerusalem, *that* **watchers** [*NIV "a besieging army"*] come from a far country [*Babylon*], and **give out their voice against** [*are enemies to*] **the cities of Judah**.

17 As keepers of a field, are they against her round about [*they will surround Judah*]; **because she hath been rebellious against me**, saith the LORD.

18 **Thy way and thy doings have procured these *things* unto thee** [*you have brought this destruction upon yourselves*]; this *is* thy wickedness, because it is bitter, because it reacheth unto thine heart [*you are wicked through and through (ripe in iniquity)*].

Verse 19, next, can describe the terror that will engulf the wicked inhabitants of Judah as the Babylonian armies descend upon them. However, it can also describe the deep anguish and sorrow in Jeremiah's heart as he sees the vision of coming destruction upon the wicked people of Judah.

19 ¶ My bowels, my bowels [*a phrase meaning "deepest anguish"*]! I am pained at my very heart [*deepest agony*]; my heart maketh a noise in me [*my heart is pounding*]; I cannot hold my peace [*I cry out*], because thou hast heard, O my soul, the sound of the trumpet, the alarm of war.

20 Destruction upon destruction is cried; for **the whole land is spoiled** [*ruined, ravaged*]: suddenly are my tents spoiled, *and* my curtains [*dwelling places*] in a moment.

21 How long shall I see the standard, *and* hear the sound of the trumpet [*how long do I have to look at this scene of horror, this scene of battle and destruction*]?

It appears that verse 22, next, could represent the feelings of the Lord about Judah at this time.

22 For **my people *is* foolish**, they have not known me [*they have apostatized, left Me*]; they *are* sottish [*senseless; do not think*] children, and they have none understanding: **they *are* wise to do evil, but to do good they have no knowledge**.

Verses 23–29 seem to describe the devastation and desolation that will come upon Judah and Jerusalem when the invading Babylonian armies finish with them.

23 I beheld the **earth, and, lo,** *it* *was* **without form, and void** [*the land was "empty and desolate"— see Abraham 4:2*]; and the heavens, and **they *had* no light** [*perhaps meaning that the dust from the battles obscured the sunlight; could also symbolize that the light of the gospel is gone*].

24 I beheld the mountains, and, lo, they trembled, and all the hills moved lightly.

25 I beheld, and, lo, *there was* no man [*the people were slaughtered or taken away into captivity*], and all the birds of the heavens were fled.

26 I beheld, and, lo, **the fruitful place** [*the once-beautiful Jerusalem and surrounding area*] *was* **a wilderness**, and all the cities thereof were broken down at the presence of the LORD, *and* **by his fierce anger**.

In verse 27, next, the Lord says that the land will be desolate, but the Jews will not be completely destroyed.

27 For thus hath the LORD said, The whole land shall be desolate; **yet will I not make a full end**.

In the context of this chapter and prophecy, verse 28, next, states emphatically that unless the people of Judah repent (verse 14), the destruction will come as described.

By the way, since the Lord is sinless, He has no need to repent. Thus, the word "repent" in this verse is not a good translation in view of the normal use of the word.

28 For this [*because of this destruction*] shall the earth mourn, and the heavens above be black: because **I have spoken** *it,* **I have purposed** *it,* **and will not repent** [*relent nor change My mind*], **neither will I turn back from it.**

29 **The whole city** [*Jerusalem*] **shall flee** for [*because of*] the noise of the horsemen and bowmen [*the Babylonian armies*]; they shall go into thickets, and climb up upon the rocks: **every city** [*of Judah*] **shall be forsaken** [*deserted*], and not a man dwell therein.

Verses 30–31 conclude this chapter with the question, "What will you do when all this happens?" And the basic answer is that Judah will still seek help from her false gods, her idols. Verse 30 is a description of a harlot attempting to make herself attractive for her lovers. The imagery is that Judah (the "harlot," symbolic of "stepping out on God," in other words, disloyalty to her covenants with Jehovah) attempts to get help from her false gods and gets none.

30 And *when* thou *art* **spoiled** [*ruined by the Babylonians*], **what wilt thou do?** Though thou clothest thyself with crimson, though thou deckest thee with ornaments of gold, though thou rentest thy face with painting [*use makeup to make your eyes look bigger—see footnote 30b, in your LDS Bible*], in vain shalt thou make thyself fair [*your attempts to make yourself look attractive won't work*]; **thy lovers** [*false gods*] **will despise thee**, they will seek thy life [*they will not help you at all against your enemies*].

Part of the imagery in verse 31, next, is that there is no way (in Jeremiah's day) to stop childbirth labor once it starts. So also, once the coming armies descend upon Jerusalem, there will be no way to stop them. The pain and anguish of a woman having her first child is compared to the anguish of the people of Judah, as the stark reality of their destruction hits them.

31 For **I have heard a voice as of a woman in travail** [*childbirth labor*], *and* the **anguish** as of her that bringeth forth her first child, the voice of the daughter of Zion [*Jerusalem*], *that* **bewaileth herself**, *that* spreadeth her hands, *saying,* **Woe** *is* **me now!** for my soul is wearied because of murderers [*my life is in the hands of murderers*].

JEREMIAH 5

Background

In this chapter, Jeremiah describes the corruption that has permeated every facet of society by this point in the history of Judah.

We will move rather quickly through this chapter, using **bold** to let the scriptures themselves point out this corruption to you. The hope is that you will gain more skill and confidence in capturing the basic meaning of Jeremiah's writing without having to understand every detail. We will intentionally add very few notes in this chapter. Try going through first, just reading the **bolded** words and phrases. Remember, we are looking for various types of corruption that can ruin society and lead to downfall and destruction, as well as the consequences of such behavior, as described by Jeremiah.

1 **RUN ye to and fro through the streets of Jerusalem, and see** now, and know, and seek in the broad places thereof, **if ye can find a man**, if there be *any* that executeth judgment, **that seeketh the truth**; and I will pardon it.

2 And **though they say, The LORD liveth; surely they swear falsely** [*break covenants and contracts; don't keep their word*].

3 O LORD, *are* not thine eyes upon the truth? **thou hast stricken them, but they have not grieved; thou hast consumed them, *but* they have refused to receive correction**: they have made their faces harder than a rock; **they have refused to return**.

4 Therefore I said, Surely these *are* poor; they are foolish: for **they know not the way of the LORD,** *nor* the judgment of their God.

5 I will get me unto the great men, and will speak unto them; for they have known the way of the LORD, *and* the judgment of their God: but **these have altogether broken the yoke** [*the covenants that bind them to Jehovah*], *and* burst the bonds.

6 **Wherefore a lion** out of the forest **shall slay them, *and* a wolf** of the evenings **shall spoil them**, a leopard shall watch over their cities: every one that goeth out thence shall be torn in pieces [*the Lord will allow their destruction*]: **because their transgressions are many**, *and* their backslidings are increased.

7 ¶ **How shall I pardon thee for this? thy children have forsaken me**, and **sworn by *them that are no gods*** [*have worshiped idols*]: when I had fed them to the full, they then **committed adultery**, and **assembled themselves by troops in the harlots' houses**.

8 **They were *as* fed horses** in the morning: **every one neighed after his neighbour's wife** [*sexual immorality is rampant throughout society*].

9 **Shall I not visit** [*punish*] **for these *things*? saith the LORD**: and shall not my soul be avenged on such a nation as this?

10 ¶ Go ye up upon her walls, and destroy; but make not a full end: take away her battlements; for they *are* not the LORD's.

11 **For the house of Israel and the house of Judah have dealt very treacherously against me**, saith the LORD.

12 **They have belied** [*lied about*] **the LORD, and said**, *It is* not he; **neither shall evil come upon us; neither shall we see sword nor famine**:

13 And **the prophets shall become wind, and the word** *is* **not in them** [*the prophecies against us will not be fulfilled*]: thus shall it be done unto them.

14 Wherefore thus saith the LORD God of hosts, **Because ye speak this word** [*verse 13*], behold, **I will make my words in thy mouth fire**, and this people wood, **and it shall devour them**.

15 Lo, **I will bring a nation upon you from far**, O house of Israel, saith the LORD: **it** *is* **a mighty nation, it** *is* **an ancient nation, a nation whose language thou knowest not, neither understandest what they say**.

16 Their quiver *is* as an open sepulchre, **they** *are* **all mighty men**.

17 And **they shall eat up thine harvest, and thy bread**, *which* thy sons and thy daughters should eat: they shall eat up **thy flocks and thine herds**: they shall eat up **thy vines and thy fig trees**: they shall impoverish thy fenced cities, wherein thou trustedst, with the sword.

18 **Nevertheless** in those days, saith the LORD, **I will not make a full end with you** [*I will preserve a remnant of Judah*].

19 ¶ And it shall come to pass, when ye shall say, Wherefore [*why*] doeth the LORD our God all these *things* unto us? then shalt thou answer them, Like as **ye have forsaken me**, and served strange gods in your land, **so shall ye serve strangers in a land** *that is* **not yours** [*you will be taken into slavery to a foreign country (Babylon)*].

20 **Declare this** in the house of Jacob [*Israel*], and **publish it in Judah**, saying,

21 Hear now this, **O foolish people**, and without understanding; which have eyes, and see not; which have ears, and hear not:

22 **Fear ye not me?** saith the LORD: **will ye not tremble at my presence**, which have placed the sand *for* the bound of the sea by a perpetual decree, that it cannot pass it: and though the waves thereof toss themselves, yet can they not prevail; though they roar, yet can they not pass over it?

23 But **this people hath a revolting and a rebellious heart**; they are revolted and gone.

24 **Neither say they in their heart, Let us now fear the LORD our God**, that giveth rain, both the former and the latter, in his season: he reserveth unto us the appointed weeks of the harvest.

25 ¶ **Your iniquities have turned away these** *things,* **and your sins have withholden good** *things* **from you**.

26 For **among my people are found wicked** *men:* they lay wait, as he that setteth snares; they set a trap, they catch men.

27 As a cage is full of birds, so *are* **their houses full of deceit**: therefore they are become great, and waxen rich.

28 **They are waxen fat** [*they have grown rich on corruption*], they shine: yea, **they overpass** [*ignore*] **the deeds of the wicked**: they judge not the cause, the cause of the fatherless, yet they prosper; and the right of the needy do they not judge.

29 **Shall I not visit** [*punish*] **for these** *things*? saith the LORD: shall not my soul be avenged on such a nation as this?

30 ¶ **A** wonderful [*astonishing*] **and horrible thing is committed in the land;**

31 **The prophets** [*false prophets*] **prophesy falsely**, and the priests bear rule by their means [*take authority unto themselves; are not authorized by God*]; and **my people love** *to have it* **so**: and what will ye do in the end thereof?

How did you do? This approach to reading the Old Testament can be quite helpful. Even though you may not understand everything, you get the big picture and can benefit much from the major messages.

JEREMIAH 6

Background
This chapter continues the theme of the destruction of Jerusalem by the Babylonians, because of gross wickedness among the covenant people. We will add a few more notes here than we did for chapter 5, in hopes that you will continue to get a better feel for the "manner of prophesying among the Jews" (2 Nephi 25:1), including the use of words and symbolism to create pictures in the minds of the readers.

1 **O YE children** [*descendants*] **of Benjamin** [*remember that the tribes of Judah and Benjamin stayed together at the time the twelve tribes split into two nations, after King Solomon died; they became known as "Judah"*], gather yourselves to **flee out of the midst of Jerusalem,** and blow the trumpet [*sound the alarm*] in Tekoa [*a Judean city, about six miles south of Bethlehem,*

which is about five miles southwest of Jerusalem], and set up a sign of fire in Beth-haccerem: **for evil appeareth out of the north, and great destruction**.

Next, the siege of Jerusalem by Babylon is described.

2 I have likened [*compared*] the **daughter of Zion** [*Jerusalem*] to a comely [*beautiful*] and delicate *woman*.

3 **The shepherds** [*the Babylonians*] with their flocks shall come unto her; they **shall pitch** *their* **tents against her round about**; they shall feed every one in his place.

4 **Prepare ye war against her** [*Jerusalem*]; arise, and let us [*Babylon*] go up at noon [*let's attack Jerusalem at noon*]. Woe unto us! for the day goeth away [*the daylight is fading*], for the shadows of the evening are stretched out [*are getting longer*].

5 Arise, and let us go by night [*let us also attack Jerusalem at night*], and **let us destroy her palaces**.

6 ¶ For thus hath the LORD of hosts said, **Hew ye down trees, and cast a mount against Jerusalem** [*throw up a mound of dirt outside the walls of Jerusalem for the siege and build battlements*]: **this** *is* **the city to be visited** [*punished*]; she *is* wholly oppression in the midst of her [*Jerusalem is completely corrupt*].

Next, Jerusalem is described as a fountain of filthy water, spewing forth wickedness all around.

7 **As a fountain** casteth out her waters, so **she casteth out her wickedness**: violence and spoil is heard in her; before me continually *is* grief and wounds.

8 **Be thou instructed** [*heed the warnings*], **O Jerusalem**, lest my soul depart from thee; **lest I make thee desolate, a land not inhabited**.

The symbolism in verse 9, next, is that of being thoroughly harvested. The "gleaners" went through the vineyards again, after the main harvest was gathered, and completely stripped the vines of any remaining grapes. Thus, the inhabitants of Jerusalem and the surrounding cities of Judah are going to be thoroughly "gleaned" by their enemies.

9 ¶ Thus saith the LORD of hosts, **They** [*the* Babylonians] **shall thoroughly glean the remnant of Israel** [*Judah*] as a vine: turn back thine hand as a grapegatherer into the baskets.

Next, the question is, in effect, who is there in all of Judah to whom this urgent message might get through? Answer: nobody.

10 **To whom shall I speak, and give warning**, that they may hear? behold, **their ear** *is* **uncircumcised**

[*they don't even recognize the word of God; they are wicked to the point that they are completely spiritually deaf*], and **they cannot hearken** [*they cannot obey because they cannot hear*]: behold, **the word of the LORD is unto them a reproach** [*they consider the word of the Lord to be a negative thing*]; **they have no delight in it**.

In verse 11, next, we are told that destruction will come upon all the inhabitants of Jerusalem, regardless of age and circumstance.

11 **Therefore** [*this is why*] **I am full of the fury of the LORD**; I am weary with holding in [*holding it back*]: I will pour it [*the fury of the Lord*] out upon the children abroad [*playing in the streets*], and upon the assembly of young men together [*simultaneously*]: for even the husband with the wife shall be taken, the aged with *him that is* full of days [*those who are bent over with age*].

12 And their houses shall be turned unto others [*others will inhabit their homes*], *with their* fields and wives together: for I will stretch out my hand upon [*I will punish*] the inhabitants of the land, saith the LORD.

Perhaps you've noticed that Jeremiah is saying the same basic thing many different ways. This is typical of prophetic utterances of his day. Repetition for emphasis is typical of Isaiah's writings also, likewise with many other prophets in the Old Testament.

Next, Jeremiah again repeats that society in and around Jerusalem is completely riddled with corruption. (This is one of the reasons Lehi and his family were commanded to leave the Jerusalem area.)

13 For from the least of them even unto the greatest of them **every one** *is* **given to covetousness**; and from the prophet [*false prophet*] even unto the priest [*false, corrupt priest*] **every one dealeth falsely**.

14 **They** [*the false prophets and false priests supported by these corrupt people*] **have healed also the hurt** *of the daughter* **of my people slightly** [*have superficially addressed the moral corruption and coming destruction and war*], saying, Peace, peace; when *there is* no peace.

Next, in verse 15, we see that the people had lost their ability to blush and be embarrassed at wickedness. It had become so common and accepted among them that it was no longer a big deal.

15 **Were they ashamed** when they had committed abomination? **nay, they were not at all ashamed, neither could they blush**: therefore they shall fall among them that fall: at the time *that* I visit [*punish*] them they shall be cast down, saith the LORD.

Once again, in verse 16, next, the

people are invited to repent. But they refuse.

16 Thus saith the LORD, Stand ye in the ways [*repent and stand in holy places; in other words, live righteously*], and see, and **ask for the old paths** [*the old ways of truth and righteousness*], where *is* the good way, **and walk therein**, **and ye shall find rest for your souls**. But **they said, We will not walk** *therein*.

Have you noticed that the Lord reminds us over and over that He has given these people plenty of warning? One of the great blessings in our lives is that we hear the same warning messages time and time again in our lives, thus giving us many opportunities to repent and continually improve.

Once again, these wicked people of Judah refuse to listen to the warning.

17 Also **I set watchmen** [*prophets*] over you, *saying,* Hearken to the sound of the trumpet [*listen to the warning of approaching danger and destruction*]. **But they** [*the people of Judah*] **said, We will not hearken**.

18 ¶ **Therefore hear, ye nations**, and know, O congregation, **what is among them** [*all nations are called to serve as witnesses against Judah*].

19 Hear, O earth: behold, **I will bring evil upon this people**, *even* the fruit [*product*] of their thoughts [*their evil thoughts have produced wicked deeds*], **because they have not hearkened unto my words, nor to my law, but rejected it**.

As you can see, the main message of verse 20, next, is that empty ritual and empty worship is of no value. The incense and offerings mentioned were part of normal religious worship under the law of Moses.

20 **To what purpose** cometh there to me incense from Sheba, and the sweet cane from a far country [*in other words, what good does your ritual and worship do*]? **your burnt offerings** *are* **not acceptable, nor your sacrifices sweet unto me**.

The theme of destruction continues in verse 21, next.

21 Therefore thus saith the LORD, Behold, I [*the Lord*] **will lay stumblingblocks** before this people, and **the fathers and the sons together shall fall upon them; the neighbour and his friend shall perish**.

More repetition. Remember, repetition for emphasis is a major component of the Jewish culture at the time of Jeremiah. Sometimes, "westerners" (including most of us) struggle a bit with such repetition, because we start thinking, "Wait a minute. He already said that. Is he saying something else here and I am missing it?" No. You are not missing it. It is just part of the manner of speaking and prophesying among the Jews.

22 Thus saith the LORD, Behold, **a people** [*the Babylonian armies*] **cometh from the north country**, and **a great nation** [*Babylon*] shall be raised **from the sides of the earth** [*the ends of the earth; in other words, from far away*].

23 **They shall lay hold on bow and spear** [*they will be well-armed*]; **they** *are* **cruel**, and have no mercy; their voice roareth like the sea; and they ride upon horses, set in array as men for war against thee, O daughter of Zion [*Jerusalem*].

24 **We have heard the fame thereof: our hands wax feeble** [*we get weak and faint just hearing about them*]: anguish hath taken hold of us, *and* pain, as of a woman in travail.

25 Go not forth into the field [*don't leave the house*], nor walk by the way; for the sword of the enemy *and* **fear** *is* **on every side**.

26 ¶ O daughter of my people, **gird** *thee* **with sackcloth** [*start mourning now*], and **wallow thyself in ashes** [*roll in ashes; putting ashes upon one's self was a sign of mourning in the Jewish culture of the day*]: **make thee mourning**, *as for* an only son, **most bitter** lamentation: for the spoiler [*Babylon*] shall suddenly come upon us.

Next, the Savior reassures Jeremiah of his calling to be a prophet (compare with Jeremiah 1:18).

27 **I have set thee** *for* **a tower** *and* a fortress among my people, that thou mayest know and try their way.

The imagery of the "tower," in verse 27, above, is that of the watchtowers which were built in those days. A person standing upon the watchtower could spot trouble coming a long way off. Our prophets, as inspired men of God, serve as "watchtowers" among us to spot coming danger and warn us of it while there is still time to prepare to defend ourselves from it.

Next, Jeremiah is reminded of the kind of people he is to serve, as one of the Lord's prophets shortly before the downfall of Jerusalem. The Lord uses the imagery of a refiner attempting to smelt precious metal from available ore to describe the wicked residents of Judah. In the normal refining process, the ore is placed in a crucible that is then heated with fire until the ore melts.

As the ore melts, the impurities float to the top and are removed as slag. The precious metal is heavier, so it sinks to the bottom of the crucible. The impurities are, in effect, burned out of the mix and all that remains is the precious metal, in other words, the desired product of the refiner's fire.

Symbolically, the Lord is the Refiner. We are the ore. We have many imperfections that need to be burned out of us in the "furnace of affliction." If we are willing, the "fire of the Holy Ghost" will burn the imperfections out of our souls. We can thus be cleansed by the Atonement of Christ, and become pure gold in the hands of the Refiner.

In the case of Israel, and Judah specifically in this example, they are not allowing the Refiner's fire to work on them successfully. They remain "brass and iron" (verse 28). In fact, they get "consumed" by the fire (verse 29), rather than refined. It is an agency choice whether to be purged and cleansed by the refiner's fire, or destroyed by it. The people of Judah have chosen to be destroyed at this time in their history.

28 **They** *are* **all grievous revolters**, walking with slanders: *they are* **brass and iron**; they *are* all **corrupters**.

29 The bellows are burned [*the bellows of the refiner's fire blow fiercely; see footnote 29a in your LDS Bible*], **the lead is consumed of** [*by*] **the fire** [*in effect, the Jews have decided they want to be "lead" rather than gold (symbolic of godliness) and thus are destroyed by the refiner's fire*]; **the founder melteth in vain** [*the Lord works in vain to redeem these people*]: for **the wicked are not plucked away** [*the

imperfections are not purged out of the people; in other words, there are not just a few wicked people of Judah, rather, the whole nation is corrupt; therefore, if the Lord takes out the "impurities," there will be almost no one left in Judah*].

30 Reprobate [*rejected*] silver shall *men* call them, because **the LORD hath rejected them**.

JEREMIAH 7

Background

Chapters 7 through 10 go together. Chapter 26 contains the same basic prophecy but is somewhat shorter. In these chapters, sometimes called "the temple sermon" or "the temple prophecy" by scholars, Jeremiah is told by the Lord to stand in the gate of the temple in Jerusalem and deliver the messages that follow.

You will see that yet another invitation to repent is given to these wicked and foolish people. It is another reminder to all of us that it is not too late to repent, but can become so. The sweet message is that we can repent still. The sad fact is that these people opt to refuse to return to the Lord. Consequently, additional detail is provided regarding the coming destruction.

Perhaps you have noticed that it is often difficult to determine who is speaking here, Jeremiah or the Lord. Sometimes it is quite clear, but in many instances it is not. We won't worry too much about this because we are familiar with the quote from the Doctrine and Covenants which says (**bold** added for emphasis):

<u>**D&C 1:38**</u>
38 What I the Lord have spoken, I have spoken, and I excuse not myself; and though the heavens and the earth pass away, my word shall not pass away, but shall all be fulfilled, **whether by mine own voice or by the voice of my servants, it is the same**.

Again, we will make frequent use of **bold** for emphasis.

1 **THE word that came to Jeremiah** from the LORD, saying,

2 **Stand in the gate of the LORD's house** [*the temple in Jerusalem*], and proclaim there this word, **and say, Hear the word of the LORD**, all *ye of* Judah, that enter in at these gates to worship the LORD.

> Did you notice that even though they are wicked, they are still "going to church," so to speak?

3 Thus saith the LORD of hosts, the God of Israel, **Amend your ways and your doings, and I will cause you to dwell in this place** [*and you can stay here*].

4 **Trust ye not in lying words**, saying, The temple of the LORD, The temple of the LORD, The

temple of the LORD, *are* these [*don't trust in the physical temple, nor in going there to worship, to save you (unless you repent)*].

5 For **if ye thoroughly** [*through and through; genuinely*] **amend your ways and your doings**; if ye throughly execute judgment [*fairness; integrity*] between a man and his neighbour;

6 *If* **ye oppress not the stranger, the fatherless, and the widow**, and **shed not innocent blood** in this place, **neither walk after other gods** [*worship idols*] to your hurt:

7 **Then will I cause you to dwell in this place**, in the land that I gave to your fathers, **for ever and ever**.

8 ¶ Behold, ye trust in lying words, that cannot profit [*you trust in the words of false prophets and priests, corrupt leaders, etc., which do you no good*].

9 **Will ye steal, murder, and commit adultery,** and **swear falsely,** and **burn incense unto Baal,** and **walk after other gods** whom ye know not;

10 **And come and stand before me in this house** [*the temple in Jerusalem*], which is called by my name, and say, We are delivered to do all these abominations [*as long as we attend the temple, we are free to be wicked*]?

11 **Is this house** [*the temple*], which is called by my name, **become a den of robbers** in your eyes? Behold, even **I have seen it, saith the LORD**.

Next, the people are told to go to Shiloh and be reminded what happened there to wicked Israel. By way of quick review, after Joshua led the children of Israel into the promised land, the Tabernacle was set up in Shiloh (about twenty miles north of Jerusalem). Thus, Shiloh, in effect, was the site of their temple. Eventually, Israel became so wicked that they set up idols and worshiped them there (Judges 18:30–31). They lost the protection of the Lord and the Philistines conquered Shiloh and took the Ark of the Covenant (1 Samuel 4:10–12).

12 But **go ye now unto my place which** *was* **in Shiloh**, where I set my name at the first, **and see what I did to it for** [*because of*] **the wickedness of my people Israel**.

13 And now, because ye have done all these works, saith the LORD, and **I spake unto you**, rising up early and speaking, **but ye heard not** [*you would not listen*]; and **I called you, but ye answered not;**

14 **Therefore will I do unto** *this* **house** [*the temple in Jerusalem*], which is called by my name, wherein ye trust, and unto the place which I gave to you and to your fathers, **as I have done to Shiloh**.

15 And **I will cast you out of my sight, as I have cast out all your brethren,** *even* **the whole seed of Ephraim** [*Israel, the lost ten tribes, which were commonly referred to as "Ephraim"*].

Verse 16, next, is a dramatic way of saying that the people are so wicked that it is hopeless for Jeremiah to try to get the Lord to save them. This can remind us of the hopeless situation Mormon faced, when his people fell to the same spiritual low as Jeremiah's people here. Let's read what Mormon said about the Nephites of his day and then look at verse 16 in Jeremiah:

Mormon 5:2

2 But behold, **I was without hope**, for I knew the judgments of the Lord which should come upon them; for they repented not of their iniquities, but did struggle for their lives without calling upon that Being who created them.

16 Therefore **pray not thou for this people**, neither lift up cry nor prayer for them, **neither make intercession to me: for I will not hear thee** [*in other words, in effect, the Lord will not be able to answer Jeremiah's prayers for them, because He cannot violate their agency; see also verse 27*].

17 ¶ **Seest thou not what they do in the cities of Judah and in the streets of Jerusalem?**

Verse 18, next, says, in effect,

that everyone in Judah is participating in idol worship, including every member of every family. Various activities involved in preparing for and performing idol worship are described.

18 The **children gather wood** [*to be used in pagan sacrifices*], and the **fathers kindle the fire**, and the **women** knead *their* dough, to **make cakes to the queen of heaven** [*the goddess of fertility, such as Ishtar, whom the Babylonians worshiped— see footnote 18a in your LDS Bible*], and to **pour out drink offerings unto other gods**, that they may provoke me to anger.

19 **Do they provoke me to anger?** saith the LORD: *do they* **not** *provoke* themselves to the confusion **of their own faces** [*aren't they bringing shame and disgrace upon themselves by so doing—see footnote 19a in your LDS Bible*]?

20 **Therefore** [*this is why*] thus saith the Lord GOD; Behold, **mine anger and my fury shall be poured out upon this place**, upon man, and upon beast, and upon the trees of the field, and upon the fruit of the ground; and it shall burn, and shall not be quenched.

Verses 21–24, next, say, in effect, that a major purpose of burnt offerings and sacrifices for the children of Israel under the law of Moses was to teach obedience to God. The problem with Judah is that the people are continuing the ritual sacrifices of the law of Moses but they are disobeying the Lord in their daily lives. Their ritual worship of Jehovah is empty and meaningless.

21 ¶ Thus saith the LORD of hosts, the God of Israel; **Put your burnt offerings unto your sacrifices, and eat flesh** [*go ahead and continue with your empty rituals, offering sacrifices and eating the meat from the animal sacrifices as always*].

22 For I spake not unto your fathers, nor commanded them in the day that I brought them out of the land of Egypt, concerning burnt offerings or sacrifices [*NIV "I did not* **just** *give them commands about burnt offerings and sacrifices"*]:

23 **But this thing commanded I them, saying, Obey my voice, and I will be your God, and ye shall be my people**: and **walk ye in all the ways that I have commanded** you, **that it may be well unto you**.

24 **But they hearkened not, nor inclined their ear** [*wouldn't listen*], but walked in the counsels *and* in the imagination of their evil heart, and **went backward, and not forward**.

Next, the Savior reminds these people that He has constantly tried to save them.

25 Since the day that your fathers [*forefathers, ancestors*] came forth out of the land of Egypt unto this

day **I have even sent unto you all my servants the prophets**, daily rising up early [*I have warned you constantly, ahead of the coming destruction*] and sending *them:*

26 **Yet they hearkened not unto me, nor inclined their ear**, but hardened their neck [*remained prideful*]: they did worse than their fathers [*they are worse than their ancestors—compare with Jeremiah 16:12*].

Next, Jehovah reminds Jeremiah that the people will not listen to him and change their ways. He gives him more specific things to say to them.

27 Therefore **thou shalt speak all these words unto them** [*the call to repentance*]**; but they will not hearken to thee**: thou shalt also call unto them; but they will not answer thee [*respond positively*].

28 **But thou shalt say unto them, This** *is* **a nation that obeyeth not the voice of the LORD** their God, nor receiveth correction [*they refuse to repent*]: truth is perished, and is cut off from their mouth [*they no longer live truth nor speak it*].

Verse 29, next, can well have several meanings. It is typical of Jeremiah, Isaiah, and others to embed several symbolic meanings into a word or phrase in their writings. For example, in verse 29, it says, in effect, that the Jews of Jeremiah's day should go into mourning now in anticipation of the coming destruction. It says for Jerusalem to cut off her hair. This can have many possible meanings:

1. Conquering armies of the day often shaved their prisoners bald, to identify them as slaves as well as to humiliate them (compare with Isaiah 3:24).

2. Shaving one's head was symbolic of grief as in Job 1:20.

3. In Jewish culture of the time, one's hair was considered to be a diadem, a crown symbolizing royalty and dignity. And having it cut off by an enemy was demeaning and a terrible insult.

4. In a religious sense, long hair could symbolize the vow of a Nazarite and his consecration to Jehovah (Numbers 6:2–8.) Intentionally cutting off one's hair could be symbolic of abandoning Jehovah and His commandments.

29 ¶ **Cut off thine hair**, *O Jerusalem,* and cast *it* away, and **take up a lamentation** [*go into mourning*] on high places; for the LORD hath rejected and forsaken the generation of his wrath [*because you are no longer under the protection of the Lord*].

Several reasons as to why the Lord can no longer bless and protect these wicked people are reviewed again in verses 30–31, next. Verse 31 informs us that they had gone so far as to sacrifice their children to their false gods.

30 **For the children of Judah** [*the Jews*] **have done evil in my sight**, saith the LORD: they **have set their abominations in the house** [*they have placed idols in the temple at Jerusalem*] which is called by my name, **to pollute it**.

31 And **they have built the high places of Tophet**, which *is* in the valley of the son of Hinnom, **to burn their sons and their daughters in the fire**; which I commanded *them* not, neither came it into my heart.

In verses 32–34, next, we see that the coming Babylonian armies will cause such slaughter that there will not be room to bury all the dead of Jerusalem and Judah.

32 ¶ Therefore, behold, the days come, saith the LORD, that **it shall no more be called Tophet, nor the valley of the son of Hinnom** [*the site where the Jews sacrificed their children to their false gods—see verse 31*], **but the valley of slaughter**: for **they shall bury in Tophet, till there be no place**.

The Bible Dictionary gives us a bit of additional information about Tophet (verse 32, above).

Bible Dictionary: Tophet
A spot in the valley of the son of Hinnom, south of Jerusalem, where human sacrifices were offered to Molech (2 Kgs. 23:10; Isa. 30:33; Jer. 7:31 f.; 19:6, 13).

33 And the carcases of this people [*the people of Judah and Jerusalem*] shall be meat [*food*] for the fowls of the heaven, and for the beasts of the earth; and none shall fray [*frighten*] *them* away.

Verse 34, next, is a prophetic description of the devastating aftermath resulting from the Babylonian captivity of the Jews.

34 **Then will I cause to cease** from the cities of Judah, and from the streets of Jerusalem, the voice of **mirth**, and the voice of **gladness**, the voice of the **bridegroom**, and the voice of the **bride**: for **the land shall be desolate**.

JEREMIAH 8

Background
Jeremiah's description of the destruction of Judah and Jerusalem continues in this chapter. Verses 1–2 describe one of the ultimate insults heaped upon a nation by its conquerors, namely the desecration of their dead by the triumphant enemies.

1 **AT that time** [*when Jerusalem and Judah are defeated*], saith the LORD, **they** [*the enemies*] **shall bring out the bones** of the kings of Judah, and the bones of his princes, and the bones of the priests, and

the bones of the prophets, and the bones of the inhabitants of Jerusalem, **out of their graves**:

2 And they shall spread them before the sun, and the moon, and all the host of heaven, whom they have loved, and whom they have served, and after whom they have walked, and whom they have sought, and whom they have worshipped: **they shall not be gathered, nor be buried; they shall be for dung upon the face of the earth**.

We will include a quote from the *Old Testament Student Manual* that helps us understand verses 1–2, above.

"In order to pour the utmost contempt upon the land, the victorious enemies dragged out of their graves, caves, and sepulchers, the bones of kings, princes, prophets, priests, and the principal inhabitants, and exposed them in the open air; so that they became, in the order of God's judgments, a reproach to them in the vain confidence they had in the sun, moon, and the host of heaven—all the planets and stars, whose worship they had set up in opposition to that of Jehovah. This custom of raising the bodies of the dead, and scattering their bones about, seems to have been general. It was the highest expression of hatred and contempt" (Adam Clarke, *The Holy Bible . . . with a Commentary and Critical Notes*, 4:276).

Verse 3, next, indicates that the fate of those who survive the slaughter will be worse than death. They will desire to die rather than to continue living in such horrible conditions.

3 And **death shall be chosen rather than life by all the residue of them that remain of this evil family** [*Judah*], **which remain in all the places whither I have driven them, saith the LORD of hosts**.

From here to the end of the chapter, we see the sins of these people described. You will no doubt see many parallels between them and the world in which we live.

In verses 4–5, next, the question is asked, in effect, "Why don't these people return to the Lord?"

4 ¶ Moreover [*in addition*] thou [*Jeremiah*] shalt say unto them, Thus saith the LORD; **Shall they fall, and not arise** [*don't people normally get up after they fall*]? **shall he turn away, and not return?**

5 **Why** *then* **is this people of Jerusalem slidden back by a perpetual backsliding** [*why do these people live lives of continual apostasy*]? **they hold fast deceit** [*they hold on tightly to wickedness and evil, to self-deception*], **they refuse to return** [*repent*].

6 **I hearkened and heard** [*the Lord*

has listened carefully for them to ask for forgiveness], **but** they spake not aright [*but they don't ask*]: **no man repented him of his wickedness, saying, What have I done?** every one turned to his course [*they all walk in their own paths*], as the horse rusheth into the battle [*like a horse running into battle*].

Next, in effect, we are told that creatures are wiser than these people. The creatures sense when to migrate, etc., and do it. But the covenant people of the Lord do not sense the coming destruction.

7 Yea, the stork in the heaven knoweth her appointed times; and the turtle and the crane and the swallow observe the time of their coming [*follow their migratory patterns*]; **but my people know not the judgment of the LORD**.

Next, in verse 8, we are told that the scribes (who interpret the laws of God among these Jews) have led them astray with their false and evil interpretations of the law of the Lord.

8 **How do ye say** [*how can you say*], **We** *are* **wise, and the law of the LORD** *is* **with us** [*we have the law of God among us*]? Lo, certainly in vain made he *it;* **the pen of the scribes** *is* **in vain** [*the scribes have misinterpreted the laws of Moses*].

9 **The wise** *men* **are ashamed** [*your supposedly wise men will be*

put to shame*], they are dismayed and taken: lo, **they have rejected the word of the LORD; and what wisdom** *is* **in them** [*why listen to them*]?

The message of verse 10, next, is that the wicked leaders of Jerusalem will be gone. Another message is that their society is completely corrupt. Greed is a major problem.

10 **Therefore will I give their wives unto others,** *and* **their fields to them** [*new owners*] **that shall inherit** *them:* for **every one from the least even unto the greatest is given to covetousness**, from the prophet [*false prophet*] even unto the priest [*corrupt priests*] **every one dealeth falsely**.

Next, we see that the leaders of the Jews at this point in their history have treated corruption and wickedness lightly, telling the people that destruction is not coming and that peace will continue. The imagery used is that of treating a serious wound as if it were just a scratch.

11 For **they have healed the hurt of the daughter of my people slightly,** saying, Peace, peace; when *there is* no peace.

Next, we see that one of the problems of this corrupt society is that nobody blushes at evil anymore.

12 **Were they ashamed when they**

had committed **abomination? nay, they were not at all ashamed, neither could they blush**: therefore shall they fall among them that fall: in the time of their visitation [*punishment*] they shall be cast down, saith the LORD.

13 ¶ **I will surely consume them, saith the LORD**: *there shall be* no grapes on the vine, nor figs on the fig tree [*none will escape*], and the leaf shall fade; and *the things that* I have given them shall pass away from them [*the Lord's former blessings will disappear*].

Verses 14–16, next, appear to be the answer from the inhabitants of Jerusalem and Judah in response to what the Lord has said above about the coming destruction. Verses 15–16 seem to be in the future, as if the Babylonian captivity is already under way or is completed.

14 **Why do we sit still** [*why are we sitting here*]? **assemble yourselves, and let us enter into the defenced cities** [*let's all retreat into our fortified cities*], **and let us be silent there** [*NIV "and perish there"*]: for the LORD our God hath put us to silence [*NIV "For the Lord our God has doomed us to perish"*], and given us water of gall [*bitter water*] to drink, **because we have sinned against the LORD**.

15 **We looked for peace** [*perhaps meaning that they looked for peace in wickedness*], **but no good** *came;*

and for a time of health, and behold trouble!

16 **The snorting of his horses** [*the enemy armies; horses are symbolic of military might and power in Jewish symbolism*] was heard from Dan [*was heard in the far north*]: **the whole land trembled at the sound of the neighing of his strong ones**; for they are come, and **have devoured the land, and all that is in it; the city, and those that dwell therein**.

17 For, **behold, I** [*the Lord*] **will send serpents, cockatrices** [*poisonous serpents; vipers; symbolic of the coming enemy armies*], **among you, which** *will* **not** *be* **charmed** [*which you cannot talk out of destroying you*], and **they shall bite you**, saith the LORD.

Opinions vary among scholars as to whether verses 18–22 represent the Lord's words or Jeremiah's. We will use verse 19 to sway us to believe that they represent the mourning of the Lord for His wayward people. But remember, it could represent Jeremiah's feelings too. We know from the record of Enoch in Moses that the Lord weeps for His people when they go astray.

Moses 7:28 (see also 28–44)
28 And it came to pass that the God of heaven looked upon the residue of the people, and he wept; and Enoch bore record of it, saying: How is it that the heavens weep, and shed forth

their tears as the rain upon the mountains?

18 ¶ *When* I would comfort myself against sorrow, **my heart *is* faint in me** [*German Bible "my heart is sick"*].

19 Behold the voice of **the cry of the daughter of my people** [*Jerusalem*] **because of them that dwell in a far country** [*apparently representing the future cries of the Jews far away in Babylonian captivity*]: *Is* not the LORD in Zion? *is* not her king in her? **Why have they provoked me to anger** with their graven images, *and* with strange vanities [*idol worship; pride, sin*]?

20 The harvest is past, the summer is ended, and we are not saved.

21 **For** [*because of*] **the hurt** [*suffering*] **of the daughter of my people** [*Judah and Jerusalem*] **am I hurt** [*I suffer*]; **I am black** [*gloomy—see footnote 21a in your Bible; I am heartbroken, in mourning*]; astonishment hath taken hold on me.

You will see the phrase, "balm in Gilead," in verse 22, next. It is a reference to a healing gum or spice found in a large area east of the Jordan River, extending north of the Dead Sea. The balm was highly prized and was used, among other things, to heal wounds. It appears to be a reference to Christ and the healing power of His Atonement. You are probably familiar with this phrase because "balm of Gilead" is used in verse 3 of our hymn, "Did You Think to Pray," which begins with "Ere you left your room this morning" (*Hymns*, no. 140).

22 **Is there** no balm in Gilead [*is healing not available*]; *is there* no physician there [*can no one heal; is the Physician (the Savior) not available*]? **why then is not the health of the daughter of my people recovered** [*perhaps meaning why don't the people turn to the Savior and be healed*]?

JEREMIAH 9

Background
Verses 1–3 of this chapter appear to be a continuation from chapter 8, bemoaning the coming destruction. Remember that the language of the Old Testament is often that of painting pictures and feelings with words. We see that here as the Lord (or possibly Jeremiah), as indicated in verse 3, expresses deep-felt sorrow for apostate Judah.

1 **OH that my head were waters, and mine eyes a fountain of tears**, that I might weep day and night for the slain of the daughter of my people [*Jerusalem and the cities of Judah*]!

2 **Oh that I had in the wilderness a lodging place of wayfaring men** [*a place where travelers could obtain temporary lodging*]; that I might leave my people, and go from them! for **they be** all adulterers, an assembly of treacherous men.

In addition to the rampant sexual immorality mentioned in verse 2, above, the people of Jerusalem and its surroundings were also filled with dishonesty. Their whole lifestyle was one of seeking greater and greater evil in which to participate, as indicated in verse 3, next.

3 And **they bend their tongues** *like* **their bow** *for* **lies**: but they are not valiant for the truth upon the earth; for **they proceed from evil to evil, and they know not me, saith the LORD**.

The next several verses point out more sins of these wicked people and give us a feel for what their wickedness has done to their society. As stated previously, this could be either the Lord or Jeremiah speaking or both. It is difficult to tell since they both share the same feelings, and also since a prophet can speak for the Lord as if the Lord were the one doing the talking (D&C 1:38).

The first thing that is pointed out is the distrust that permeates a dishonest society.

4 Take ye heed [*beware*] every one of his neighbour, and **trust ye not in any brother**: for every brother will utterly supplant [*deceive you at every opportunity to do so*], and every neighbour will walk with slanders [*gossips*].

5 And **they will deceive every one his neighbour, and will not speak the truth**: they have taught their tongue to speak lies, *and* weary themselves [*wear themselves out*] to commit iniquity.

6 **Thine habitation** *is* **in the midst of deceit** [*you are surrounded by deception*]; **through deceit they refuse to know me, saith the LORD**.

Verse 7, next, says, in effect, that the Lord will have to send them through the "refiner's fire" in order to once again have a pure people.

7 Therefore thus saith the LORD of hosts, Behold, **I will melt them** [*as a refiner does with gold ore in order to extract impurities and have pure gold as the end product of the refining process*], and try them; **for how shall I do for the daughter of my people** [*what else can I do in light of the sins of My people in Jerusalem*]?

8 **Their tongue** *is as* **an arrow shot out; it speaketh deceit** [*they are constantly shooting off their mouths with lies*]: *one* **speaketh peaceably to his neighbour with his mouth, but in heart he layeth his wait** [*he sets a trap for him; he says one thing but thinks another*].

9 ¶ **Shall I not visit** [*punish*] **them for these** *things*? **saith the LORD**: shall not my soul be avenged [*should not the law of justice take over*] on such a nation as this?

Verses 10–11, next, prophesy

emptiness and desolation, rubble and loneliness where a once-prosperous people lived.

10 **For the mountains will I take up a weeping and wailing, and for the habitations of the wilderness a lamentation** [*I will mourn for the mountains and wilderness where many people once lived and traveled*], **because they are burned up** [*they have become like a barren desert*], **so that none can pass through** *them;* neither can *men* hear the voice of **the cattle**; both **the fowl** of the heavens **and the beast** are fled; they **are gone**.

11 And **I will make Jerusalem heaps** [*a pile of rubble*], **and a den of dragons** [*a place where desert animals (jackals) live*]; and **I will make the cities of Judah desolate, without an inhabitant**.

12 ¶ **Who** *is* **the wise man, that may understand this** [*who is wise enough to get the picture*]**?** and **who is he to whom the mouth of the LORD hath spoken, that he may declare it** [*who can explain why this has happened*], for what [*why*] the land perisheth *and* is burned up like a wilderness [*has become like a desert*], that none passeth through?

In verse 12, above, the Lord asked a question, in effect, "Who can explain why this happened to Jerusalem?" In verses 13–16, He now answers His own question. In effect, He says, "I will tell you why."

13 And the LORD saith, **Because they have forsaken my law which I set before them, and have not obeyed my voice, neither walked therein**;

14 **But have walked after the imagination of their own heart**, and after Baalim [*Baal worship, an extremely wicked form of idol worship*], which their fathers taught them:

15 **Therefore** thus saith the LORD of hosts, the God of Israel; Behold, **I will feed them**, *even* this people, **with wormwood** [*extremely bitter*], and **give them water of gall to drink** [*in other words, the Lord will give them bitter medicine*].

16 **I will scatter them** also among the heathen [*foreign nations*], whom neither they nor their fathers have known: and I will send a sword after them, till I have consumed them.

"Consumed," as used in verse 16, above, does not mean to become extinct. We will quote from the *Old Testament Student Manual* for clarification on this:

"To be consumed does not mean to become extinct. Being consumed and destroyed, in the context of the prophecies of the scattering of Israel, meant to be utterly disorganized and disbanded so that Israel's power, influence, and cohesiveness as a nation was gone. Moses, in

Deuteronomy 4:26, told all Israel that they would 'utterly be destroyed.' Yet the verses following show that Israel still existed as homeless individuals" (*Old Testament Student Manual*, page 238).

Next, these unrepentant people are told to get ready to mourn.

17 ¶ Thus saith the LORD of hosts, Consider ye, and **call for the mourning women**, that they may come; and **send for cunning *women*** [*skilled mourners*], that they may come:

18 And let them make haste [*have them hurry, you will need them soon*], and **take up a wailing** [*mourning*] **for us**, that our eyes may run down with tears, and our eyelids gush out with waters [*tears*].

As stated previously, part of the "manner of prophesying among the Jews" (2 Nephi 25:1) was to speak of the future as if it had already taken place. Verse 19, next, is an example of this. It speaks of the coming destruction of Jerusalem as if it had already occurred.

19 For **a voice of wailing is heard out of Zion** [*Jerusalem and the other cities of Judah*], **How are we spoiled** [*see how completely we are ruined*]! **we are greatly confounded**, because we have forsaken the land, because our dwellings have cast *us* out.

20 Yet hear the word of the LORD, O ye women, and let your ear receive the word of his mouth, and **teach your daughters wailing**, and every one her neighbour lamentation.

21 For **death is come** up into our windows, *and* is entered into our palaces, to cut off the children from without, *and* the young men from the streets.

22 Speak, Thus saith the LORD, Even **the carcases of men shall fall as dung** [*animal droppings*] **upon the open field**, and as the handful [*the few remaining*] after the harvestman, and none shall gather *them*.

Do you know what the backward "P" at the beginning of verse 23, next, (and many other places throughout the King James Version of the Bible—the version we use in English) means? It indicates that the Bible is now turning to another topic or a new aspect of the topic already under consideration.

In this case, it is a very short course in how to avoid wickedness.

23 ¶ Thus saith the LORD, **Let not the wise *man* glory in his wisdom** [*avoid being prideful*], **neither let the mighty *man* glory in his might** [*let powerful people avoid pride*], **let not the rich *man* glory in his riches**:

24 **But let him** that glorieth **glory in this, that he understandeth and knoweth me, that I** *am* **the LORD** which exercise lovingkindness, judgment, and righteousness, in the earth: for in these *things* I delight, saith the LORD.

The topic now turns to hypocrisy, claiming to be the Lord's people through outward ordinances, but inwardly being the "natural man" (Mosiah 3:19). The Lord says that the day is coming when His people, who have been circumcised according to the law of Moses (a token of loyalty and dedication to the Lord, from Abraham to the end of the Old Testament), will be punished by other wicked nations, referred to as "the uncircumcised" at the end of verse 25. The cause of this punishment is given at the end of verse 26.

25 ¶ **Behold, the days come, saith the LORD, that I will punish all** *them which are* **circumcised** [*who have entered into outward covenants with the Lord, but are wicked*] **with the uncircumcised**;

26 Egypt, and Judah, and Edom, and the children of Ammon, and Moab, and all *that are* in the utmost corners, that dwell in the wilderness: for **all** *these* **nations** *are* **uncircumcised**, and **all the house of Israel** *are* **uncircumcised in the heart** [*are not faithful to God*].

The point in verses 25–26, above, seems to be that even though the people of Judah, as part of Israel, are outwardly the Lord's covenant people, they are in fact no better off than any other nation or people because they have broken their covenants with God.

JEREMIAH 10

Background
In this chapter, the people are counseled to learn to distinguish between false gods and the true God. Jeremiah points out how absurd idol worship is and teaches the people to worship the Lord. We will quote from the *Old Testament Student Manual*:

"In a profound and yet simple chain of reasoning, Jeremiah showed the stupidity and sheer illogic of worshiping an idol. Men take such materials as wood and precious metals which they work and shape at their own will, making all kinds of objects of service. Then they take those same materials, make them into an idol by the work of their own hands, and suddenly expect the idol to be filled with supernatural power and be able to provide miraculous aid for the person who made it" (*Old Testament Student Manual*, pages 238–39).

1 HEAR ye the word which the LORD speaketh unto you, O house of Israel:

2 **Thus saith the LORD, Learn not the way of the heathen** [*don't join with the heathen in their false*

religions, including idol worship], and **be not dismayed** [*terrified*] **at the signs of heaven** [*at signs in the sky, such as eclipses and falling stars*]; for the heathen are dismayed at them.

Watch now as Jeremiah points out how ridiculous it is to make idols with their own hands and then worship them.

By the way, some have interpreted verse 3, next, to be a direct reference to Christmas trees in our day, and have thus come to the conclusion that the Bible is against them. Not so. The word of the Lord here is against idols, as a replacement for the true God. Trees were often cut down and idols made from the wood.

3 For the customs of the people *are* vain [*useless*]: for *one* cutteth a tree out of the forest, **the work of the hands of the workman**, with the axe.

4 **They deck it with silver and with gold**; they **fasten it with nails** and with hammers, **that it move not** [*so that it doesn't fall over*].

5 **They** [*the idols*] *are* upright as the palm tree, but **speak not**: they **must needs be borne** [*they have to be carried from place to place*], **because they cannot go** [*because they can't move themselves*]. **Be not afraid of them; for they cannot do evil, neither also** *is it* **in them to do good**.

Next, in verses 7–8, Jeremiah points out that neither idols nor the greatest among men can begin to compare with the true God.

6 Forasmuch as ***there is* none like unto thee, O LORD**; thou *art* great, and thy name *is* great in might.

7 Who would not fear [*revere and respect*] thee, O King of nations? for to thee doth it appertain [*reverence and honor are properly due You*]: forasmuch as among all the wise *men* of the nations, and in all their kingdoms, ***there is* none like unto thee**.

8 **But they** [*people who make and worship idols*] **are altogether brutish** [*are completely without sense*] **and foolish**: the stock [*the idol made from a portion of a tree trunk or limb*] *is* a doctrine of vanities [*is a worthless doctrine*].

9 Silver spread into plates is brought from Tarshish, and gold from Uphaz, the work of the workman, and of the hands of the founder: blue and purple *is* their clothing: **they** [*idols*] **are all the work of cunning** *men* [*skilled craftsmen*].

10 **But the LORD** *is* **the true God, he** *is* **the living God, and an everlasting king**: at his wrath the earth shall tremble, and the nations [*wicked* nations] shall not be able to abide his indignation.

11 Thus shall ye say unto them, **The**

gods [*idols and other false gods*] that have not made the heavens and the earth, *even* they **shall perish from the earth**, and from under these heavens.

12 **He** [*Jehovah; Jesus Christ*] **hath made the earth by his power**, he hath established the world by his wisdom, and hath stretched out the heavens by his discretion.

Verse 13, next, gives a very brief summary of the creation. The point is that when the Living God speaks, He is obeyed by nature. Contrast this to the lack of power in idols, as described in verse 14.

13 **When he uttereth his voice**, *there is* a multitude of waters in the heavens [*see Genesis, chapter 1*], and he causeth the vapours to ascend from the ends of the earth; he maketh lightnings with rain, and bringeth forth the wind out of his treasures.

14 Every man is brutish [*behaving like an animal*] in *his* knowledge [*every man who makes and then worships an idol, is totally without common sense in applying knowledge*]: every founder [*goldsmith, silversmith, etc., who shapes precious metal overlays for idols*] is confounded [*put to shame*] by the graven image: for his molten image *is* falsehood [*the resulting idol is a lie*], and *there is* no breath in them [*idols*].

15 They *are* vanity [*worthless*], *and* the work of errors [*the product of false doctrine*]: in the time of their visitation [*when God's punishments come*] they shall perish.

16 **The portion of Jacob** [*Jehovah, the God of Israel*] *is* **not like them** [*idols*]: for **he** *is* **the former** [*creator*] **of all** *things;* and Israel *is* the rod [*NIV "tribe"*] of his inheritance: **The LORD of hosts** *is* **his name**.

In verse 17, next, the people of Judah are told to gather their belongings in preparation for the coming siege. And in verse 18, they are told that after the siege (verse 17), they will be scattered.

17 ¶ **Gather up thy wares** out of the land, O inhabitant of the fortress [*the besieged city*].

18 For **thus saith the LORD**, Behold, **I will sling out the inhabitants of the land** at this once [*the Jews will be scattered by the Babylonians*], and will distress them, that they may find *it so* [*and will cause that they can be captured*].

Verses 19–22, next, describe the mourning and devastation that will accompany the conquering and scattering of the Jews at this point in their history.

19 ¶ Woe is me for my hurt! **my wound is grievous**: but I said, Truly this *is* a grief, and I must bear it.

20 **My tabernacle** [*dwelling*] **is**

spoiled, and all my cords [*the ropes that hold the tent up*] are broken [*in other words, economic and spiritual support are gone*]: **my children are gone forth of me** [*scattered*], and they *are* not [*they are gone*]: *there is* none to stretch forth my tent any more, and to set up my curtains.

We will use verses 19–20, above, as a reminder that there is more than one way in which Jeremiah's writings can be interpreted. We will mention three possibilities for these verses. No doubt there are more.

One
If it is Jeremiah who is speaking, then we might interpret them as follows:

19 ¶ Woe is me [*Jeremiah*] for my hurt! my wound is grievous [*it makes me very sad to see this happen to my people*]: but I said, Truly this *is* a grief, and I must bear it.

20 My tabernacle is spoiled [*my home and homeland are ruined*], and all my cords are broken [*all the support for my people is gone*]: my children are gone forth of me [*my family and followers are scattered*], and they *are* not [*they are gone*]: *there is* none to stretch forth my tent any more, and to set up my curtains [*no one is left in the land*].

Two
These two verses could represent the mourning of the Lord for His people.

19 ¶ Woe is me [*the Lord*] for my hurt! my wound is grievous [*it makes Me very sad to see this happen to My people*]: but I said, Truly this *is* a grief, and I must bear it.

20 My tabernacle is spoiled [*My temple in Jerusalem is ruined*], and all my cords are broken [*all the covenants with My people have been broken*]: my children are gone forth of me [*my people have been scattered*], and they *are* not [*they are gone*]: *there is* none to stretch forth my tent any more, and to set up my curtains [*there are none left in Jerusalem and the cities of Judah to establish My Church*].

Three
These two verses could even represent the mourning of Jerusalem for her people. Such personification of a city or land is often found in ancient writings.

19 ¶ Woe is me [*Jerusalem*] for my hurt! my wound is grievous [*it makes me very sad to see this happen to my people*]: but I said, Truly this *is* a grief, and I must bear it.

20 My tabernacle is spoiled [*my land is devastated*], and all my cords are broken [*I have fallen down, crumbled*]: my children are gone forth of me [*my inhabitants have been scattered*], and they *are* not [*they are gone*]: *there is* none to stretch forth my tent any more, and to set up my curtains [*no one is left in me*].

As you continue to read and study the writings of the Old Testament prophets, keep in mind that many of their writings can be understood in more than one way. Such is the beauty as well as the difficulty of writings that involve much use of symbolism.

We will continue now with some possible explanations of these next verses.

21 For **the pastors** are become brutish, and **have not sought the LORD** [*the leaders of the Jews are senseless and have not come to the Lord for guidance*]: **therefore they shall not prosper, and all their flocks shall be scattered** [*the scattering of the Jews*].

22 Behold, the noise of the bruit [*news*] is come [*the news of the coming armies has arrived*], and **a great commotion out of the north country, to make the cities of Judah desolate**, *and* a den of dragons [*jackals; in other words, jackals will move into the ruins of Jerusalem and Judah; symbolic of the desolation and emptiness left by the invading armies*].

Verse 23, next, says, in effect, that man, when he opts to do things on his own, without God, is not capable of governing himself successfully. Most scholars consider verses 23–25 to be Jeremiah speaking.

23 ¶ O LORD, I know that **the way of man** *is* **not in himself:** *it is* **not in man that walketh to direct his steps**.

Joseph Smith explained the principle in verse 23, above. He taught (**bold** added for emphasis):

"It has been the design of Jehovah, from the commencement of the world, and is His purpose now, to regulate the affairs of the world in His own time, to stand as a head of the universe, and take the reins of government in His own hand. When that is done, judgment will be administered in righteousness; anarchy and confusion will be destroyed, and 'nations will learn war no more.' **It is for want of this great governing principle, that all this confusion has existed; 'for it is not in man that walketh, to direct his steps;'** this we have fully shown" (*Teachings of the Prophet Joseph Smith*, pages 250–51).

In verse 24, next, Jeremiah humbly requests that the Lord correct him as needed. This attitude is described by the word "contrite." It appears that what Jeremiah has seen in vision by way of the coming punishments that will come upon Jerusalem has caused him to be a bit concerned about the anger of the Lord. Thus, he asks that he not be punished in anger. We know that the Lord does not punish righteous people in anger, but it may be that Jeremiah is still learning.

24 O LORD, correct me, but with judgment [*justice; fairness*]; **not in thine anger**, lest thou bring me to nothing [*perhaps meaning "for fear that Thou destroy me too"*].

The enemies of Israel and Judah were cruel and wicked people themselves. In verse 25, next, Jeremiah invites the Lord to exercise punishment upon them too.

25 Pour out thy fury upon the heathen [*referring to the enemies of Israel, in this context*] that know thee not, and upon the families that call not on thy name: for **they have eaten up Jacob** [*they have destroyed the house of Israel*], and devoured him, and consumed him, **and have made his habitation desolate**.

JEREMIAH 11

Background
In this chapter we see emphasis on the fact that, anciently, Israel was chosen to be the Lord's covenant people, but they rejected Him and the covenant. Remember, the covenant involved being blessed themselves with the blessings of potential exaltation, and the responsibility of taking the priesthood and the blessings of the gospel to all people (Abraham 2:9–11).

As we begin, the people of Judah are reminded that they and their ancestors rejected the covenant through their wickedness. (Remember that the people of Judah, which includes part of the small tribe of Benjamin, are all that remain of the Israelites, as a group in the Holy Land, since the ten tribes were conquered and carried away captive about one hundred years ago at this point of Jeremiah's prophesying.)

1 THE word that came to Jeremiah from the LORD, saying,

2 Hear ye the words of this covenant, and **speak unto the men of Judah**, and to the inhabitants of Jerusalem;

3 And say thou unto them, Thus saith the LORD God of Israel; **Cursed** [*stopped in progression*] *be* **the man that obeyeth not the words of this covenant,**

The covenant (known to us as the Abrahamic covenant) is briefly described in verses 4–5, next.

4 Which I commanded your fathers [*ancestors*] in the day *that* I brought them forth out of the land of Egypt, from the iron furnace [*symbolic of affliction*], saying, **Obey my voice**, and do them [*keep the commandments—see verse 3, above*], according to all which I command you: **so shall ye be my people, and I will be your God**:

5 That I may perform the oath [*in other words, as you obey the commandments, you enable the Lord to keep His part of the bargain— compare with D&C 82:10*] which I have sworn [*promised*] unto your fathers, **to give them a land flowing with milk and honey** [*symbolic of prosperity on earth and eventual celestial exaltation*], as *it is* this day. **Then answered I** [*the children of Israel answered—compare with Deuteronomy 26:17; Exodus 6:7*], and said, **So be it, O LORD.**

We see yet another invitation to the wicked people of Judah to repent and renew their covenant, delivered through Jeremiah by the Lord, in verse 6, next.

6 Then the LORD said unto me, Proclaim all these words in the cities of Judah, and in the streets of Jerusalem, saying, **Hear ye the words of this covenant, and do them**.

Verse 7, next, reminds us that the Lord had given these rebellious Israelites many, many chances to repent and return to Him.

7 For **I earnestly protested** [*witnessed—see footnote 7a in your Bible*] **unto your fathers** [*ancestors*] in the day *that* I brought them up out of the land of Egypt, *even* **unto this day**, rising early and protesting, **saying, Obey my voice**.

8 **Yet they obeyed not**, nor inclined their ear, **but walked every one in the imagination of their evil heart**: therefore **I will bring upon them all the words of this covenant** [*they will be held accountable for breaking this covenant*], which I commanded *them* to do; but they did *them* not.

9 And the LORD said unto me [*Jeremiah*], **A conspiracy** [*deliberate disobedience*] **is found among the men of Judah**, and among the inhabitants of Jerusalem.

10 **They are turned back to the iniquities of their forefathers**, which refused to hear my words; and they **went after other gods** to serve them: **the house of Israel and the house of Judah have broken my covenant** which I made with their fathers.

11 ¶ **Therefore** thus saith the LORD, Behold, **I will bring evil upon them**, which they shall not be able to escape; and **though they shall cry unto me, I will not hearken unto them** [*it will get to the point that it is too late to be saved by the Lord from their enemies*].

12 **Then shall the cities of Judah and inhabitants of Jerusalem** go, and **cry unto the gods** [*their idols*] unto whom they offer incense: **but they shall not save them at all** in the time of their trouble.

Next, we see that Jewish society of the day was completely riddled with idolatry. They had idols for every city, with altars to them in every street. Baal was worshiped everywhere. Remember that Baal worship involved sexual immorality with temple prostitutes. Sexual immorality destroys societies as well as individuals.

13 For *according to* the number of

thy cities were thy gods, O Judah; and *according to* **the number of the streets of Jerusalem have ye set up altars** to *that* shameful thing, *even* altars to burn incense unto Baal.

The hopelessness of Judah's situation is again symbolized by the Lord's requesting that Jeremiah no longer pray for these people.

14 **Therefore pray not thou for this people**, neither lift up a cry or prayer for them: for I will not hear *them* in the time that they cry unto me for their trouble.

15 **What hath my beloved to do in mine house** [*in effect, what is Judah thinking?*], *seeing* **she hath wrought lewdness** [*adultery*] **with many** [*in other words, has stepped out on God with spiritually illicit relationships with many false gods, as well as literal adultery*], and the holy flesh [*righteous, acceptable sacrifices—see footnote 15a in your Bible*] is passed from thee? **when thou doest evil, then thou rejoicest**.

Verses 16–17, next, remind us of the allegory of the tame and wild olive trees, taught by Zenos and quoted by Jacob in the Book of Mormon, in Jacob, chapter 5. We wonder in fact if Zenos lived before Jeremiah and these verses are a reference to his writings. We don't know the answer, but the question is interesting.

We will continue by giving one possible interpretation of verses 16–17, next.

16 The LORD called thy name, **A green olive tree, fair, *and* of goodly fruit** [*Judah is compared to an olive tree that once produced good people*]: **with the noise of a great tumult** [*with the coming destruction at the hands of the Babylonians*] **he** [*the Lord*] **hath kindled fire upon it** [*has destroyed Judah*], **and the branches of it are broken** [*the Jews are broken and scattered*].

17 For the LORD of hosts, **that planted thee** [*who established you as part of covenant Israel*], **hath pronounced evil against thee** [*the punishments of God are upon you*], **for** [*because of*] **the evil of the house of Israel and of the house of Judah**, which **they have done against themselves** to provoke me to anger in offering incense unto Baal [*they have brought great evil upon themselves because of their apostasy*].

Did you notice, in verse 17, above, that when we sin against God, we sin against ourselves?

<u>Major Message</u>
(Verse 17)
When we sin against God, we sin against ourselves.

Next, Jeremiah reports to us that the men of his hometown, Anathoth, hatched a plot to kill him.

He was unaware of it until the Lord revealed it to him.

18 ¶ And the LORD hath given me knowledge *of it,* and I know *it:* **then thou shewedst me their doings** [*the plot devised by the men of Anathoth—see verse 21*].

19 But **I** *was* **like a lamb** *or* **an ox** *that* **is brought to the slaughter**; and **I knew not that they had devised devices against me,** *saying,* Let us destroy the tree with the fruit thereof, and let us cut him off from the land of the living, that his name may be no more remembered.

20 But, O LORD of hosts, that judgest righteously, that triest the reins [*kidneys; symbolic, in Jewish culture of the day, of the deepest thoughts and feelings*] and the heart, let me see thy vengeance on them: for unto thee have I revealed my cause.

Verse 21, next, tells us that the men of Jeremiah's hometown threatened to kill him if he did not stop prophesying.

21 Therefore thus saith the LORD of **the men of Anathoth**, that seek thy life, **saying, Prophesy not in the name of the LORD, that thou die not by our hand:**

22 Therefore **thus saith the LORD** of hosts, Behold, **I will punish them**: the young men shall die by the sword; their sons and their

daughters shall die by famine:

23 And **there shall be no remnant of them** [*they will be wiped out*]: for **I will bring evil** [*punishment*] **upon the men of Anathoth**, *even* the year of their visitation [*the day of their punishment will come*].

JEREMIAH 12

Background

In this chapter, Jeremiah asks a question that many people would like to hear the Lord's answer to. It is important to understand correct doctrine on this matter. The question is, in effect, why do the wicked prosper and the righteous suffer? (The same question is asked in Habakkuk, chapter 1, and answered in Habakkuk 2:1–4.)

We appreciate that Jeremiah's relationship with the Savior was such that he could be open about his concerns on this issue. In the heading to chapter 12, in your LDS Bible, you will note that the wording is "Jeremiah complains of the prosperity of the wicked." Let's dive right in and see how the Lord responds to his concerns about fairness.

1 **RIGHTEOUS** *art* **thou, O LORD**, when I plead with thee: **yet let me talk with thee of** *thy* **judgments** [*in effect, "I have a concern about how You are running things*]: **Wherefore** [*why*] **doth the way of the wicked prosper** [*why do the wicked prosper*]? *wherefore* **are all they happy that deal very**

treacherously [*why are the wicked so happy*]?

2 **Thou hast planted them** [*You established them in this land*], yea, they have taken root: they grow, yea, **they bring forth fruit** [*they prosper*]: **thou *art* near in their mouth** [*they do lip service to You*], **and far from their reins** [*but You are far from their inner thoughts and desires*].

3 **But thou, O LORD, knowest me**: thou hast seen me, and tried [*tested*] mine heart toward thee: pull them out like sheep for the slaughter, and prepare them for the day of slaughter [*a prophecy of coming destruction for the wicked in Judah*].

In verse 4, next, and also in verse 11, below, Jeremiah's concerns remind us of Enoch's witness of the earth's mourning because of the suffering she goes through due to the wickedness upon her.

Moses 7:48
48 And it came to pass that Enoch looked upon the earth; and he heard a voice from the bowels thereof, saying: Wo, wo is me, the mother of men; I am pained, I am weary, because of the wickedness of my children. When shall I rest, and be cleansed from the filthiness which is gone forth out of me? When will my Creator sanctify me, that I may rest, and righteousness for a season abide upon my face?

4 **How long shall the land mourn**, and the herbs of every field wither [*because of famine sent to punish the wicked*], **for** [*because of*] **the wickedness of them that dwell therein?** the beasts are consumed, and the birds; **because they said, He shall not see our last end** [*because the wicked say that God will not punish and destroy them*].

In verses 5–17, the Lord answers Jeremiah's question as to why the wicked seem to prosper. In effect, He says that punishment will come upon the wicked, in the Lord's due time. He also reminds Jeremiah that He does know what is going on.

5 ¶ **If thou hast run with the footmen, and they have wearied thee, then how canst thou contend with horses** [*perhaps saying to Jeremiah that he is getting in a bit over his head in wondering if the Lord is slipping up where the wicked are concerned*]? **and *if* in the land of peace, *wherein* thou trustedst, *they wearied thee*, then how wilt thou do in the swelling of Jordan** [*perhaps saying, in effect, to Jeremiah that if he is having trouble while peace is still upon the land, how will he handle it when the flood of enemies takes over the land*]?

6 For **even thy brethren, and the house of thy father** [*the members of your own family*], even they **have dealt treacherously with thee; yea, they have called a multitude after thee** [*it sounds like a mob came

after Jeremiah]: **believe them not,** though they speak fair words unto thee [*even though they try to convince you that you are in no danger from them*].

Next, it appears that the Lord is saying that Jeremiah is not the only one who has been deserted by his family. The Lord's people have likewise deserted Him, causing Him not to be able to bless them.

7 ¶ I have forsaken mine house, I have left mine heritage; **I have given the dearly beloved of my soul into the hand of her enemies.**

8 **Mine heritage** [*My people*] is unto me as a lion in the forest; it **crieth out against me** [*they cry loudly, like the roar of a lion, against Me*]: **therefore have I hated it** [*I could no longer bless them*].

When you see the phrase "the Lord hated them," or something to that effect in the scriptures, it often means "He could no longer bless them," rather than that He literally hates them.

Have you ever seen birds, for example, baby chicks, peck at one that is odd or wounded, until they kill it? This seems to be the imagery used in verse 9, next, where the "speckled bird" (Judah, which should be different than other people because she is the covenant people of the Lord) is attacked by other birds (enemies).

9 **Mine heritage** [*the Jews and the land of Judah*] **is** unto me **as a speckled bird**, the **birds round about** *are* **against her**; come ye, assemble all the beasts of the field [*symbolic of the armies of Babylon—see footnote 9a in your Bible*], **come to devour.**

Verse 10, next, points out the damage done to a society by false political and religious leaders.

10 **Many pastors have destroyed my vineyard,** they have trodden my portion under foot, they have **made my pleasant portion** [*Jerusalem and the land of Judah*] **a desolate wilderness.**

11 They have made it desolate, *and being* desolate **it mourneth unto me**; the whole land is made desolate, because no man layeth *it* to heart [*no one pays attention—see footnote 11a in your Bible*].

12 The spoilers [*enemies*] are come upon all high places through the wilderness: for **the sword of the LORD shall devour from the *one* end of the land even to the *other*** end of the land: no flesh shall have peace.

13 They have sown wheat, but shall reap thorns [*they will harvest disappointment*]: they have put themselves to pain [*they work hard to be wicked*], *but* shall not profit: and they shall be ashamed of your

revenues [*they will be put to shame because of the products of their wickedness*] because of the fierce anger of the LORD [*the law of justice*].

Next, in verses 14–17, we see a prophecy that the gospel will eventually be taught to all people, including the nations who attack the Lord's people. This reminds us that all people will have a completely fair chance to be taught the gospel, understand it, and accept it or reject it, before the day of final judgment.

14 ¶ Thus saith the LORD against all mine evil neighbours [*all enemies of the Lord's covenant people*], that touch the inheritance which I have caused my people Israel to inherit; Behold, I will pluck them out of their land, and pluck out the house of Judah from among them [*the gathering of the Jews*].

15 And it shall come to pass, after that I have plucked them out **I will return, and have compassion on them**, and will bring them again, every man to his heritage, and every man to his land.

16 **And it shall come to pass** [*a prophecy*], **if they** [*all people in the world*] **will diligently learn the ways of my people** [*will learn the gospel of Jesus Christ*], to **swear by my name** [*make covenants with God*], The LORD liveth; as they taught my people to swear by Baal [*in place of the counterfeit cove-*

nants *of false philosophies and false religions*]; **then shall they be built in the midst of my people** [*then they too will become the Lord's chosen people*].

17 **But if they will not obey, I will utterly pluck up and destroy that nation**, saith the LORD.

JEREMIAH 13

Background

Have you noticed by now that the same basic messages are being repeated over and over in these chapters of Jeremiah? One of the benefits of studying some chapters in considerable detail is that it prepares you to understand the basic messages in other chapters, even though you may not understand all the details.

One of my friends recently observed that although he did not understand everything he was listening to in Isaiah (on a portable recorder while walking), he discovered that he understood far more than he anticipated, just by paying attention to the main messages and words of the Lord and thinking how they might apply to him and the world today. This approach can be of great help to all of us as we study the writings of Old Testament prophets.

In this chapter, Israel and Judah are compared to a linen girdle or sash (verse 1) which is hidden or buried in a crevice of some rocks and later dug up (verse 7). Through this treatment, it becomes useless. We don't know if what the Lord commanded Jeremiah to do here, with respect to the linen sash, is literal, or if it is symbolic, a type of parable. Either way, the lesson is the same: Israel and Judah have become so marred by "hiding" from the Lord that they have basically become of no use as the covenant people.

1 THUS saith the LORD unto me [*Jeremiah*], **Go and get thee a linen girdle, and put it upon thy loins** [*put it around your waist*], and put it not in water.

2 **So I got a girdle** according to the word of the LORD, **and put** *it* **on my loins**.
3 And the word of the LORD came unto me the second time, saying,

4 **Take the girdle** that thou hast got, which *is* upon thy loins, **and arise, go to Euphrates, and hide it there in a hole of the rock**.

It may be that "Euphrates," in verse 4, above, symbolizes Babylon, since a river by that name flows through that country. If so, this could symbolize the Babylonian captivity of Judah, which is just around the corner at this time in the history of the Jews.

5 **So I went, and hid it by Euphrates**, as the LORD commanded me.

6 And it came to pass **after many days**, that **the LORD said** unto me,

Arise, **go to Euphrates, and take the girdle from thence**, which I commanded thee to hide there.

7 Then **I went to Euphrates, and digged, and took the girdle from the place where I had hid it**: and, **behold, the girdle was marred, it was profitable for nothing** [*it was ruined, good for nothing*].

8 Then the word of the LORD came unto me, saying,

The meaning of verses 1–7 is given in the next verses.

9 Thus saith the LORD, **After this manner will I mar the pride of Judah, and the great pride of Jerusalem**.

10 **This evil people**, which refuse to hear my words, which walk in the imagination of their heart [*pridefulness, stubbornness*], and walk after other gods, to serve them, and to worship them, **shall even be as this girdle, which is good for nothing**.

In verse 11, next, the Lord explains the symbolism. Just as a sash or girdle is wrapped around a man's waist, so also the house of Israel was invited to be the Lord's covenant people, and to "stick to Him" tightly, just as a girdle sticks tightly to the person wearing it. But when a girdle rots (see heading to this chapter in your Bible), it is of no use. Israel (the northern ten tribes in this context) and Judah (the tribes of Judah and Benjamin) could have been a glorious people, a credit to the Lord and to themselves, but they refused.

11 For **as the girdle cleaveth to the loins of a man, so have I caused to cleave unto me the whole house of Israel and the whole house of Judah**, saith the LORD; that they might be unto me for a people, and for a name, and for a praise, and for a glory: **but they would not hear**.

Verses 12–14, next, basically say that these people will become drunk with wickedness, in other words, out of control with wickedness, and will be destroyed.

12 ¶ Therefore thou shalt speak unto them this word; Thus saith the LORD God of Israel, Every bottle [*symbolic of every person in Jerusalem and the other cities of Judah*] shall be filled with wine: and they shall say unto thee, Do we not certainly know that every bottle shall be filled with wine?

13 Then shalt thou say unto them, Thus saith the LORD, Behold, **I will fill all the inhabitants of this land, even the kings that sit upon David's throne, and the priests** [*false priests*]**, and the prophets** [*false prophets*]**, and all the inhabitants of Jerusalem, with drunkenness**.

14 **And I will dash them one against another**, even the fathers

and the sons together, saith the LORD: I will not pity, nor spare, nor have mercy, but **destroy them**.

Next, the Lord issues yet another invitation to these people to repent, before it is too late and destruction comes upon them.

15 ¶ **Hear ye**, and give ear; **be not proud**: for the LORD hath spoken.

16 **Give glory to the LORD your God**, before he cause darkness, and before your feet stumble upon the dark mountains, and, while ye look for light, he turn it into the shadow of death, *and* make *it* gross darkness.

17 **But if ye will not hear** it, **my soul shall weep** in secret places **for *your* pride; and mine eye shall weep sore, and run down with tears, because the LORD's flock is carried away captive**.

18 Say unto the king and to the queen, **Humble yourselves**, sit down: for your principalities shall come down, *even* the crown of your glory [*if you don't repent*].

19 The cities of the south shall be shut up, and none shall open *them:* **Judah shall be carried away captive all of it**, it shall be wholly carried away captive.

20 Lift up your eyes, and behold them [*the Babylonian armies*] that come from the north: where *is* the

flock *that* was given thee, thy beautiful flock?

Verse 21, next, in effect asks the question "What will you have to say for yourselves, how will you explain your foolishness in ignoring the call from the Lord to repent, when all that is prophesied happens to you?"

21 **What wilt thou say when he shall punish thee?** for thou hast taught them *to be* captains, *and* as chief over thee: shall not sorrows take thee, as a woman in travail? [*In other words, unless you repent, the coming sorrows and destructions are as sure as the labor of a woman who is expecting a child.*]

22 ¶ And **if thou say in thine heart, Wherefore come these things upon me** [*why am I being punished*]? **For the** [*the answer is because of the*] **greatness of thine iniquity** are thy skirts discovered, *and* thy heels made bare [*you will be ravished and reduced to bondage*].

23 **Can the Ethiopian change his skin, or the leopard his spots?** *then* **may ye also do good, that are accustomed to do evil** [*in effect, if the impossible can happen, then people like you can do good who are completely caught up in wickedness*].

Next, we see another direct prophecy of the scattering of the Jews.

24 **Therefore** [*because of the above-mentioned wickedness*] **will I scatter them** as the stubble that passeth away by the wind of the wilderness.

25 **This** *is* **thy lot** [*this is what you have coming*], the portion of thy measures from me, saith the LORD; **because thou hast forgotten me, and trusted in falsehood.**

26 Therefore will **I discover thy skirts upon thy face** [*I will pull your skirts up over your face*], **that thy shame may appear** [*in effect, your protection, your false façade will be taken off and your sins will be exposed for all to see*].

Verse 27, next, contains a very brief summary of the sins of Judah, which will lead to Babylonian captivity. They are already spiritually in bondage to the devil.

27 I have seen thine **adulteries,** and thy **neighings** [*chasing after other men's wives—see Jeremiah 5:8*], the **lewdness** of thy **whoredom,** *and* thine **abominations on the hills** [*symbolic of idol worship*] in the fields. **Woe unto thee, O Jerusalem!** wilt thou not be made clean? **when** *shall it* **once** *be* [*when will the day finally come*]?

JEREMIAH 14

Background

This chapter deals with a devastating drought that will come to the

Jerusalem area. Verses 1–6 describe how serious the drought will be and the famine that will ensue.

1 THE word of the LORD that came to Jeremiah **concerning the dearth** [*famine*].

2 **Judah mourneth**, and the gates thereof languish [*are wasting away*]; they are black [*dejected, discouraged*] unto the ground; and the cry of Jerusalem is gone up [*their desperate cry is heard everywhere*].

3 And their nobles have sent their little ones to the waters: they came to the pits [*wells*], *and* **found no water**; they returned with their **vessels empty**; they were ashamed [*dismayed*] and confounded [*in deep despair*], and covered their heads.

4 Because **the ground is chapt** [*cracked, parched*], for there was **no rain** in the earth, the plowmen were ashamed [*dismayed, desperate to know what to do*], they covered their heads.

5 Yea, **the hind** [*deer*] also **calved** [*had its baby*] in the field, **and forsook** *it* [*deserted its newborn fawn*], because there was **no grass**.

6 And the wild asses did stand in the high places, they snuffed up the wind [*pant*] like dragons [*jackals; wild dogs*]; their eyes did fail, because *there was* **no grass**.

In the next several verses, Jeremiah prays for his people, but is told that the Lord cannot answer his prayers because of the wickedness of Judah. In verse 7, it appears that Jeremiah humbly includes himself with his people.

7 ¶ **O LORD, though our iniquities testify against us, do thou** *it* [*please turn Thy wrath aside*] **for thy name's sake** [*for the sake of Your reputation as a merciful God*]: **for our backslidings are many; we have sinned against thee**.

8 O the **hope of Israel** [*another name for the Savior*], the **saviour thereof in time of trouble**, why shouldest thou be as a stranger in the land [*must You be far from us in our time of need*], and as a wayfaring [*traveling*] man *that* turneth aside to tarry for a night?

9 **Why shouldest thou be** as a man astonied [*astonished, paralyzed with surprise, unable to act*], **as a mighty man** *that* **cannot save** [*why can't You show your power for us*]? yet thou, O LORD, *art* in the midst of us, and we are called by thy name; **leave us not**.

Next, the Lord answers the questions raised above and explains why He cannot help them while they are wicked with no intent to repent.

10 ¶ Thus saith the LORD unto this people, **Thus have they loved to wander** [*in sin*], **they have not**

refrained their feet [*they have not stopped wandering in the paths of sin*], **therefore the LORD doth not accept them**; he will now remember their iniquity, and visit [*punish*] their sins.

11 **Then said the LORD** unto me [*Jeremiah*], **Pray not for this people** for *their* good.

12 When they fast, **I will not hear their cry**; and when they offer burnt offering and an oblation, **I will not accept them**: but **I will consume them** by the sword, and by the famine, and by the pestilence.

13 ¶ Then said I, Ah, Lord GOD! behold, **the prophets** [*the false prophets among the Jews*] **say unto them, Ye shall not see the sword, neither shall ye have famine**; but I will give you assured peace in this place [*in effect, the false prophets have told the people that sin is not really sin and that there can be peace in wickedness*].

Sometimes we think of false prophets, such as those in verse 13, above, as being various religious leaders gone astray. But we would do well to think of political leaders, media idols, philosophers, teachers, in fact any who lead us away from the teachings of the gospel of Jesus Christ, as being false prophets also.

In verse 14, next, the Savior delivers a stern rebuke against such false prophets.

14 Then the LORD said unto me, **The prophets prophesy lies in my name** [*in other words, there are many who teach falsehoods in the name of God*]: **I sent them not**, neither have I commanded them, neither spake unto them: **they prophesy unto you a false vision** and divination, and a thing of nought, **and the deceit of their heart** [*they teach the wicked thoughts and intents of their own hearts as the word of God*].

15 **Therefore thus saith the LORD concerning the prophets that prophesy in my name, and I sent them not** [*in other words, concerning false prophets*], yet they say, Sword and famine shall not be in this land; **By sword and famine shall those prophets be consumed**.

16 **And the people to whom they prophesy shall be cast out in the streets of Jerusalem because of the famine and the sword**; and they shall have none to bury them, them, their wives, nor their sons, nor their daughters: **for I will pour their wickedness upon them**.

In verses 17–18, we see that the Lord weeps when His people become wicked.

17 ¶ Therefore thou shalt say this word unto them; **Let mine eyes run down with tears night and day**, and let them not cease: **for the virgin daughter of my people** [*Jerusalem*] **is broken with a great**

breach [*is conquered*], with a very grievous blow.

18 If I go forth into the field, then **behold the slain** with the sword! and if I enter into the city, then **behold them that are sick with famine!** yea, both the prophet and the priest [*false prophets and priests*] go about into a land that they know not [*will be taken captive into a foreign land*].

Next, Jeremiah asks heartrending questions. He has the ability to love the wicked even though he has been told that they will be destroyed because of their rejecting the Lord.

19 **Hast thou utterly rejected Judah?** hath thy soul lothed [*loathed*] Zion? why hast thou smitten us, and *there is* no healing for us? we looked for peace, and *there is* no good; and for the time of healing, and behold trouble!

20 **We acknowledge, O LORD, our wickedness,** *and* the iniquity of our fathers: for **we have sinned against thee**.

21 **Do not abhor** *us,* for thy name's sake, do not disgrace the throne of thy glory: remember, break not thy covenant with us.

22 **Are there** *any* among the vanities [*false gods*] **of the Gentiles that can cause rain?** or can the heavens give showers? *art* not thou he, **O LORD our God?** therefore

we will wait upon thee: for thou hast made all these *things*.

JEREMIAH 15

Background

This chapter gives more prophetic detail about the destruction and scattering of the Jews in Jeremiah's day. Because of their intentional rebellion, there is no stopping the coming famine and captivity.

First, in verse 1, the Lord tells Jeremiah that even if the great prophets Moses and Samuel asked Him to stop the coming destruction upon Judah, it would not happen. We are seeing the law of justice in action. One of the lessons we are taught here is that mercy cannot "rob justice" (see Alma 42:25).

Major Message
Mercy cannot rob justice

1 THEN said the LORD unto me, **Though Moses and Samuel stood before me,** *yet* **my mind** *could* **not** *be* **toward this people** [*in other words, He could not bless them*]: cast *them* out of my sight, and let them go forth [*they will be scattered*].

As mentioned several times already in this study guide, the "manner of speaking and prophesying among the Jews" is to repeat things many times for emphasis and to use words skillfully to paint pictures in our minds and create deep emotion in our hearts. We see this again in the next several verses.

2 And it shall come to pass, **if they say unto thee, Whither shall we go forth** [*if they ask you, "Where are we going"*]? then thou shalt **tell them**, Thus saith the LORD; Such as *are* for death, **to death**; and such as *are* for the sword, **to the sword**; and such as *are* for the famine, **to the famine**; and such as *are* for the captivity, **to the captivity**.

3 And I will appoint over them four kinds, saith the LORD: **the sword to slay**, and **the dogs to tear**, and **the fowls** [*carrion birds, such as vultures*] **of the heaven, and the beasts** of the earth, **to devour and destroy**.

4 And I will cause them to be **removed into all kingdoms of the earth** [*scattered to all nations of the earth*], because of Manasseh [*a very wicked king of Judah*] the son of Hezekiah king of Judah, for *that* which he did in Jerusalem.

5 For **who shall have pity upon thee, O Jerusalem?** or who shall bemoan thee? or who shall go aside to ask how thou doest?

6 **Thou hast forsaken me, saith the LORD,** thou art gone backward [*have gone away from the Lord*]: therefore will I stretch out my hand against thee, and destroy thee; **I am weary with repenting** [*since the Lord has no need to repent, this*

phrase is saying, in effect, I am tired of "relenting" and giving you chance after chance to repent; it doesn't do a bit of good].

7 And **I will fan them with a fan** in the gates of the land [*I will scatter them, as a fan scatters chaff from wheat*]; I will bereave *them* of children [*they will lose their children*], **I will destroy my people, *since* they return not from their ways** [*since they refuse to repent*].

8 **Their widows are increased** to me above the sand of the seas [*there will be more widows than you can count*]: I have brought upon them against the mother of the young men **a spoiler at noonday** [*the enemy armies will be so powerful that they don't have to sneak up on you, rather, they can approach in broad daylight*]: I have caused *him* to fall upon it suddenly, and terrors upon the city.

9 She that hath borne seven languisheth [*grows weak*]: she hath given up the ghost [*has died*]; her sun is gone down while *it was* yet day [*all her hopes are suddenly dashed to pieces*]: she hath been ashamed and confounded [*confused and stopped*]: and the residue of them [*those who don't die of the famine*] will I deliver to the sword before their enemies, saith the LORD.

Next, Jeremiah laments the fact that he was born to be such a focal point of contention to the wicked. Even though he has lived righteously, everyone hates him.

10 ¶ **Woe is me**, my mother, that thou hast borne me **a man of strife and a man of contention to the whole earth**! I have neither lent on usury, nor men have lent to me on usury [*in effect, I have faithfully kept the laws of God*]; *yet* **every one of them** [*the wicked*] **doth curse me**.

Verse 11, next, could have several fulfillments. It could refer to Jeremiah, or it could be a prophecy that many of the Jews who are captured and carried away will be treated such that they survive. It could also be a prophecy about the return of the Jews from Babylonian captivity, or all of the above.

If it refers to Jeremiah, then it can remind us of the words of the Lord to Joseph Smith when he was in Liberty Jail (D&C 121 and 122). He will eventually be delivered from his enemies. This can be literal on earth or literal in eternity.

If it refers to the Jews and their eventual return, then it prophesies that their captors will eventually take pity on them and allow them to return.

11 The LORD said, **Verily it shall be well with thy remnant**; verily I will cause the enemy to entreat thee *well* in the time of evil and in the time of affliction.

12 Shall iron break the northern iron and the steel?

The Martin Luther German Bible roughly translates verse 12, above, as saying, "Don't you know that such iron exists that can break iron and brass from the north?" Perhaps this could mean, in effect, that the Lord has power over the strong "iron hand" of nations (including Babylon who came from the north) who hold the Jews captive, and He can cause their captors to treat them well and eventually let them go free.

Verse 13, next, seems to refer to the Jews and be yet another reminder as to why many of them are to be slaughtered and the remainder carried away into captivity at this point of their history.

13 Thy substance and thy treasures will I give to the spoil without price, and *that* **for all thy sins**, even in all thy borders [*the whole nation of Judah is riddled with wickedness*].

Verse 14, next, tells Jeremiah that he too will be carried away captive into a foreign country. He was eventually taken by a group of Jews to Egypt as they escaped the conquerors of Jerusalem, and then, according to tradition, stoned to death by them. (See Bible Dictionary under "Jeremiah." It appears that Jeremiah is being reminded that the righteous also suffer when the wicked rule and incur the wrath of God [compare with D&C 98:9].)

14 And **I will make** *thee* **to pass with thine enemies into a land** *which* **thou knowest not**: for a fire is kindled in mine anger, *which* shall burn upon you.

Verse 15, next, reminds us of the words of the Prophet Joseph Smith in Liberty Jail, as he pled with the Lord. He said:

D&C 121:5
5 Let thine anger be kindled against our enemies; and, in the fury of thine heart, with thy sword **avenge us of our wrongs**.

15 ¶ O LORD, thou knowest: remember me, and visit [*bless*] me, and **revenge me of my persecutors**; take me not away in thy long-suffering: know that for thy sake I have suffered rebuke.

16 **Thy words were found** [*were given to me*], **and I did eat them** [*internalized them, made them a part of me*]; and **thy word was unto me the joy and rejoicing of mine heart**: for I am called by thy name, O LORD God of hosts.

17 **I sat not in the assembly of the mockers, nor rejoiced** [*I did not join in wickedness and take pleasure in it with the wicked*]; **I sat alone** because of thy hand: for thou hast filled me with indignation [*against sin and wickedness*].

18 **Why is my pain perpetual, and my wound incurable**, *which* refuseth to be healed? wilt thou be altogether unto me as a liar, *and as* waters *that* fail [*perhaps meaning, in effect, "Are You not going to keep Your word? Why aren't Your promises of peace and protection and help fulfilled?"*]? [*Perhaps similar to Joseph Smith's pleading—see D&C 121:1–6.*]

The Lord responds to Jeremiah's pleading.

19 ¶ Therefore thus saith the LORD, If thou return, then will I bring thee again, *and* **thou shalt stand before me**: and if thou take forth the precious from the vile, **thou shalt be as my mouth**: let them return unto thee; but return not thou unto them [*perhaps meaning for Jeremiah to stand firm, and if the people want the word of the Lord, let them come to him*].

The Lord's word to Jeremiah, in verses 20–21, next, seems to be that of being saved spiritually rather than physically. Spiritual salvation is the only thing that counts in the perspective of eternity.

20 And I will make thee unto this people a fenced brasen wall [*a fortified wall of brass or bronze*]: and **they shall fight against thee, but they shall not prevail against thee**: for I *am* with thee to save thee and to deliver thee, saith the LORD.

21 And **I will deliver thee out of the hand of the wicked, and I will redeem thee out of the hand of the terrible**.

JEREMIAH 16

Background

This chapter contains a prophecy that is quite often referred to in our lessons and talks on missionary work in the last days. It is verse 16. We will say more about it when we get there.

Verse 2, if taken literally, would mean that Jeremiah was told not to marry. As we proceed, we will take the viewpoint that this was symbolic, rather than literal. One possible message is that Jerusalem has become so polluted with wickedness that it is no longer a safe place to attempt to raise children. Another possible message is that the coming enemy armies from Babylon will show no mercy to the inhabitants, including children.

1 THE word of the LORD came also unto me, saying,

2 **Thou shalt not take thee a wife, neither shalt thou have sons or daughters in this place.**

We will quote from the *Old Testament Student Manual* for help with verse 2, above (**bold** added for emphasis):

"Jeremiah's day was a sad one for Judah. To symbolize that truth, the Lord told his prophet three things that he was not to do:

"1.　He was not to marry or father children (see Jeremiah 16:2). So universal was the calamity bearing down upon the people that God did not want children to suffer its outrage. **This commandment**, however, like the one to Hosea (see Hosea 10), who was commanded to take a wife of whoredoms, **was probably not a literal one; rather, it probably was allegorical, that is, Jeremiah was not to expect that his people would marry themselves to the covenant again, nor was he to expect to get spiritual children (converts) from his ministry**.

"2.　He was not to lament those in Judah who died by the sword or famine (see Jeremiah 16:5), since they brought these judgments upon themselves.

"3.　He was not to feast or eat with friends in Jerusalem (see verse 8), since feasting was a sign of celebration and eating together a symbol of fellowship.

"In addition, Jeremiah was commanded to explain very clearly to the people the reasons for his actions as well as the reasons for their coming punishment" (*Old Testament Student Manual*, page 241).

3 For thus saith the LORD **concerning the sons and concerning the daughters that are born in this place,** and concerning their mothers that bare them, and concerning their fathers that begat them in this land;

4 **They shall die of grievous deaths**;
they shall not be lamented; **neither
shall they be buried**; *but* they shall
be as dung upon the face of the
earth: and they shall be **consumed
by the sword**, and by **famine**; and
their carcases shall be **meat for the
fowls of heaven, and for the beasts
of the earth**.

Verse 5, next, is another reminder
that if people do not repent, the
law of mercy cannot take over
from the law of justice.

5 For thus saith the LORD, Enter
not into the house of mourning,
neither go to lament nor bemoan
them: for **I have taken away my
peace from this people, saith the
LORD,** *even* **lovingkindness and
mercies**.

6 Both **the great** [*the famous and
prominent in their society*] **and the
small shall die in this land**: they
shall **not be buried** [*implying a terrible slaughter*], neither shall *men*
lament for them, **nor cut themselves, nor make themselves bald
for them** [*signs of deep mourning
and grief in their culture*]:

Verses 6 and 7, here, seem to
indicate that everyone will be in
such distress because of their
own circumstances that they will
not take time nor have inclina-
tion to mourn for others being
ravished by the famines and conquering enemy armies.

7 Neither shall *men* tear *themselves*

for them in mourning, to comfort
them for the dead [*no one will comfort those who mourn*]; neither shall
men give them the cup of consola-
tion to drink for their father or for
their mother.

8 Thou shalt not also go into the
house of feasting, to sit with them
to eat and to drink.

In verse 9, next, Jeremiah is told
that these terrible devastations
will come upon the Jews in his
lifetime.

9 For thus saith the LORD of hosts,
the God of Israel; Behold, I will
cause to cease out of this place in
your eyes, and **in your days**, the
voice of mirth, and the voice of
gladness, the voice of the bridegroom, and the voice of the bride.

Verse 10, next, warns Jeremiah
that the wicked people against
whom he preaches will act as
if they are righteous and do not
deserve such warnings and con-
demnation.

10 ¶ And it shall come to pass,
when thou shalt shew this people
all these words, and they shall say
unto thee, **Wherefore** [*why*] **hath
the LORD pronounced all this
great evil against us? or what** *is*
our iniquity [*what have we done
wrong*]? or what *is* our sin that we
have committed against the LORD
our God?

11 **Then shalt thou say** unto them,

Because your fathers [*parents; ancestors*] **have forsaken me**, saith the LORD, and have walked after other gods, and have served them, and have worshipped them, and have forsaken me, **and have not kept my law**;

12 **And ye have done worse than your fathers**; for, behold, ye walk every one after the imagination of his evil heart, that they may not hearken unto me:

13 **Therefore will I cast you out of this land** into a land that ye know not, *neither* ye nor your fathers; and there shall ye serve other gods day and night; where I will not shew you favour [*I will not be able to bless you with the choicest gospel blessings*].

Next, we see a major prophecy concerning the gathering of Israel in the last days. The prophecy includes the fact that the deliverance of the children of Israel from Egypt, by the Lord, will no longer be the most spectacular event spoken of among the people. Rather, the gathering of Israel from all nations will become the focus of effort and conversation.

Major Prophecy
The Lord will gather scattered Israel in the last days.

14 ¶ Therefore, behold, **the days come, saith the LORD**, that **it shall no more be said, The LORD liveth, that brought up the** children of Israel out of the land of Egypt;

15 **But, The LORD liveth, that brought up the children of Israel** from the land of the north, and **from all the lands whither he had driven them**: and I will bring them again into their land that I gave unto their fathers.

Notice the order of the missionary work in the last days, as given in verse 16, next. First, large numbers of converts will come into the Church, in various nations. This is represented by "fishers" who fish with nets and catch large numbers with them. These mass conversions are followed by missionaries who are depicted as "hunters" who search the once-fertile mission field for anyone else who will join the Church.

16 ¶ Behold, **I will send for many fishers**, saith the LORD, and **they shall fish them**; and **after will I send for many hunters**, and they shall hunt them [*converts*] **from every mountain**, and from every **hill**, and out of the **holes of the rocks**.

One example of "fishers," in verse 16, above, might be Wilford Woodruff and other early missionaries who baptized thousands of converts in England in the early days of the Church. Another example could be the missionary work in South America in our day, where tens of thousands of converts are being baptized. Yet other examples might be found in any one of several countries or areas, including Africa, where initial missionary efforts have resulted in abundant baptisms in our day.

Now, though, in some areas of the world, convert baptisms are very few in number. The missionaries serving in such areas might be considered to be the "hunters," prophesied of by Jeremiah, who search everywhere for just a few who are willing to be taught the gospel.

Next, the topic turns to the fact that the Lord sees all, including the supposedly "secret" doings of the wicked.

17 For **mine eyes** *are* **upon all their ways: they are not hid from my face**, neither is their iniquity hid from mine eyes.

18 **And first** [*before the great latter-day gathering*] **I will recompense** [*punish*] **their iniquity** and their sin double; because they have defiled my land [*polluted it with wickedness*], they have filled mine inheritance with the carcases of their detestable and abominable things [*such as idol worship*].

Next, in verse 19, we see a prophecy that Gentiles from all nations will join the Church also in the last days.

19 O LORD, my strength, and my fortress, and my refuge in the day of affliction, **the Gentiles shall come unto thee from the ends of the earth**, and **shall say, Surely our fathers have inherited lies, vanity, and** *things* **wherein** *there is* **no profit** [*these converts will discard the false traditions and beliefs of their parents and ancestors in order to join the Church*].

Verse 20, next, is yet another reminder that it is completely ridiculous to make idols with one's own hands, and then worship them.

20 **Shall a man make gods unto himself, and they** *are* **no gods?**

The Lord says, in verse 21, next, that through the coming punishments, the wicked will know once and for all that there is just one true God.

21 Therefore, behold, **I will this once cause them to know**, I will cause them to know mine hand and my might; and they shall know **that my name** *is* **The LORD** [*that I am the only true God, in other words, that their idols are not gods*].

JEREMIAH 17

Background

This chapter continues emphasizing the sins that will lead to the destruction of Jerusalem and the cities of Judah as a nation in Jeremiah's day. Among other things, we are shown comparison and contrast between the lives of the wicked and the righteous.

First, in verse 1, we are told that they are hardened sinners, and that the deepest desire of their hearts is to be wicked.

1 **THE sin of Judah** *is* **written with a pen of iron,** *and* **with the point of a diamond** [*the fact that they are deeply wicked is irrefutable*]: *it is* **graven upon the table of their heart** [*the innermost desire of their heart is to be wicked*], and **upon the horns of your altars** [*their religions are dedicated to wickedness, rather than protection and blessings from the Lord*];

> The "horns of the altar," mentioned in verse 1, above, served as a place of protection and refuge for anyone who was being pursued by another. If they could get to the altar, and grab hold of one of the horns built on the four corners of it, they were safe from their enemy (see 1 Kings 1:50).

2 **Whilst their children remember their altars and their groves by the green trees upon the high hills** [*the children have been led astray by their idol-worshiping parents*].

> Verse 3, next, says, in effect, that everything the people of Judah treasure in their wicked hearts will be given to their enemies.

3 **O my mountain in the field, I will give thy substance** *and* **all thy treasures to the spoil** [*to your enemies*], *and* **thy high places for sin, throughout all thy borders.**

4 **And thou, even thyself, shalt discontinue from thine heritage that I gave thee** [*you will be taken from the Holy Land*]; **and I will cause thee to serve thine enemies in the land which thou knowest not**: for ye have kindled a fire in mine anger, *which* shall burn for ever.

5 ¶ Thus saith the LORD; **Cursed** *be* **the man that trusteth in man, and maketh flesh his arm, and whose heart departeth from the LORD.**

6 For **he shall be like the heath** [*juniper tree—see footnote 6a in your Bible*] **in the desert**, and shall not see when good cometh; but **shall inhabit the parched places in the wilderness**, *in* a salt land and not inhabited.

> The "wilderness," spoken of in verse 6, above, is obviously literal, representing their trials in the land of Babylon. But it can also be symbolic of their apostasy, living in a "spiritual wilderness" without the gospel of Jesus Christ.

> Verses 7–8, next, are a beautiful representation of the blessings of living the true gospel, in contrast to the devastations of apostasy depicted above.

7 **Blessed** *is* **the man that trusteth**

in the LORD, and whose hope the LORD **is**.

8 For he shall be as a tree planted by the waters, and *that* **spreadeth out her roots by the river, and shall not see when heat cometh, but her leaf shall be green; and shall not be careful in the year of drought, neither shall cease from yielding fruit**.

Verse 9, next, is a reminder of how devastating a heart that is filled with wicked desires can be. A question is asked and an answer is given.

Question
9 ¶ The heart *is* deceitful above all *things,* and desperately wicked: **who can know it** [*who can tell what is in it*]?

Answer
10 **I the LORD search the heart**, *I* try the reins [*the innermost thoughts and feelings*], even to give every man according to his ways, *and* according to the fruit of his doings.

11 As the partridge sitteth *on eggs,* and hatcheth *them* not; *so* **he that getteth riches, and not by right** [*dishonestly*], shall leave them in the midst of his days, and at **his end shall be a fool**.

Next, Jeremiah praises the Lord.

12 ¶ **A glorious high throne from the beginning** *is* **the place of our sanctuary** [*the Lord is above all*

and is the only safe refuge].

13 O LORD, the hope of Israel, **all that forsake thee shall be ashamed** [*will come up empty; will be disappointed, put to shame*], *and* they that depart from me shall be written in the earth, **because they have forsaken the LORD, the fountain of living waters**.

14 **Heal me, O LORD, and I shall be healed; save me, and I shall be saved: for thou** *art* **my praise**.

In verses 15–18, next, Jeremiah stands firm and faithful before the Lord, and prays for protection from his enemies.

15 ¶ Behold, **they** [*Jeremiah's enemies*] **say unto me, Where** *is* **the word of the LORD** [*where are all the destructions you have prophesied*]? **let it come now**.

16 As for me, **I have not hastened from** *being* **a pastor** to follow thee [*I have been faithful to my calling*]: neither have I desired the woeful day [*the coming destruction*]; **thou knowest: that which came out of my lips was** *right* **before thee**.

17 **Be not a terror unto me: thou** *art* **my hope in the day of evil**.

18 **Let them be confounded that persecute me, but let not me be confounded**: let them be dismayed, but let not me be dismayed: bring upon them the day of evil, and

destroy them with double destruction.

Next, in verses 19–22, we are reminded of the importance of keeping the Sabbath holy.

Major Message
Keep the Sabbath Day holy.

19 ¶ Thus said the LORD unto me; **Go and stand in the gate** [*entrance*] **of the children of the people, whereby the kings of Judah come in, and by the which they go out, and in all the gates of Jerusalem** [*in other words, chose locations where everyone can hear your message*];

20 And say unto them, **Hear ye the word of the LORD**, ye kings of Judah, and all Judah, and **all the inhabitants of Jerusalem**, that enter in by these gates:

21 Thus saith the LORD; Take heed to yourselves, and **bear no burden on the sabbath day**, nor bring *it* in by the gates of Jerusalem;

22 Neither carry forth a burden out of your houses on the sabbath day, **neither do ye any work, but hallow ye the sabbath day**, as I commanded your fathers.

The reaction of the people to Jeremiah's message about the Sabbath is given in verse 23, next.

23 **But they obeyed not**, neither inclined their ear [*wouldn't listen*], but made their neck stiff [*they were full of pride, not humble enough to be taught*], that they might not hear, nor receive instruction.

Verses 24–26 explain the great blessings which could have come to these people, had they listened and repented.

24 And it shall come to pass, **if ye diligently hearken unto me, saith the LORD**, to bring in no burden through the gates of this city on the sabbath day, but **hallow the sabbath day, to do no work therein**;

25 Then shall there enter into the gates of this city kings and princes sitting upon the throne of David, riding in chariots and on horses, they, and their princes, the men of Judah, and the inhabitants of Jerusalem: and **this city shall remain for ever** [*in other words, great prosperity, protection and peace will be yours*].

26 **And they shall come** from the cities of Judah, and from the places about Jerusalem, and from the land of Benjamin, and from the plain, and from the mountains, and from the south, **bringing burnt offerings, and sacrifices, and meat offerings, and incense, and bringing sacrifices of praise, unto the house of the LORD**.

27 **But if ye will not hearken unto me to hallow the sabbath day**, and

not to bear a burden, even entering in at the gates of Jerusalem on the sabbath day; **then will I kindle a fire in the gates thereof, and it shall devour the palaces of Jerusalem, and it shall not be quenched**.

Did you see the message in the above verses about the importance of keeping the Sabbath day holy? Among other things, when individuals and nations keep the Sabbath holy, it serves to remind them of God and the importance of keeping His commandments in their daily living. When people forget the Sabbath, they tend to forget God.

JEREMIAH 18

Background
A problem comes up in this chapter where the King James version (the Bible we use for English-speaking areas of the Church) has the Lord repenting in verses 8 and 10. The Lord does not repent since He does not sin. As you will see, when you come to these two verses, the JST makes corrections in both instances.

This chapter starts out by using the symbolism of a potter creating a pot from clay on a potter's wheel. While the clay is pliable, he can form it according to his plans. He can even start over with the clay, if necessary. This symbolizes what the Lord (the Potter) desires to do with His people (the clay). He desires to mold and shape

them to become His people.

Jeremiah is told to go to the potter's house in his neighborhood where this message and lesson from the Lord can be demonstrated.

1 **THE word which came to Jeremiah from the LORD**, saying,

2 Arise, and **go down to the potter's house, and there I will cause thee to hear my words**.

3 Then I went down to the potter's house, and, behold, he wrought a work on the wheels [*the potter was making a clay pot on a potter's wheel*].

4 And **the vessel that he made of clay was marred** [*damaged; was not shaping according to plan*] in the hand of the potter: **so he made it again** another vessel [*so he started over with it and made another pot with it*], as seemed good to the potter to make *it*.

Next, the Lord explains the symbolism of the potter throwing (making) a pot.

5 **Then the word of the LORD came to me**, saying,

6 O house of Israel [*the twelve tribes of Israel; the Lord's covenant people*], cannot I do with you as this potter? saith the LORD. Behold, **as the clay *is* in the potter's hand,**

so *are* ye in mine hand, O house of Israel.

Next, the Lord explains that He, as the Potter, will do whatever it takes to shape and form His covenant people, even if it means destroying them in order to start over with them. If they will then use their agency to repent (see verse 8), He will be enabled to form them into a covenant people, in other words, a people whom He can bless with exaltation.

7 *At what* instant [*NIV "if at any time"*] I shall speak concerning a nation, and concerning a kingdom, to pluck up, and to pull down, and to destroy *it* [*like a potter as he starts over with a failed pot by kneading it back into lump of clay*];

As mentioned in the Background to this chapter, the idea that the Lord "repents" on occasions is not correct. We will first read verse 8, next, and will then use the JST to correct the translation.

(By the way, someone asked me recently where I get these JST quotes from, since they are not all in the footnotes or in the back of our LDS Bible. The answer is that there is not room in our LDS Bible to include all the JST corrections. You can see all of them in Joseph Smith's "New Translation" of the Bible, published by Herald Publishing House, Independence, Missouri. I use the 1970 edition. Most LDS bookstores have it or can get it for you.)

8 If that nation, against whom I have pronounced, turn from their evil, I will repent of the evil that I thought to do unto them.

JST Jeremiah 18:8
8 If that nation, against whom I have pronounced, turn from their evil, I will withhold the evil that I thought to do unto them.

9 And *at what* instant [*whenever*] I shall speak concerning a nation, and concerning a kingdom, to build and to plant *it;*

10 If it do evil in my sight, that it obey not my voice, then I will repent of the good, wherewith I said I would benefit them.

JST Jeremiah 18:10
10 If it do evil in my sight, that it obey not my voice, then I will withhold the good, wherewith I said I would benefit them.

Next, in verse 11, the Lord instructs Jeremiah to once again invite these wicked people to repent.

<u>Major Message</u>
Even when it may appear that it is far too late to repent, there can still be hope.

11 ¶ Now therefore go to, speak to the men of Judah, and to the inhabitants of Jerusalem, saying, Thus saith the LORD; Behold, I frame evil against you, and devise a device against you [*your*

destruction looms before you]: **return ye now every one from his evil way, and make your ways and your doings good** [*please repent*].

As we look at the phrase "there is no hope" in the context of verse 12, next, we understand that the people are not saying that there is no hope for them. Rather, they are saying, in effect, "Don't get your hopes up. There is no reason for us to repent. We like wickedness and we want to continue the way we are going."

12 And they said, There is no hope: but **we will walk after our own devices, and we will every one do the imagination of his evil heart**.

The basic question in verses 13–14, next, is "Have you ever heard of such a thing as a people leaving a God who has power to bless them?" Even the heathen are wiser than that!

13 Therefore thus saith the LORD; Ask ye now among the heathen, **who hath heard such things: the virgin of Israel** [*Jerusalem*] **hath done a very horrible thing**.

14 Will *a man* leave the snow of Lebanon *which cometh* from the rock of the field? *or* shall the cold flowing waters that come from another place be forsaken?

JST Jeremiah 18:14

14 Will you not leave the snow of the fields of Lebanon; shall not the cold flowing waters that come

from another place from the rock, be forsaken?

It may be that verse 14, above, in the context of verse 13, is saying, in effect, "Would you not be better off not to leave a sure thing, like the God of Israel?"

The Lord goes on to describe the "horrible thing" mentioned in verse 13.

15 Because **my people hath forgotten me**, they have **burned incense to vanity** [*idols*], and **they** [*their false gods and idols*] **have caused them to stumble in their ways** *from* the ancient paths, to walk in paths, *in* a way not cast up [*in a path which has not been graded and maintained*];

16 **To make their land desolate** [*their choices are setting up their land for destruction*], *and* a perpetual hissing; every one that passeth thereby shall be astonished, and wag his head [*there will be much negative and derisive gossip in the future about what happened to Judah and Jerusalem*].

17 **I will scatter them** as with an east wind [*symbolic of rapid and terrible devastation*] before the enemy: I will shew them the back, and not the face [*the Lord will turn His back to them*], in the day of their calamity.

The people don't like what Jeremiah is saying, so they plot to discredit him (verse 18). Verse 23 indicates that they plotted to kill him.

18 ¶ Then said they, **Come, and let us devise devices against Jeremiah**; for the law shall not perish from the priest, nor counsel from the wise, nor the word from the prophet [*the things he is prophesying will not come to pass*]. **Come, and let us smite him with the tongue**, and let us not give heed to any of his words.

Next, Jeremiah petitions the Lord for help and protection against his enemies. He asks that the Lord's punishments be upon them.

19 **Give heed to me**, O LORD, **and hearken to the voice of them that contend with me** [*be sure to hear the threats my enemies are giving out against me*].

20 Shall evil be recompensed for good? for **they have digged a pit for my soul**. Remember that **I stood before thee to speak good for them, *and* to turn away thy wrath from them** [*I have tried to save them*].

Verse 21, next, can serve to remind us of the application of the law of justice. It may also reflect the Lord's law of self-defense, as described in D&C 98.

21 Therefore deliver up their children to the famine, and pour out their *blood* by the force of the sword;

and let their wives be bereaved of their children, and *be* widows; and let their men be put to death; *let* their young men *be* slain by the sword in battle.

22 Let a cry be heard from their houses, when thou shalt bring a troop suddenly upon them: for **they have digged a pit to take me, and hid snares for my feet**.

23 Yet, LORD, **thou knowest all their counsel against me to slay *me:*** forgive not their iniquity, neither blot out their sin from thy sight, but **let them be overthrown before thee; deal *thus* with them in the time of thine anger**.

As mentioned in our note before verse 21, above, D&C 98 may shed some light on verses 21–23, above. Jeremiah's life has been in danger and his enemies have tried to stop him a number of times by now. It may be that the "one, two, three" of D&C 98:23–27 have, in effect, been fulfilled, and he is now seeking to stop them, according to the law of self-defense that the Lord gave to the ancient prophets (D&C 98:32). We will quote some relevant verses from the Doctrine and Covenants, using **bold** for emphasis:

D&C 98:23–35
23 Now, I speak unto you concerning your families—**if men will smite you, or your families, once**, and ye bear it patiently and revile not against them,

neither seek revenge, ye shall be rewarded;

24 But if ye bear it not patiently, it shall be accounted unto you as being meted out as a just measure unto you.

25 And again, if your enemy shall smite you **the second time**, and you revile not against your enemy, and bear it patiently, your reward shall be an hundred fold.

26 And again, if he shall smite you **the third time**, and ye bear it patiently, your reward shall be doubled unto you four–fold;

27 And these three testimonies shall stand against your enemy if he repent not, and shall not be blotted out.

28 And now, verily I say unto you, if that enemy shall escape my vengeance, that he be not brought into judgment before me, then ye shall **see to it that ye warn him in my name**, that he come no more upon you, neither upon your family, even your children's children unto the third and fourth generation.

29 And then, **if he shall come upon you or your children**, or your children's children unto the third and fourth generation, **I have delivered thine enemy into thine hands**;

30 And then if thou wilt spare him, thou shalt be rewarded for thy righteousness; and also thy children and thy children's children unto the third and fourth generation.

31 Nevertheless, thine enemy is in thine hands; and if thou rewardest him according to his works thou art justified; **if he has sought thy life, and thy life is endangered by him, thine enemy is in thine hands and thou art justified**.

32 Behold, **this is the law I gave unto my servant Nephi, and thy fathers, Joseph, and Jacob, and Isaac, and Abraham, and all mine ancient prophets and apostles**.

33 And again, this is the law that I gave unto mine ancients, that they should not go out unto battle against any nation, kindred, tongue, or people, save I, the Lord, commanded them.

34 And if any nation, tongue, or people should proclaim war against them, they should first lift a standard of peace unto that people, nation, or tongue;

35 And **if that people did not accept the offering of peace, neither the second nor the third time, they should bring these testimonies before the Lord**;

JEREMIAH 19

Background

In this chapter, we see that the inhabitants of Jerusalem and the cities of Judah had arrived at the point where they were sacrificing their own children to idols. Such sacrifice is the ultimate blasphemy against the voluntary sacrifice of the Son of God for our sins.

Again, as in the case of the potter and the potter's wheel (chapter 18), Jeremiah is requested by the Lord to go to a certain place to obtain this message. This time, he is asked to pick up a clay jar and go to the "valley of the son of Hinnom" (verse 2), and await the word of the Lord. This valley was just south of Jerusalem and was the site of human sacrifices (see Bible Dictionary under "Topheth.") These sacrifices included their own children (verse 5). The breaking (verse 10) of the clay jar (mentioned in verse 1) is symbolic of the destruction of Jerusalem.

1 THUS saith the LORD, **Go and get a potter's earthen bottle** [*a clay jar*], and *take* of the ancients of the people, and of the ancients of the priests [*take some of the city elders and old priests with you*];

2 And **go forth unto the valley of the son of Hinnom**, which *is* by the entry of the east gate, and proclaim there the words that I shall tell thee,

3 **And say**, Hear ye the word of the LORD, O kings of Judah, and inhabitants of Jerusalem; **Thus saith the LORD** of hosts, the God of Israel; Behold, **I will bring evil upon this place**, the which whosoever heareth, his ears shall tingle [*whoever hears about it will hardly believe their ears*].

4 **Because they have forsaken me, and have estranged this place** [*have desecrated this place; made it no longer a "Holy Land"*], and **have burned incense in it unto other gods** [*worshiped idols*], whom neither they nor their fathers have known, nor the kings of Judah, and **have filled this place with the blood of innocents** [*have offered human sacrifices, including children*];

5 They have built also the high places of Baal [*they have built altars to Baal*], to **burn their sons with fire *for* burnt offerings unto Baal**, which I commanded not, nor spake *it,* neither came *it* into my mind:

Verses 6–9 are yet another prophecy concerning the coming destruction of Jerusalem and the surrounding area.

6 **Therefore** [*because of gross wickedness*], behold, **the days come**, saith the LORD, **that this place shall no more be called** Tophet, nor **The valley of the son of Hinnom, but The valley of slaughter.**

7 And **I will make void the counsel of Judah and Jerusalem in this place** [*they will no longer have political clout*]; and **I will cause**

them to fall by the sword before their enemies, and by the hands of them that seek their lives: **and their carcases will I give to be meat for the fowls of the heaven, and for the beasts of the earth**.

8 And **I will make this city desolate,** and an hissing [*an object of scorn and gossip*]; every one that passeth thereby shall be astonished and hiss [*deride them*] because of all the plagues thereof.

Next, in verse 9, we see a frightful prophecy of cannibalism during the coming siege of Jerusalem.

9 And **I will cause them to eat the flesh of their sons and the flesh of their daughters, and they shall eat every one the flesh of his friend** in the siege and straitness [*dire circumstances*], wherewith their enemies, and they that seek their lives, shall straiten them.

The above prediction of hunger and cannibalism was fulfilled during the siege of Jerusalem by Nebuchadnezzar, king of Babylon. We read of it in Lamentations:

Lamentations 4:8–10
8 Their visage is blacker than a coal; they are not known in the streets: **their skin cleaveth to their bones; it is withered, it is become like a stick**.

9 *They that be* slain with the sword are better than *they that be* **slain with hunger**: for these

pine away, stricken through for *want of* the fruits of the field.

10 The hands of the pitiful **women have sodden** [*boiled, cooked*] **their own children: they were their meat** [*food*] in the destruction of the daughter of my people [*during the destruction of Jerusalem*].

Next, Jeremiah is instructed to break the clay jar (representing the people of Judah) that he was instructed (in verse 1) to take with him to the site of human sacrifices.

10 **Then shalt thou break the bottle** [*symbolic of the "breaking" of Jerusalem and the scattering of the Jews in pieces—see verse 11*] **in the sight of the men** [*the city elders and leaders—see verse 1*] that go with thee,

11 And shalt **say unto them, Thus saith the LORD of hosts; Even so will I break this people and this city, as** *one* **breaketh a potter's vessel**, that cannot be made whole again: and they shall bury *them* in Tophet [*a spot in the Valley of Hinnon—see verse 2*], till *there be* no place to bury [*in other words, there will be a great slaughter of the Jews in that valley*].

12 **Thus will I do unto this place, saith the LORD**, and to the inhabitants thereof, and *even* make this city as Tophet [*a place of great slaughter*]:

There is symbolism in the phrase "make this city as Tophet" in verse 12, above. As noted above, Tophet was a place in the valley, south of Jerusalem, where human sacrifice was practiced, including the sacrifice of children to the fire god Molech. (See Bible Dictionary under "Molech.") Therefore, to make Jerusalem like Tophet means that the wicked will be sacrificed to their wickedness, just like they wickedly sacrificed others to their false gods.

13 And **the houses of Jerusalem**, and the houses [*palaces*] of the kings of Judah, **shall be defiled as the place of Tophet**, because of all the houses upon whose roofs they have burned incense unto all the host of heaven [*all the false gods and idols imaginable*], and have poured out drink offerings unto other gods.

14 **Then came Jeremiah from Tophet**, whither the LORD had sent him to prophesy; **and he stood in the court of the LORD's house** [*the outer courtyard of the Jerusalem Temple*]; **and said to all the people**,

15 Thus saith the LORD of hosts, the God of Israel; **Behold, I will bring** upon this city and upon all her towns **all the evil that I have pronounced** [*prophesied*] against it, **because they have hardened their necks** [*refused to humble themselves*], **that they might not hear my words**.

JEREMIAH 20

Background

In this chapter, Pashur, the senior officer or chief overseer of the temple in Jerusalem, vents his anger against Jeremiah because of the things he is teaching and prophesying about the wickedness of the Jews and their leaders (see, for example, Jeremiah 19:14–15). He beats Jeremiah (verse 2) and has him placed in the stocks.

1 NOW **Pashur** the son of Immer the priest, who *was* also **chief governor in the house of the LORD, heard that Jeremiah prophesied these things**.

2 **Then Pashur smote Jeremiah** the prophet, **and put him in the stocks** that *were* in the high gate of Benjamin, which *was* by the house of the LORD.

We will quote from the *Old Testament Student Manual* for a description of being "put in the stocks." We will add **bold** for emphasis.

"Jeremiah 19:14–15 records Jeremiah's standing in the court of the temple, again reminding the people of the troubles that lay ahead because of their wickedness. When Pashur, the chief overseer of the temple, heard of the incident, he had Jeremiah beaten and placed in stocks. **Stocks were an instrument of torture by which the body was forced into an unnatural** position, much as the wooden stocks of medieval times confined certain parts of the body, such as the arms, legs, or head, by means of wooden beams that locked the parts of the body into place" (*Old Testament Student Manual*, page 245).

In verse 3, next, Jeremiah, under the direction of the Lord, uses the common technique (in their culture) of changing a person's name as a means of confirming a change in status, either good or bad. In this case, it is bad. "Pashur" means "free." But watch what the change of names denotes for Pashur's future, at the end of the verse.

3 And it came to pass **on the morrow** [*the next day*], that **Pashur brought forth Jeremiah out of the stocks**. Then said Jeremiah unto him, **The LORD hath not called thy name Pashur, but Magormissabib** ["terror all around"—see footnote 3a in your Bible].

4 For thus saith the LORD, **Behold, I will make thee a terror to thyself, and to all thy friends**: and **they shall fall by the sword** of their enemies, and **thine eyes shall behold** *it* [*you will see this prophecy fulfilled*]: and **I will give all Judah into the hand of the king of Babylon, and he shall carry them captive into Babylon, and shall slay them with the sword**.

5 **Moreover** [*in addition*] **I will deliver all the strength of this city**, and all the labours thereof, and **all the precious things** thereof, and **all the treasures** of the kings of Judah will I give **into the hand of their enemies**, which shall spoil them, and take them, and carry them to Babylon.

6 **And thou, Pashur, and all that dwell in thine house shall go into captivity**: and thou shalt come **to Babylon, and there thou shalt die**, and shalt be buried there, thou, and all thy friends, to whom thou hast prophesied lies.

The scene in verse 6, above, reminds us of Abinadi in King Noah's court (Mosiah 17:16–18).

The word, "deceived," in verse 7, next, can be a problem. We will read it and then get some help on the matter.

7 ¶ O LORD, thou hast **deceived** me, and I was deceived: thou art stronger than I, and hast prevailed: I am in derision daily, every one mocketh me.

"The great stress the prophetic calling caused Jeremiah is particularly discernible in Jeremiah 20:7–8, 14–18. The **Hebrew word translated in verse 7 as "deceived" means literally "enticed" or "persuaded."** The power that persuaded the prophet to continue to preach God's word at such great personal cost was 'as a burning fire shut up in [his] bones' (verse 9).

It could not be stayed. Verses 14–18 reflect Jeremiah's despair over the lonely ministry he was given" (*Old Testament Student Manual*, page 245).

We will now repeat verse 7, above, and incorporate the helps given in the student manual. We catch a glimpse of Jeremiah's personality.

Jeremiah 20:7 (repeated)

¶ O LORD, thou hast deceived me [*persuaded me to serve as a prophet*], and I was deceived [*and I have been successfully persuaded*]: thou art stronger than I, and hast prevailed [*You win*]: I am in derision daily, every one mocketh me [*this is a most difficult calling*].

8 **For since I spake, I cried out, I cried violence and spoil** [*ever since I began to prophesy, I have had to say much about violence and devastation*]; **because the word of the LORD was made a reproach unto me, and a derision, daily** [*and it has caused me to be mocked and brought much personal pain*].

We continue to see insights into Jeremiah's personality. He is without guile and rather straightforward with the Lord. Next, he confesses that he considered not delivering the messages, but his burning testimony compelled him to be faithful to his calling as a prophet.

9 **Then I said, I will not make**

mention of him, nor speak any more in his name [*I said to myself, "I will not do any more prophesying for the Lord"*]. **But *his word* was in mine heart as a burning fire shut up in my bones, and I was weary with forbearing, and I could not *stay*** [*I just could not hold back any more*].

Jeremiah continues, sharing his frustrations and confirming his absolute commitment to be true to the Lord. According to the first part of verse 10, next, it appears that there were many attempts to discredit Jeremiah through slander against his name. People were constantly watching to catch him in any kind of slip up.

10 ¶ For **I heard the defaming** [*slander*] **of many**, fear on every side [*paranoia everywhere*]. Report, *say they,* and we will report it. **All my familiars** [*close acquaintances*] **watched for my halting** [*watched, hoping to see me slip up*], *saying,* **Peradventure he will be enticed** [*perhaps he will compromise his standards*], **and we shall prevail against him, and we shall take our revenge on him**.

11 But **the LORD *is* with me** as a mighty terrible one [*NIV "like a mighty warrior"*]: **therefore my persecutors shall stumble, and they shall not prevail**: they shall be greatly ashamed [*disgraced*]; for **they shall not prosper**: *their* everlasting confusion shall never be forgotten.

Again, we see Jeremiah plead with the Lord for help against his enemies, much the same as Joseph Smith did as recorded in D&C 121:2–5.

12 But, O LORD of hosts, that triest [*tests*] the righteous, *and* seest the reins and the heart [*and sees the innermost feelings and desires of the heart*], **let me see thy vengeance on them: for unto thee have I opened my cause**.

Next, Jeremiah reaffirms his faith that the Lord has power to deliver him from the wicked.

13 Sing unto the LORD, praise ye the LORD: for **he hath delivered the soul of the poor** [*those in need*] **from the hand of evildoers**.

This seems to be a low point in Jeremiah's life (understatement). We feel his discouragement and frustration in verses 14–18.

14 ¶ **Cursed *be* the day wherein I was born**: let not the day wherein my mother bare me be blessed.

15 **Cursed *be* the man who brought tidings to my father, saying, A man child is born unto thee**; making him very glad.

16 And let that man be as the cities which the LORD overthrew, and repented not: and **let him hear the cry in the morning, and the shouting at noontide** [*in other words, in effect, if the man who told my father*

that I was born could just hear what I hear everyday, he would be sorry he even announced my birth];

17 Because he slew me not from the womb; **or that my mother might have been my grave, and her womb *to be* always great *with me*** [*if I could just not have been born; if my mother could have remained pregnant with me forever*].

18 **Wherefore came I forth out of the womb** [*why did I have to be born*] to see labour and sorrow, that my days should be consumed with shame [*perhaps meaning "that my life should be spent as a social outcast"*]?

JEREMIAH 21

Background

As mentioned in the introduction to the Book of Jeremiah, in this study guide, Jeremiah served during the reigns of five different kings of Judah. The last king was Zedekiah. He was the wicked king who ruled when Lehi and his family left Jerusalem in 600 B.C. (see 1 Nephi 1:4).

In this chapter, wicked King Zedekiah (who was twenty-one years old when he began his reign and reigned for eleven years until the Babylonians took him prisoner) sends a servant to Jeremiah to see what the Lord has to say about the coming Babylonian armies.

1 **THE word** which came unto

Jeremiah **from the LORD, when king Zedekiah sent unto him Pashur** [*not the same man as the "Pashur" in chapter 20, verse 1*] the son of Melchiah, and Zephaniah the son of Maaseiah the priest, **saying,**

2 **Enquire, I pray thee, of the LORD for us; for Nebuchadrezzar king of Babylon maketh war against us**; if so be that the LORD will deal with us according to all his wondrous works, that he may go up from us [*in other words, is there a possibility that the Lord will cause Nebuchadnezzar and his armies to go away without attacking Jerusalem?*].

Perhaps you noticed a technical detail in verse 2, above. We usually refer to this powerful Babylonian king as "Nebuchadnezzar" (see, for example, Daniel 3:1–3), but in verse 2, it is spelled "Nebuchadrezzar" (with an "r" instead of an "n"). The spelling used in verse 2 is a Hebrew variation of the spelling.

Jeremiah's answer to the question of protection from the Lord, for this wicked king and his wicked people, is given in verses 3–14, next.

3 ¶ **Then said Jeremiah unto them** [*the messengers sent by king Zedekiah, of Jerusalem*], Thus shall ye say to Zedekiah:

4 **Thus saith the LORD** God of Israel; Behold, **I will turn back** [*make ineffective*] **the weapons of war that** *are* **in your hands**, wherewith ye fight against the king of Babylon, and *against* the Chaldeans [*another name for the Babylonians, in this context*], which besiege you without [*outside of*] the walls, and I will assemble them into the midst of this city [*I will bring your enemies right into the middle of Jerusalem*].

5 And **I** [*the Lord*] **myself will fight against you** with an outstretched hand and with a strong arm, even in anger, and in fury, and in great wrath.

6 And **I will smite the inhabitants of this city**, both man and beast: they shall die of a great pestilence.

7 And afterward, saith the LORD, **I will deliver Zedekiah king of Judah, and his servants, and the people**, and such as are left in this city from the pestilence, from the sword, and from the famine, **into the hand of Nebuchadrezzar king of Babylon**, and into the hand of their enemies, and into the hand of those that seek their life: and he shall smite them with the edge of the sword; **he shall not spare them, neither have pity, nor have mercy.**

In fulfillment of the above prophecy, King Zedekiah was captured by Nebuchadnezzar's armies, his sons (except for Mulek—see Helaman 6:10) were killed before his eyes, and then his eyes were put out and he was carried as a trophy of war to Babylon (see Jeremiah 52:8–11).

Next, the Lord instructs Jeremiah to tell the inhabitants of Jerusalem how they can avoid being killed by the invading armies.

8 ¶ And **unto this people thou shalt say**, Thus saith the LORD; Behold, **I set before you the way of life, and the way of death** [*you can either live or die in the coming siege*].

9 **He that abideth** [*remains*] **in this city** [*Jerusalem*] **shall die by the sword, and by the famine, and by the pestilence**: but **he that goeth out** [*leaves the city*], **and falleth** [*surrenders*] **to the Chaldeans** [*Babylonian armies*] that besiege you, he **shall live**, and **his life shall be unto him for a prey** [*in other words, you will be taken captive and put in bondage—that's the condition under which you will remain alive*].

10 For **I have set my face against this city for** [*because of their*] **evil**, and not for good, saith the LORD: **it shall be given into the hand of the king of Babylon, and he shall burn it with fire**.

Next, in verses 11–14, the Lord tells the royal family as well as the people that there is one way they can yet be preserved as a nation. It is if they will repent and turn to righteousness.

11 ¶ And **touching** [*concerning*] **the house of the king of Judah** [*the royal family*], *say,* Hear ye the word of the LORD;

12 O house of David, thus saith the LORD; **Execute judgment** [*be fair and righteous*] in the morning, and **deliver** *him that is* **spoiled out of the hand of the oppressor** [*conduct the business of the kingdom with integrity*], lest my fury go out like fire, and burn that none can quench *it,* because of the evil of your doings.

13 **Behold, I** *am* **against thee**, O inhabitant of the valley, *and* rock of the plain, saith the LORD; **which say**, Who shall come down against us [*who can conquer us*]? or who shall enter into our habitations [*what enemies could possibly come into our land*]?

14 But **I will punish you according to the fruit of your doings** [*according to your wicked deeds*], saith the LORD: and **I will kindle a fire in the forest thereof** [*in other words, the Lord will burn their trees; trees are often symbolic of people, in Old Testament symbolism*], and it shall **devour all things round about it**.

JEREMIAH 22

Background
In this chapter, Jeremiah is given yet another uncomfortable task. He is to go to the palace of the king and deliver a prophecy.

Verses 1–9 are a general invitation to the kings of Judah to repent and do right, and a warning about the ultimate consequences of their wickedness if they choose to continue doing evil.

1 THUS saith the LORD; **Go down to the house** [*palace*] **of the king of Judah, and speak there this word**,

2 And say, **Hear the word of the LORD, O king of Judah**, that sittest upon the throne of David [*who occupies the office of king, once held by King David*], **thou, and thy servants, and thy people** that enter in by these gates:

3 Thus saith the LORD; **Execute ye judgment and righteousness** [*be fair and exercise righteousness in your reign as king*], and **deliver the spoiled out of the hand of the oppressor** [*redeem the oppressed*]: and **do no wrong**, do no violence to the stranger [*foreigners*], the fatherless [*orphans*], nor the widow, neither shed innocent blood in this place.

4 For **if ye do this thing** indeed, then shall there enter in by the gates of this house kings sitting upon the throne of David, riding in chariots and on horses, he, and his servants, and his people [*in other words, if you do what is right, the nation of Judah will continue and will thrive*].

5 **But if ye will not** hear these words, I swear by myself, saith the LORD, that **this house shall become a desolation** [*the royal family will be destroyed, along with its subjects*].

For verse 6, next, it is helpful to know that "Gilead" had the richest soil in Israel, and "Lebanon" had the highest mountain and the finest trees in the surrounding area. Remember that trees often represent people in Old Testament symbolism. The message seems to be that Israel was planted in the best gospel soil (the promised land) and its people (the covenant people) were to be the very best "trees." The Lord knows their potential, and the stewardship of the kings of Judah was to foster righteousness and loyalty to God among their citizens.

6 For thus saith the LORD unto the king's house of Judah; **Thou** *art* **Gilead unto me,** *and* **the head of Lebanon** [*you have the potential to be the very best*]: *yet* **surely** [*if you don't repent*] **I will make thee a wilderness** [*I will cut down all your "trees"*]**,** *and* **cities** *which* **are not inhabited**.

7 And **I will prepare destroyers against thee**, every one with his weapons: and they shall cut down thy choice cedars [*your people*], and cast *them* into the fire.

8 And **many nations shall pass by this city** [*travelers from many

nations will see the ruins of Jerusalem], and **they shall say every man to his neighbour**, Wherefore hath the LORD done thus unto this great city [*what did they do to deserve such destruction*]?

9 Then they shall **answer,** Because they have forsaken the covenant of the LORD their God, and worshipped other gods, and served them.

Verses 10–12, next, are a very specific prophecy, directed to Jehoahaz, who succeeded his righteous father, King Josiah. Josiah reigned from about 641 B.C. to 610 B.C., when he died of a wound received in the Battle of Megiddo. His wicked son, Jehoahaz became the next king of Judah, and ruled for just three months. People were mourning King Josiah's death at the time of this prophecy.

10 ¶ **Weep ye not for the dead** [*King Josiah*], neither bemoan him: **but weep sore for him** [*Jehoahaz*] **that goeth away**: for **he shall return no more, nor see his native country**.

After just three months as king, Jehoahaz was captured and taken away to Egypt where he died.

11 For **thus saith the LORD touching Shallum** [*Jehoahaz*] the son of Josiah king of Judah, **which reigned instead of** [*in the place of*] **Josiah his father**, which went

forth out of this place; **He shall not return thither any more** [*will never return to Jerusalem*]:

12 **But he shall die in the place** [*Egypt*] **whither they have led him captive**, and shall see this land no more.

In verses 13–19, next, Jeremiah rebukes Jehoiakim, also a son of righteous King Josiah, for his tyranny and self-centeredness as king. He ruled from about 609 B.C. to 598 B.C.

13 ¶ **Woe unto him** [*Jehoiakim— see verse 18*] **that buildeth his house by unrighteousness,** and his chambers by wrong; *that* **useth his neighbour's service without wages, and giveth him not for his work;**

14 That saith, **I will build me a wide house** [*a large palace*] and large chambers, and cutteth him out windows; and *it is* cieled [*paneled*] with cedar, and painted with vermilion [*bright red to red orange*].

15 Shalt thou reign, because thou closest *thyself* in cedar? **did not thy father** [*righteous King Josiah*] eat and drink, and **do judgment and justice,** *and* then *it was* **well with him?**

16 **He judged the cause of the poor and needy** [*he was a righteous judge over his people*]; then *it was* well *with him*: **was not this to know me** [*isn't this what the gospel*

is all about]? saith the LORD.

17 **But thine eyes and thine heart** *are* **not but for thy covetousness** [*you are self-centered and greedy*], and for **to shed innocent blood** [*you are a murderer*], and for **oppression**, and for **violence**, to do *it*.

18 **Therefore thus saith the LORD concerning Jehoiakim** the son of Josiah king of Judah; **They shall not lament for him**, *saying,* Ah my brother! or, Ah sister! they shall not lament for him, *saying,* Ah lord! or, Ah his glory!

19 **He shall be buried with the burial of an ass** [*a phrase in Jeremiah's day which meant to be dumped in an open field without burial*]**, drawn and cast forth beyond the gates of Jerusalem** [*when he dies his carcass will be treated like that of a dead donkey, dragged outside the city and dumped*].

The Jewish historian, Josephus, recorded that Nebuchadnezzar killed Jehoiakim and commanded that he be thrown out without a burial. (See *Antiquities of the Jews*, 10.6.3.)

Lebanon and Bashan, in verse 20, next, are a prophetic description of the route of the captives of Judah as they were taken to Babylon.

20 ¶ **Go up to Lebanon, and cry**; and **lift up thy voice in Bashan, and cry from the passages** [*as you*

pass through that country]: **for all thy lovers** [*false gods with whom you have committed spiritual adultery*] **are destroyed**.

21 **I spake unto thee in thy prosperity;** *but* **thou saidst, I will not hear** [*I invited you to repent when you were prosperous, but you refused*]. This *hath been* thy manner from thy youth, that thou obeyedst not my voice [*you have been this way for a long time*].

22 **The wind** [*the hot, dry east wind, symbolic of destruction*] **shall eat up all thy pastors** [*your wicked leaders*]**, and thy lovers** [*false gods; also, sexual immorality was rampant among the Jews at this time in their history*] **shall go into captivity**: surely then shalt thou be ashamed and confounded for all thy wickedness.

Verse 23, next, can best be understood if you know that the cedars of Lebanon were often used as symbols of prideful people, in the vocabulary of the day. Here they represent the proud, rebellious leaders of Judah.

23 **O inhabitant of Lebanon** [*Judah's proud, haughty leaders*], that makest thy nest in the cedars [*whose lives are filled with pride*], **how gracious shalt thou be when pangs** [*the pains of Babylonian captivity*] **come upon thee**, the pain as of a woman in travail [*which are as unavoidable now for you as the pains of a woman in labor*]!

Next, Jeremiah turns his attention to Jehoiachin, another wicked king of Judah, whose wicked reign lasted only a few months. He and his mother will be carried captive into Babylon (verses 26–27) and none of his posterity will ever sit on the throne of King David (verses 28–30).

24 *As* I live, saith the LORD, though [*even if*] Coniah [*Jehoiachin*] the son of Jehoiakim king of Judah **were the signet** [*the signet ring*] **upon my right hand**, yet **would I pluck thee thence** [*I would take you off and throw you to Babylon*];

25 And **I will give thee into the hand** of them that seek thy life, and into the hand *of them* whose face thou fearest, even into the hand **of Nebuchadrezzar** [*another spelling of "Nebuchadnezzar"—see Jeremiah 27:8*] **king of Babylon**, and into the hand of the Chaldeans [*the Babylonians*].

26 And **I will cast thee out, and thy mother that bare thee, into another country** [*Babylon*], where ye were not born; and **there shall ye die**.

27 **But to the land whereunto they desire to return** [*Jerusalem and the land of Judah*], **thither** [*there*] **shall they not return**.

Next, as a technique for emphasizing what has already been said, several questions are asked

by Jeremiah about Jehoiachin (Coniah).

28 *Is* **this man Coniah a despised broken idol** [*is he like a despicable broken idol*]? *is he* **a vessel wherein** *is* **no pleasure** [*is he an empty vessel*]? **Wherefore** [*why*] **are they cast out** [*of Jerusalem*], he and his seed [*his posterity*], and are cast **into a land which they know not**?

29 O earth, earth, earth [*everyone listen up*], hear the word of the LORD.

30 Thus saith the LORD, **Write ye this man childless** [*consider this man to be childless, as far as ever having a son who will rule as king in Jerusalem*], a man *that* shall not prosper in his days: for **no man of his seed shall prosper, sitting upon the throne of David**, and ruling any more in Judah.

JEREMIAH 23

Background

For us, probably the most significant thing about this chapter is that it contains a marvelous prophecy of the gathering of Israel in the last days (verses 3–8). We are part of the fulfillment of that prophecy. The most important aspect of the "gathering" for each of God's children is to be converted to the gospel of Jesus Christ, to be baptized, and then to remain faithful to all covenants made in the Church. In other words, the top priority of the "gathering of Israel" is to "gather" each one of us to Christ, if we are willing.

The rest of the chapter lists and describes the terrible sins of the Jewish religious leaders, including false priests and false prophets of Jeremiah's day.

Jeremiah begins with a powerful denunciation of the wicked religious leaders of his day. This rebuke can apply to any, including political leaders, media personalities, and individuals, who lead people away from the Lord at anytime.

1 **WOE be unto the pastors** [*false religious leaders*] **that destroy and scatter the sheep** [*Israel*] of my pasture! saith the LORD.

2 Therefore thus saith the LORD God of Israel against the pastors that feed my people; **Ye have scattered my flock, and driven them away**, and have not visited [*taken good care of*] them: behold, **I will visit upon you the evil of your doings** [*you will be punished for the evil you have done*], saith the LORD.

Next, in verse 3, we see a great prophecy concerning the gathering of Israel in the last days.

3 And **I will gather the remnant of my flock** [*Israel*] **out of all countries whither I have driven them**, and will bring them again to their

folds [*various lands*]; and they shall be fruitful and increase.

4 And **I will set up shepherds** [*righteous religious leaders*] **over them which shall feed them**: and they shall fear no more, nor be dismayed, neither shall they be lacking [*because they will have the true gospel of Jesus Christ*], saith the LORD.

Elder Bruce R. McConkie explained the gathering, spoken of in the above verses. He taught:

"The gathering of Israel consists of receiving the truth, gaining again a true knowledge of the Redeemer, and coming back into the true fold of the Good Shepherd. In the language of the Book of Mormon, it consists of being 'restored to the true church and fold of God,' and then being 'gathered' and 'established' in various 'lands of promise.'" (2 Ne. 9:2; "Come: Let Israel Build Zion," *Ensign*, May 1977, p. 117)

President Spencer W. Kimball also instructed us on this important topic.

"He (the Lord) said through Nephi, 'The house of Israel (sooner or later will) be scattered upon all the face of the earth.' (1 Nephi 22:3) And now He says, 'I will gather the remnant of my flock out of all countries whither I have driven them.' (Jeremiah 23:3)

"The gathering of Israel is now in progress. Hundreds of thousands of people have been baptized into the Church. Millions more will join the Church. And this is the way that we will gather Israel. The English people will gather in England. The Japanese people will gather in the Orient. The Brazilian people will gather in Brazil. So that important element of the world history is already being accomplished.

"It is to be done by missionary work. It is your responsibility to attend to this missionary work." (In Conference Report, Sao Paulo Brazil Area Conference, Feb.–Mar. 1975, p. 73)

Verses 5–6, next, prophesy of the millennial reign of the Savior (see footnote 5d in your Bible).

5 ¶ Behold, the days come, saith the LORD, that I will raise unto David a righteous Branch [*Christ*], and **a King shall reign and prosper** [*Jesus Christ will rule during the Millennium as King of kings and Lord of lords"—see Revelation 117:14*], **and shall execute judgment and justice in the earth**.

6 **In his days Judah shall be saved, and Israel shall dwell safely**: and this *is* his name whereby he shall be called, THE LORD OUR RIGHTEOUSNESS.

Verses 7–8, next, prophesy more about the gathering of Israel

in the last days, leading up to the Millennium. At that time, the much-talked-about event will no longer be the miraculous deliverance of the children of Israel from Egypt. Rather, the "buzz" will be about missionary work and the exciting gathering of Israel in all nations and lands.

7 Therefore, behold, **the days come, saith the LORD, that they shall no more say, The LORD liveth, which brought up the children of Israel out of the land of Egypt;**

8 **But, The LORD liveth**, which brought up and **which led the seed of the house of Israel** [*the descendants of scattered Israel*] out of the north country, and **from all countries whither I had driven them; and they shall dwell in their own land**.

From here to the end of the chapter, the main message is the terrible damage done by dishonest and wicked leaders of false religions among the Jews of Jeremiah's day.

9 ¶ **Mine heart within me is broken because of the** [*false*] **prophets**; all my bones shake; I am like a drunken man, and like a man whom wine hath overcome, because of the LORD, and because of the words of his holiness [*perhaps meaning that Jeremiah is heartbroken and almost out of his mind because of what he knows about the true gospel in contrast to what the false prophets*

among the Jews are teaching].

10 For **the land is full of adulterers**; for because of swearing [*because of the curse of the Lord*] **the land mourneth**; the pleasant places of the wilderness are dried up, and **their course is evil, and their force *is* not right** [*their influence leads people astray*].

11 **For both** [*false*] **prophet and** [*false*] **priest are profane** [*are not religious themselves—see footnote 11c in your Bible*]; yea, **in my house** [*in the temple in Jerusalem*] **have I found their wickedness**, saith the LORD.

12 Wherefore [*therefore*] **their way** [*their evil course in life*] **shall be unto them as slippery *ways*** [*will become treacherous*] in the darkness [*spiritual darkness*]: **they shall be driven on, and fall therein**: for I will bring evil upon them, *even* **the year of their visitation** [*the time when the Lord's punishment catches up with them*], saith the LORD.

By now you are probably quite used to seeing repetition as a means of driving home a particular point or message in Jeremiah's writing. We will see much of this repetition for emphasis in the next several verses.

The reason we bring this up is that occasionally students of the Old Testament will begin to wonder if perhaps they are

missing something as they read such repetitions. They have already caught the message and wonder if maybe the prophet isn't saying something else instead of repeating and they are missing it. They are not.

Verse 13, next appears to refer specifically to the false prophets among the northern ten tribes (who were led away captive by Assyria about 722 B.C.) who led Israel away from the worship of Jehovah into the worship of Baal.

13 And **I have seen folly** [*wickedness*] in **the prophets of Samaria** [*the former capital of the ten tribes (Israel)*]; **they prophesied in Baal, and caused my people Israel to err.**

14 I have seen also in **the** [*false*] **prophets of Jerusalem** an horrible thing: they **commit adultery**, and **walk in lies**: they strengthen also the hands of evildoers [*they support wickedness*], that none doth return from his wickedness: **they are all of them unto me as Sodom, and the inhabitants thereof as Gomorrah** [*they have become just like the residents of Sodom and Gomorrah*].

15 **Therefore thus saith the LORD** of hosts **concerning the** [*false*] **prophets**; Behold, **I will feed them with wormwood** [*a terribly bitter herb—see Bible Dictionary under "Wormwood"*], **and make them drink the water of gall** [*in other*

words, these false prophets will have a bitter fate]: for from the prophets of Jerusalem is profaneness [lack of being truly religious] gone forth into all the land.

Next, we see a warning to avoid heeding the words of false prophets. Remember, "false prophets" can be anyone, including religious leaders, politicians, media personalities, philosophers, atheists, gang leaders, and friends whose influence tends to lead people away from God.

16 Thus saith the LORD of hosts, **Hearken not unto the words of the** [*false*] **prophets that prophesy unto you**: they make you vain [*they make you miss the truth*]: they speak a vision of their own heart [*they teach their own beliefs*], *and* not out of the mouth of the LORD.

17 **They say** still **unto them that despise me**, The LORD hath said, **Ye shall have peace**; and they say unto every one that walketh after the imagination of his own heart, No evil shall come upon you [*in other words, they teach that you can have peace in wickedness*].

18 For **who** [*which of these false prophets*] **hath stood in the counsel of the LORD, and hath perceived and heard his word?** who hath marked his word [*in his heart and daily life*], and heard *it* [*in other words, which of these false prophets and teachers has embraced the true gospel and is attempting to live it*]?

19 Behold, **a whirlwind** of [*destruction from*] the LORD is gone forth in fury, even a grievous whirlwind: it **shall fall grievously upon the head of the wicked**.

20 **The anger of the LORD shall not return** [*turn away*], **until he have executed, and till he have performed the thoughts of his heart** [*until the prophesied destruction takes place*]: in the latter days [*NIV "in days to come"*] ye shall consider [*understand*] it perfectly.

21 **I have not sent these** [*false*] **prophets**, yet they ran [*took over quickly*]: I have not spoken to them, yet they prophesied.

22 But **if they had stood in my counsel** [*if they had understood and followed My counsel*], and had caused my people to hear my words, **then they should have turned them from their evil way**, and from the evil of their doings.

23 *Am* I a God at hand, saith the LORD, and not a God afar off [*perhaps meaning "Am I not a God who knows all things, near and far—see verse 24*]?

24 **Can any hide himself** in secret places **that I shall not see him?** saith the LORD. **Do not I fill heaven and earth?** saith the LORD.

25 **I have heard what the** [*false*] **prophets said, that prophesy lies in my name**, saying, I have

dreamed, I have dreamed [*the false prophets claim to have had dreams from God*].

26 **How long shall *this* be in the heart of the prophets that prophesy lies?** yea, *they are* prophets of the deceit of their own heart [*they teach according to the deceitfulness in their own hearts*];

27 **Which think to cause my people to forget my name** by their dreams which they tell every man to his neighbour, as their fathers [*ancestors*] have forgotten my name for [*because of*] Baal.

28 **The** [*true*] **prophet that hath a dream, let him tell a dream**; and **he** [*true prophets, such as Jeremiah and Lehi*] **that hath my word, let him speak my word faithfully**. What *is* the chaff to the wheat [*what is the word of false prophets compared to the true word of God*]? saith the LORD.

The power of the true word of God to burn out false doctrines and destroy the false philosophies of men is described in verse 29, next. We often see this power of the word described in scriptures as a two-edged sword, able to cut in all directions through falsehood and deception.

29 *Is* **not my word like as a fire?** saith the LORD; and **like a hammer *that* breaketh the rock in pieces?**

30 Therefore, behold, **I *am* against the prophets**, saith the LORD, **that steal my words every one from his neighbour** [*in other words, against the false prophets who borrow lies and falsehoods from one another to teach their followers*].

31 Behold, **I *am* against the** [*false*] **prophets**, saith the LORD, **that use their tongues, and say, He saith** [*who claim to be teaching the will of God*].

32 Behold, **I *am* against them that prophesy false dreams**, saith the LORD, and do tell [*preach*] **them**, and **cause my people to err by their lies**, and **by their lightness** [*failure to take the true words of God seriously*]; yet **I sent them not**, nor commanded them: therefore they shall not profit this people at all, saith the LORD.

The word, "burden," as used in the context of the next verses, basically means "prophesy," especially "message of doom." Thus, the Lord is telling Jeremiah what to say when people sarcastically come up to him and ask him what the next message of doom for them from God is.

33 ¶ And when this people, or the [*false*] prophet, or a [*false*] priest, shall ask thee, saying, **What *is* the burden of the LORD? thou shalt then say** unto them, What burden? **I will even forsake you, saith the LORD.**

34 And *as for* the prophet, and the

priest, and the people, that shall say, The burden of the LORD, **I will even punish that man and his house**.

Next, in verse 35, Jeremiah is instructed to tell the wicked to spread the word that the Lord will forsake them (verse 33) because of their willful failure to repent.

35 **Thus shall ye say every one to his neighbour**, and every one to his brother, What hath the LORD answered [*what was the Lord's answer to our question [verse 33]*]? and, What hath the LORD spoken?

36 **And the burden of the LORD shall ye mention no more: for every man's word shall be his burden** [*you don't need to talk about the fact that the Lord has forsaken you, because you yourselves are your own worst enemies*]; for **ye have perverted** [*twisted and corrupted*] **the words of the living God**, of the LORD of hosts our God.

37 **Thus shalt thou say to the** [*false*] **prophet**, What hath the LORD answered thee? and, **What hath the LORD spoken** [*what has the Lord revealed to you*]?

38 But **since ye say, The burden of the LORD; therefore thus saith the LORD** [*since you claim to speak for the Lord*]; Because ye say this word, The burden of the LORD, and I have sent unto you, saying, **Ye shall not say, The burden of the LORD**;

39 **Therefore**, behold, I, even I, will utterly forget you, and **I will forsake you, and the city** that I gave you and your fathers, *and cast you out of my presence*:

The phrase "I will utterly forget you," in verse 39, above, does not mean that the Lord actually forgets the wicked. Of course, His memory is perfect. It means that He will withdraw His blessings from them and will bring punishments upon them.

40 And **I will bring an everlasting reproach upon you** [*you will be looked down upon by other nations*], and a perpetual shame, which shall not be forgotten.

JEREMIAH 24

Background

Ultimately, as prophesied by Jeremiah, the Jews were taken captive into Babylon (sometimes referred to in these scriptures as "Chaldea"). After about seventy years, a remnant of them was allowed to return to Jerusalem to rebuild it.

In this chapter, Jeremiah has a vision of "two baskets of figs" (verse 1), one good and one bad (verse 2). The good figs represent the remnant of the Jews who will be brought back to Jerusalem by the Lord (verses 5–6) after seventy years.

The bad figs represent wicked King Zedekiah and the evil leaders of the Jews as well as many of their people (verses 8–10).

Jeremiah's vision in verse 1 shows the actual captivity of Jerusalem and the carrying of the captives into Babylon (roughly the location of modern Iraq). This is an interactive vision, where Jeremiah is asked questions and gives answers (starting with verse 3). In a way, it reminds us of Nephi's vision, beginning with 1 Nephi, chapter 11, where he is asked many questions as to what he sees in his vision.

1 **THE LORD shewed me**, and, behold, **two baskets of figs** *were* set before the temple of the LORD, **after** that **Nebuchadrezzar king of Babylon had carried away captive** Jeconiah the son of Jehoiakim king of Judah, and the princes [*leaders*] of Judah, with the carpenters and smiths [*in other words, with the skilled craftsmen*], from Jerusalem, **and had brought them to Babylon**.

2 **One basket** *had* **very good figs**, *even* like the figs *that are* first ripe: **and the other basket** *had* **very naughty figs**, which could not be eaten, they were so bad.

3 Then said the LORD unto me, **What seest thou, Jeremiah?** And I said, Figs; the good figs, very good; and the evil, very evil, that cannot be eaten, they are so evil.

Next, the Lord explains the meaning of the two baskets of figs. One thing we learn from this vision is that there were some good people among the Jews who were taken captive. It was not just the wicked that suffered because of the corrupt leaders who were among the people at this time.

4 ¶ Again **the word of the LORD came unto me, saying,**

5 Thus saith the LORD, the God of Israel; **Like these good figs, so will I acknowledge them that are carried away captive of Judah**, whom I have sent out of this place into the land of the Chaldeans **for** *their* **good**.

6 For I will set mine eyes upon them **for good**, and **I will bring them again to this land** [*Jerusalem and the surrounding territory of Judah*]: **and I will build them** [*they will rebuild Jerusalem and the surrounding country*], and not pull *them* down; and **I will plant them, and not pluck** *them* **up**.

7 And **I will give them an heart to know me, that I** *am* **the LORD**: and **they shall be my people**, and I will be their God: for **they shall return unto me with their whole heart**.

8 ¶ And as **the evil figs**, which cannot be eaten, they are so evil; surely thus saith the LORD, So will I give **Zedekiah the king of Judah, and his princes, and the residue of Jerusalem**, that remain in this land [*who are left behind*], and them that dwell in the land of Egypt:

9 And **I will deliver them to be removed** [*scattered*] **into all the kingdoms of the earth** for *their* hurt, ***to be* a reproach and a proverb, a taunt and a curse** [*to be looked down upon and disparaged*], **in all places whither I shall drive them**.

10 And **I will send the sword**, the **famine**, and the **pestilence**, among them, **till they be consumed from off the land** [*the Holy Land*] that I gave unto them and to their fathers [*ancestors; the children of Israel whom Joshua led into the promised land*].

JEREMIAH 25

Background

In this chapter, we learn that the captives of Judah will serve in Babylon for seventy years (verse 11). At the end of that time, Babylon will be conquered and will serve other kings and nations (verses 12–14). The Lord also has Jeremiah prophesy against all wicked nations, warning them that all who are wicked and do not repent will eventually be punished by the Lord (verses 15–29).

The last part of the chapter "prophetically leaps forward to the time of the battle of Armageddon" in the last days (see *Old Testament Student Manual*, page 246).

In verse 1, Jeremiah identifies the time of this prophecy as about 605

B.C. Be aware that almost all dates given in Old Testament chronology are approximations. Thus, you will see slight variations in dates given for specific events, depending on the sources used.

The first part of this prophecy is directed at the people of Judah.

1 **THE word that came to Jeremiah concerning all the people of Judah in the fourth year of Jehoiakim** [*about 605 B.C.*] **the son** of Josiah king of Judah, that *was* **the first year of Nebuchadrezzar king of Babylon**;

2 The which Jeremiah the prophet spake **unto all the people of Judah, and to all the inhabitants of Jerusalem**, saying,

In verse 3, next, Jeremiah tells us when he was first called to be a prophet. Remember, as stated above, dates vary a bit, depending on the sources. Thus, we often see anywhere from 628 to 626 B.C. given for the beginning of Jeremiah's service as a prophet.

3 **From the thirteenth year of Josiah** [*about 628 B.C.—see chronology chart in Bible Dictionary*] the son of Amon king of Judah, even **unto this day**, that *is* the three and twentieth year [*the twenty-third year that I have been serving as a prophet*], **the word of the LORD hath come unto me, and I have spoken unto you**, rising early and

speaking; **but ye have not hearkened**.

Next, in verse 4, Jeremiah informs us that the Lord sent many prophets to the people of Judah, including Jerusalem, at this time in history. This is confirmed in the Book of Mormon. We read (**bold** added for emphasis):

1 Nephi 1:4
4 For it came to pass in the commencement of the first year of the reign of Zedekiah, king of Judah, (my father, Lehi, having dwelt at Jerusalem in all his days); and **in that same year there came many prophets**, prophesying unto the people that they must repent, or the great city Jerusalem must be destroyed.

Included in these "many prophets" were Jeremiah, Lehi, Nahum, Habakkuk, Zephaniah, and perhaps Ezekiel.

4 And **the LORD hath sent unto you all his servants the prophets**, rising early and sending *them* [*sending them way ahead of your pending destruction*]; **but ye have not hearkened, nor inclined your ear to hear**.

5 **They** [*the true prophets*] **said, Turn ye again now every one from his evil way**, and from the evil of your doings [*in other words, repent*], and dwell in the land that the LORD hath given unto you and to your fathers for ever and ever:

6 And **go not after other gods** to serve them, and to worship them, and provoke me not to anger with the works of your hands [*idols*]; and I will do you no hurt.

7 Yet **ye have not hearkened unto me, saith the LORD**; that ye might provoke me to anger with the works of your hands [*including idols*] to your own hurt [*you are damaging yourselves*].

8 ¶ **Therefore** thus saith the LORD of hosts; **Because ye have not heard my words,**

In verse 9, next, we see an illustration of something Mormon taught. He said:

Mormon 4:5
5 But, behold, the judgments of God will overtake the wicked; and **it is by the wicked that the wicked are punished**; for it is the wicked that stir up the hearts of the children of men unto bloodshed.

This principle applies to Nebuchadnezzar (spelled "Nebuchadrezzar" here), the wicked king whom the Lord uses to punish the wicked people of Judah.

9 Behold, **I will send and take all the families of the north** [*in other words, I will bring hordes of enemies upon you, and they will come in from the north*], saith the LORD, **and Nebuchadrezzar the king of**

Babylon, my servant [*the instrument of destruction which the Lord will use against Judah*], **and will bring them against this land, and against the inhabitants thereof**, and against all these nations round about [*the Babylonians will conquer and devastate many surrounding nations also*], **and will utterly destroy them, and make them an astonishment** [*objects of startled horror*], and an **hissing** [*objects of scorn*], and perpetual **desolations** [*leave in ruins*].

10 **Moreover** [*in addition*] **I will take from them** the voice of **mirth** [*lighthearted pleasantness*], and the voice of **gladness** [*happiness*], the voice of the **bridegroom**, and the voice of the **bride**, the sound of the **millstones** [*grinding grain; in other words, economic well-being*], and the **light of the candle** [*pleasant evenings*].

11 And **this whole land shall be a desolation**, *and* an astonishment; and **these nations shall serve the king of Babylon seventy years**.

Next, Jeremiah tells us what will happen when the seventy years of captivity and servitude are over.

12 ¶ And it shall come to pass, **when seventy years are accomplished** [*are over*], *that* **I will punish the king of Babylon**, **and that nation**, saith the LORD, **for their iniquity** [*for their wickedness*], and the land

of the Chaldeans [*another name for Babylonia, sometimes used to refer to southeastern Babylon, where Abraham came from—see Abraham 1:1*], and will make it perpetual desolations.

Verse 12, above, is rather important because it clears up any confusion about the phrase "the king of Babylon, my servant," reminding us that "servant," in this context, means an instrument used by the Lord to accomplish His purposes.

13 And **I will bring upon that land all my words which I have pronounced against it**, *even* all that is written in this book, **which Jeremiah hath prophesied against all the nations**.

14 For many nations and great kings shall serve themselves of them also: and **I will recompense** [*punish*] **them according to their deeds**, and according to the works of their own hands [*all the wicked will eventually be punished (unless they repent when given ample opportunity to do so)*].

The "cup of fury" is commonly used imagery to represent the anger of the Lord, in other words, the law of justice as it descends upon the unrepentant wicked. We see this imagery next, in verses 15–17, as the Lord tells Jeremiah to give the wicked nations what they have asked for.

15 ¶ For **thus saith the LORD God of Israel unto me** [*Jeremiah*]; **Take the wine cup of this fury at my hand, and cause all the nations, to whom I send thee** [*to whom you are called to prophesy*], **to drink it** [*in effect, "give them the punishments they have asked for from Me and have them drink them in"*].

16 And **they shall drink** [*the Lord's punishments will come upon them*], **and be moved** [*will stagger*], **and be mad** [*will be out of their mind with anguish*], **because of the sword** [*symbolic of destruction*] that I will send among them.

Next, Jeremiah testifies that he has obeyed the Lord and carried out His instructions. He is a witness against the wickedness of the people to whom he preaches.

17 **Then took I the cup at the LORD's hand** [*the cup of fury (the punishments of the Lord upon the wicked)*], **and made all the nations to drink, unto whom the LORD had sent me:**

As indicated in our note at the beginning of verse 18, next, "to wit" means "namely." In other words, Jeremiah is now going to list several of the nations implicated in his prophecy of punishment and destruction. He starts out by naming Jerusalem, and then goes on to name several other nations and peoples who will eventually drink the "fury" of the Lord.

18 *To wit* [*namely—see footnote 18a in your Bible*], **Jerusalem**, and **the cities of Judah**, and **the kings** thereof, and **the princes** [*political and religious leaders*] thereof, to make them a desolation, an astonishment, an hissing, and a curse; as *it is* this day;

As pointed out previously, "princes" is a word that generally means "leaders." You will see this use of the word quite often in your Old Testament study.

19 Pharaoh king of **Egypt**, and his servants, and his princes, and all his people;

20 And all the mingled people, and all the kings of the land of **Uz**, and all the kings of the land of the **Philistines**, and **Ashkelon**, and **Azzah**, and **Ekron**, and the remnant of **Ashdod**,

21 **Edom**, and **Moab**, and the **children of Ammon**,

22 And all the kings of **Tyrus** [*NIV "Tyre"*], and all the kings of **Zidon**, and the kings of the **isles** [*other nations*] **which** *are* **beyond the sea**,

23 **Dedan**, and **Tema**, and **Buz**, and **all** *that are* **in the utmost corners**,

24 And all the kings of **Arabia**, and all the kings of **the mingled people** [*foreigners*] **that dwell in the desert**,

25 And all the kings of **Zimri**, and all the kings of **Elam**, and all the kings of the **Medes**,

26 And **all the kings of the north**, far and near, one with another, and **all the kingdoms of the world**, which *are* **upon the face of the earth**: and the king of **Sheshach** [*NIV "Babylon"—see also Jeremiah 51:41*] shall drink after them [*NIV "will drink it too"*].

No doubt you noticed that Jeremiah did not leave out any of the wicked anywhere. The message is clear: It is impossible for the wicked, who chose not to repent when given ample opportunity to do so, to escape the punishments of God.

Next, the fact that all have agency to choose is emphasized. Just like a person can choose to get drunk and throw up (verse 27), so also can nations and people choose to get drunk, or out of control with wickedness, where they lurch and stagger from one form of evil to another, until they fall and are destroyed.

27 Therefore thou shalt say unto them, Thus saith the LORD of hosts, the God of Israel; **Drink ye, and be drunken** [*symbolic of wickedness; in other words, you have agency to choose to be out of control with wickedness*], and **spue** [*NIV "vomit"*], and **fall,** and **rise no more**, because of the sword [*destruction*] which I will send among you.

Verse 28, next, reminds us that it is impossible for the unrepentant wicked to avoid the law of justice.

28 And it shall be, **if they refuse to take the cup at thine hand to drink** [*if they think they can stop the punishments of* God], then shalt thou **say unto them**, Thus saith the LORD of hosts; **Ye shall certainly drink**.

29 For, lo, **I begin to bring evil on the city which is called by my name** [*I am beginning even now to punish the inhabitants of Jerusalem*], and **should ye be utterly unpunished? Ye shall not be unpunished**: for I will call for a sword upon all the inhabitants of the earth [*none of the wicked anywhere will ultimately escape their punishment*], saith the LORD of hosts.

As mentioned in the background to this chapter in this study guide, the final verses here seem to point to the last days and eventually to the Battle of Armageddon. Evil and wickedness will spread throughout the earth, and nations will gather in a concerted effort against the work of the Lord and His people.

30 **Therefore prophesy thou against them** [*the wicked*] **all these words,** and say unto them, **The LORD shall roar** [*everyone will hear it; "roar" can also symbolize the destructive power of a lion when it falls upon its prey, as*

mentioned in verse 38, below] from on high, and **utter his voice** from his holy habitation; he shall mightily roar upon his habitation; he shall give a shout, as they that tread *the grapes,* **against all the inhabitants of the earth**.

The imagery in the phrase "tread the grapes" in verse 30, above, can symbolize the destruction of the wicked. This symbolism is also used to represent the destruction of the wicked at the time of the Second Coming. The red on the Savior's clothing symbolizes the blood of the wicked as they are destroyed at His coming. We will quote from the Doctrine and Covenants:

D&C 133:48–51
48 And **the Lord shall be red in his apparel**, and his garments **like him that treadeth in the wine-vat**.

49 And so great shall be the glory of his presence that the sun shall hide his face in shame, and the moon shall withhold its light, and the stars shall be hurled from their places.

50 And his voice shall be heard: I have trodden the wine–press alone, and have brought judgment upon all people; and none were with me;

51 And **I have trampled them** *[the wicked]* **in my fury**, and I did tread upon them in mine anger, and **their blood have I sprinkled upon my garments,**

and stained all my raiment *[the blood of the wicked is symbolically spattered upon the Savior's clothing, dying it red]*; for this was the day of vengeance which was in my heart *[this was the execution of the law of justice, which is in His heart as a vital part of the Plan of Salvation]*.

31 **A noise shall come** *even* **to the ends of the earth**; for the LORD hath a controversy with the nations, he will **plead** with all flesh *[in effect, "He will bring all people to His court of law]*; **he will give them** *that are* **wicked to the sword**, saith the LORD.

32 Thus saith the LORD of hosts, Behold, **evil shall go forth from nation to nation**, and a great whirlwind shall be raised up from the coasts of the earth.

33 And **the slain of the LORD** *[the wicked who are destroyed]* **shall be at that day from** *one* **end of the earth even unto the** *other* end of the earth: they shall not be lamented, neither gathered, nor buried; they shall be dung upon the ground.

Next, Jeremiah targets the wicked leaders throughout the earth who lead the people astray.

34 ¶ **Howl, ye shepherds**, and cry; and **wallow yourselves** *in the ashes* *[a sign of great anguish and mourning in the culture of Jeremiah's day]*, ye principal *[leaders]* of the

flock: for **the days of your slaughter and of your dispersions are accomplished** [*the time for you to be punished has arrived*]; and ye shall fall like a pleasant vessel [*you will be shattered like fine pottery*].

35 And **the shepherds shall have no way to flee**, nor the principal of the flock to escape [*there is no escaping the Lord's punishments for you*].

As you have no doubt noticed, Jeremiah is definitely using the technique of repetition for emphasis here.

36 A voice of **the cry of the shepherds** [*the anguish of the evil leaders*], and an **howling of the principal** [*leaders*] of the flock, *shall be heard:* **for the LORD hath spoiled their pasture**.

37 And **the peaceable habitations** [*the pleasant living conditions*] **are cut down because of the fierce anger of the LORD**.

38 **He** [*the Lord*] **hath forsaken his covert, as the lion** [*He has come out of hiding like a lion*]: for **their land is desolate** because of the fierceness of the oppressor, and because of his fierce anger.

JEREMIAH 26

Background

It is helpful to understand that the book of Jeremiah is not all arranged in chronological order. For example,

chapter 25 fits in the fourth year of the reign of King Jehoiakim (see Jeremiah 25:1), whereas chapter 26 fits chronologically in the first year of his reign as king (see verse 1, next).

The JST makes important changes to seven verses in this chapter (verses 3, 5, 6, 13, 18, 19, and 20). We will include the JST text for each of these verses as we go along.

You have seen several prophecies about the destruction of Jerusalem so far in Jeremiah, and this chapter contains that same message. After he delivers this prophecy, Jeremiah will be arrested (verse 8) and tried in court for his life. The scene reminds us of Abinadi the prophet, arrested and tried in wicked King Noah's court because of the things he prophesied against the king and the people (Mosiah 12:9).

1 **IN the beginning of the reign of Jehoiakim** [*about 609 B.C.*] the son of Josiah king of Judah **came this word from the LORD** [*to Jeremiah*], saying,

2 Thus saith the LORD; Stand in the court of the LORD's house [*the outer courtyard of the temple in Jerusalem*], and **speak unto all the cities of Judah**, which come to worship in the LORD's house, **all the words that I command thee to speak unto them; diminish not a word** [*don't leave out a thing*]:

Verse 3, next, contains an invitation to the people to repent. And the JST makes an important correction, showing that it is the people who need to repent, not the Lord.

3 **If so be they will hearken, and turn every man from his evil way** [*if they will repent*], that I may repent me of the evil, which I purpose to do unto them because of the evil of their doings.

JST Jeremiah 26:3
3 If so be they will hearken, and turn every man from his evil way, **and repent, I will turn away the evil** which I purpose to do unto them because of the evil of their doings.

4 And thou shalt say unto them, Thus saith the LORD; **If ye will not hearken to me, to walk in my law**, which I have set before you,

5 **To hearken to the words of my servants the prophets, whom I sent** unto you, both rising up early, and sending *them,* **but ye have not hearkened**;

JST Jeremiah 26:5
5 To hearken to the words of my servants, the prophets, whom I sent unto you, **commanding them to rise up early**, and sending them;

In order to understand the comparison between the temple in Jerusalem and Shiloh, in verse 6, next, it helps to know that Shiloh

(about twenty miles northeast of Jerusalem) was the final resting place for the tabernacle after the children of Israel settled in the promised land. Due to the eventual wickedness of the Israelites, the Lord allowed the Philistines to desecrate the tabernacle and destroy it. So also will the Lord allow the Babylonians to destroy the Jerusalem Temple and ravish Jerusalem.

6 Then will I make this house [*the temple in Jerusalem*] **like Shiloh, and will make this city a curse** to all the nations of the earth.

The JST adds an important phrase to verse 6, above.

JST Jeremiah 26:6
6 Then will I make this house like Shiloh, and will make this city a curse to all the nations of the earth; **for ye have not hearkened unto my servants the prophets**.

7 So the priests and the prophets and all the people heard Jeremiah speaking these words in the house of the LORD.

8 ¶ Now it came to pass, **when Jeremiah had made an end of speaking** all that the LORD had commanded *him* to speak unto all the people, that **the priests and the** [*false*] **prophets and all the people took him** [*arrested him*], **saying, Thou shalt surely die.**

9 **Why hast thou prophesied** in the

name of the LORD, **saying, This house shall be like Shiloh, and this city shall be desolate without an inhabitant?** And all the people were gathered against Jeremiah in the house of the LORD.

Next, beginning with verse 10, we see that a court was convened to try Jeremiah. The trial was held near the temple in a public place where large crowds could watch the proceedings.

10 ¶ **When the princes** [*leaders*] of Judah **heard these things, then they came** up from the king's house unto the house of the LORD, **and sat down in the entry of the new gate of the LORD's** *house*.

11 Then spake the priests and the prophets unto the princes and to all the people, saying, **This man** *is* **worthy to die; for he hath prophesied against this city, as ye have heard with your ears.**

12 ¶ **Then spake Jeremiah** unto all the princes and to all the people, saying, **The LORD sent me to prophesy against this house and against this city all the words that ye have heard**.

13 Therefore now **amend your ways and your doings** [*in other words, repent*], and obey the voice of the LORD your God; and the LORD will repent [*see JST changes, next*] him of the evil that he hath pronounced against you.

JST Jeremiah 26:13

13 Therefore now, amend your ways and your doings, and **obey the voice of the Lord your God, and repent, and the Lord will turn away the evil that he hath pronounced against you**.

14 **As for me**, behold, I *am* in your hand: **do with me as seemeth good and meet** [*appropriate*] **unto** you.

15 **But** know ye for certain, that **if ye put me to death**, ye shall surely bring innocent blood upon yourselves, and upon this city, and upon the inhabitants thereof: for of a truth the LORD hath sent me unto you to speak all these words in your ears [*compare with Abinadi's words in Mosiah 17:9–10*].

Next, we see that controversy arose concerning what to do with Jeremiah.

16 ¶ **Then said the princes and all the people** unto the [*false*] priests and to the [*false*] prophets; **This man** *is* **not worthy to die**: for he hath spoken to us in the name of the LORD our God.

17 Then rose up **certain of the elders** [*older, wiser men*] of the land, and **spake to all the assembly** of the people, saying,

18 **Micah** the Morasthite **prophesied** [*see Micah, chapter 1*] in the days of Hezekiah king of Judah, and spake to all the people of Judah, saying, Thus saith the LORD of

hosts; **Zion shall be plowed** *like* **a field, and Jerusalem shall become heaps**, and the mountain of **the house** [*Temple*] **as** the high places of **a forest**.

JST Jeremiah 26:18

18 Micah the Morasthite prophesied in the days of Hezekiah king of Judah, and spake to all the people of Judah, saying, Thus saith the Lord of hosts; Zion shall be ploughed like a field, and Jerusalem shall become heaps, and the mountain of the house **of the Lord** as the high places of a forest.

19 **Did Hezekiah king of Judah and all Judah put him at all to death** [*did they even come close to putting Micah to death for what he prophesied*]**?** did he not fear the LORD, and besought the LORD, and the LORD repented him of the evil which he had pronounced against them? Thus might we procure great evil against our souls [*we could lose our souls if we execute Jeremiah*].

JST Jeremiah 26:19

19 Did Hezekiah, king of Judah, and all Judah put him at all to death? Did he not fear the Lord and beseech the Lord and repent? **and the Lord turned away the evil** which he had pronounced against them. **Thus by putting Jeremiah to death** we might procure great evil against our souls.

Next, in verses 20–24, we catch a glimpse of how wicked King Jehoiakim was and thus understand that Jeremiah's life was indeed in danger. In these verses, a case from the past is brought up at Jeremiah's trial, detailing what had happened to Urijah, one of the Lord's prophets who had previously prophesied against the King and his wicked people.

20 And **there was also a man** that prophesied in the name of the LORD, **Urijah** the son of Shemaiah of Kirjath-jearim, **who prophesied against this city** and against this land according to all the words of Jeremiah [*just like Jeremiah has done*]:

You will see many changes made here by the Prophet Joseph Smith.

JST Jeremiah 26:20

20 But there was a man among the priests, rose up and said, that, Urijah the son of Shemaiah of Kirjath-jearim, prophesied in the name of the Lord, who also prophesied against this city, and against this land, according to all the words of Jeremiah;

21 **And when Jehoiakim the king, with all his mighty men, and all the princes, heard his words, the king sought to put him to death**: **but** when **Urijah** heard it, he was afraid, and **fled**, and went **into Egypt**;

22 **And Jehoiakim the king sent men into Egypt,** *namely,* Elnathan

the son of Achbor, and *certain* men with him into Egypt.

23 **And they fetched forth Urijah out of Egypt, and brought him unto Jehoiakim the king; who slew him with the sword** [*King Jehoiakim personally killed Urijah*], and cast his dead body into the graves of the common people.

The implication in verse 24, next, is that the officials of the court tried to turn Jeremiah over to the people to take him and kill him. But a man by the name of Ahikam protected him and saved his life. We will probably have to wait until we pass through the veil to get the rest of this story.

24 **Nevertheless** the hand of **Ahikam** the son of Shaphan **was with Jeremiah, that they should not give him into the hand of the people to put him to death**.

JEREMIAH 27

Background
In this chapter, we see clearly that Judah is not the only nation that will be conquered by the coming armies of King Nebuchadnezzar of Babylon. We saw this same basic message in chapter 25.

As the Lord sends Jeremiah to deliver this message, He instructs him to use visual aids to help get the message across.

There appears to be a contradiction within the chapter as to when this prophecy was given. Verse 1 indicates that it came at the beginning of Jehoiakim's reign, but verses 3 and 12 suggest that it was given during King Zedekiah's reign several years later. We will quote from the *Old Testament Student Manual* for some helpful background.

"Ambassadors from several neighboring countries had come to Zedekiah with the proposal that unitedly they could defeat Babylon. **Jeremiah was instructed to take bonds and yokes and wear them to symbolize that it was the Lord's will that they submit to their would-be conquerors**. The message that they not try to change the decrees of God was also given by Jeremiah. Their lands were assigned to Babylon until that country ripened in iniquity and reaped its own reward. A specific promise to Judah was given in verse 11 that submission was their only hope of retaining their lands" (*Old Testament Student Manual*, page 247).

1 IN the beginning of the reign of Jehoiakim the son of Josiah [*should say "Zedekiah the son of Josiah"— see verse 3; also NIV, Jeremiah 27:1; this is probably an error made by a scribe somewhere along the way*] king of Judah came this **word unto Jeremiah from the LORD, saying**,

Can you imagine how unpopular Jeremiah's message of surrender was, which he gives in the next verses? He would be viewed as a coward and as a traitor.

2 Thus saith the LORD to me; **Make thee bonds and yokes, and put them upon thy neck** [*in other words, the Lord says for you to prepare to surrender*],

3 **And send them to the king of Edom**, and to the king of **Moab**, and to the king of the **Ammonites**, and to the king of **Tyrus** [*Tyre*], and to the king of **Zidon**, by the hand of the messengers [*the ambassadors*] which come to Jerusalem unto Zedekiah king of Judah;

4 And **command them to say unto their masters**, **Thus saith the LORD** of hosts, the God of Israel; Thus shall ye say unto your masters;

5 **I have made the earth**, the man and the beast that *are* upon the ground, by my great power and by my outstretched arm, **and have given it unto whom it seemed meet** [*good, appropriate*] unto me.

6 And **now have I given all these lands into the hand of Nebuchadnezzar the king of Babylon**, my servant [*an instrument temporarily in the hands of the Lord through whom to accomplish His purposes*]; and the beasts of the field have I given him also to serve him.

7 **And all** [*these*] **nations shall serve** him, and his son, and his son's son, until the very time of his land [*JST "of their end"*] **come**: and then many nations [*JST "and after that many nations"*] and great kings shall serve themselves of him [*will conquer him and be served by him*].

8 And it shall come to pass, *that* **the nation and kingdom which will not serve** the same **Nebuchadnezzar** the **king of Babylon**, and **that will not put their neck under the yoke of the king of Babylon** [*those who will not surrender to him*], **that nation will I punish**, saith the LORD, with the sword, and with the famine, and with the pestilence, until I have consumed them by his hand.

When we combine verse 9, next, with verse 14, below, we come up with one scriptural definition of the term "false prophets."

9 Therefore **hearken not ye to your** [*false*] **prophets**, nor to your **diviners** [*fortune tellers who predict the future*], nor to your **dreamers**, nor to your **enchanters**, nor to your **sorcerers**, **which speak** unto you, **saying, Ye shall not serve the king of Babylon** [*who prophesy to you, saying that you will not come into bondage to Babylon*]:

10 For they **prophesy a lie unto you**, to remove you far from your land; and that I should drive you out, and ye should perish.

11 **But the nations that bring**

their neck under the yoke of [*voluntarily surrender to*] **the king of Babylon**, and serve him, those **will I let remain still in their own land, saith the LORD; and they shall till it, and dwell therein**.

Next, in verses 12–15, Jeremiah tells us that he personally delivered this message of surrender to King Zedekiah.

12 ¶ **I spake also to Zedekiah** king of Judah according to all these words, **saying, Bring your necks under the yoke of the king of Babylon, and serve him and his people, and live**.

13 **Why will ye die**, thou and thy people, by the sword, by the famine, and by the pestilence, **as the LORD hath spoken against the nation that will not serve the king of Babylon?**

14 Therefore **hearken not unto the words of the** [*false*] **prophets** [*such as those described in verse 9, above*] **that speak** unto you, **saying, Ye shall not serve** [*you will not come into bondage to*] **the king of Babylon**: for they prophesy **a lie** unto you.

15 For **I have not sent them**, saith the LORD [*in other words, they are false prophets*], yet **they prophesy a lie in my name**; that I might drive you out, and that ye might perish, ye, and the prophets that prophesy unto you.

Next, Jeremiah reports that he has also delivered this same message to the false priests and to the people.

16 **Also I spake to the priests and to all this people, saying**, Thus saith the LORD; **Hearken not to the words of your** [*false*] **prophets** that prophesy unto you, saying, Behold, the vessels of the LORD's house shall now shortly be brought again from Babylon: **for they prophesy a lie unto you**.

Apparently, according to verse 16, above, some of the false prophets had told the people that the furnishings and adornments of the temple in Jerusalem would be taken to Babylon but would be returned to Jerusalem shortly thereafter.

17 **Hearken not unto them**; **serve** [*surrender to*] **the king of Babylon, and live**: wherefore should this city be laid waste?

Next, Jeremiah issues a challenge to the people to test their false prophets as to whether or not they are sent from God.

18 But **if they** *be* **prophets**, and if the word of the LORD be with them, **let them now make intercession to the LORD of hosts** [*let them use their influence with the true God*], **that the vessels** [*the treasures*] which are left in the house of the LORD, and *in* the house of the king of Judah, and at

Jerusalem, **go not to Babylon**.

Perhaps you sensed from the above verses that some of the Jews have already been taken to Babylon by this time. This is indeed the case. The conquest came in waves. For example, Daniel was taken to Babylon with many others in about 606 B.C. (see verse 20, below). The temple had not yet been completely looted, as indicated in verses 19–20, next.

19 ¶ For thus saith the LORD of hosts concerning the **pillars** [*of brass—see 2 Kings 25:13*], and concerning the **sea** [*the brass basin*], and concerning the **bases** [*stands*], and concerning the **residue of the vessels** [*furnishings, etc.*] that **remain in this city** [*Jerusalem*],

20 **Which Nebuchadnezzar king of Babylon took not, when he carried away captive Jeconiah** the son of Jehoiakim king of Judah from Jerusalem to Babylon, **and all the nobles of Judah and Jerusalem**;

We get a bit more information about the above-indicated wave of conquest from Daniel, which took place about 606 B.C., including a definition of "the nobles of Judah" (verse 20, above).

Daniel 1:1–6
1 IN the third year of the reign of Jehoiakim king of Judah came Nebuchadnezzar king of Babylon unto Jerusalem, and besieged it.

2 And the Lord gave Jehoiakim king of Judah into his hand, with **part of the vessels of the house of God**: which he carried into the land of Shinar [*Babylon*] to the house of his god; and he brought the vessels into the treasure house of his god.

3 ¶ And the king spake unto Ashpenaz the master of his eunuchs, that he should **bring certain of the children of Israel, and of the king's seed, and of the princes**;

4 Children **in whom *was* no blemish, but well favoured, and skilful in all wisdom, and cunning in knowledge, and understanding science, and such as *had* ability in them** to stand in the king's palace, and **whom they might teach the learning and the tongue of the Chaldeans**.

5 And the king appointed them a daily provision of the king's meat, and of the wine which he drank: so nourishing them three years, that at the end thereof they might stand before the king.

6 Now **among these were** of the children of Judah, **Daniel, Hananiah, Mishael, and Azariah** [*Shadrach, Meshach, and Abednego—see Daniel 3:12*]:

21 Yea, **thus saith the LORD of hosts, the God of Israel, concerning the vessels that remain** *in* the house of the LORD, and *in* the house of the king of Judah and of Jerusalem;

22 **They shall be carried to Babylon, and there shall they be until the day that I visit them** [*bring the Jews back to Jerusalem, in about seventy years*], saith the LORD; then will I bring them up, and restore them to this place [*treasures will be brought back to Jerusalem*].

JEREMIAH 28

Background

In this chapter we see Hananiah, a false prophet, go head-to-head with Jeremiah. It gets rather dramatic as Hananiah breaks the yoke (symbolic of slavery and forced labor— see Jeremiah 27:2) off of Jeremiah's neck and shoulders. In so doing, Hananiah emphasized his prophecy that those of Judah who had already been taken to Babylon would be back within two years, rather than in seventy years, as Jeremiah had prophesied (see Jeremiah 25:11).

Hananiah chooses a very public place to make his claim and challenge Jeremiah (verse 1). Let's see what happens.

1 AND it came to pass the same year, **in the beginning of the reign of Zedekiah** king of Judah, in the fourth year, *and* in the fifth month, *that* **Hananiah** the son of Azur the prophet, which *was* of Gibeon, **spake unto me** [*Jeremiah*] in the house of the LORD, **in the presence of the priests and of all the people**, saying,

2 **Thus speaketh the LORD** of hosts, the God of Israel, saying, **I have broken the yoke of the king of Babylon**.

3 **Within two full years** will I bring again into this place **all the vessels** of the LORD's house, **that Nebuchadnezzar king of Babylon took away from this place**, and carried them to Babylon:

4 And **I will bring again to this place** Jeconiah the son of Jehoiakim king of Judah, **with all the captives of Judah, that went into Babylon**, saith the LORD: for **I will break the yoke** [*power*] **of the king of Babylon**.

Imagine the exited anticipation among the onlookers as Jeremiah responded to Hananiah's challenge.

5 ¶ **Then the prophet Jeremiah said unto the** [*false*] **prophet Hananiah** in the presence of the priests, and in the presence of all the people that stood in the house of the LORD,

6 Even the prophet **Jeremiah said, Amen: the LORD do so: the LORD perform thy words which thou hast prophesied**, to bring again the vessels of the LORD's house, and all that is carried away captive, from Babylon into this place.

Did Jeremiah's response, above, catch you a little off guard? It might appear that he is giving in and agreeing with Hananiah, in front of the crowds of people. But he is not. The following quote helps us understand what is going on:

"In verse 6, **Jeremiah's 'Amen, the Lord do so,' is sarcastic**, a challenge to see whose prophecies would be fulfilled. Moses taught that one test of a true prophet is whether his words come to pass (see Deuteronomy 18:22). Jeremiah had prophesied destruction and captivity; Hananiah, return and restoration. Jeremiah's response was simply that the prophet whose words come to pass is the one chosen by the Lord (see verse 9)" (*Old Testament Student Manual*, page 247).

7 Nevertheless **hear thou now this word that I** [*Jeremiah*] **speak** in thine ears, and in the ears of all the people;

Next, Jeremiah points out that many true prophets of old have prophesied misery and destruction against wicked nations.

8 The **prophets** that have been before me and before thee **of old prophesied both against many countries, and against great kingdoms**, of war, and of evil, and of pestilence.

As mentioned above, the test of a true prophet is whether or not his prophecies come true. Jeremiah points this out, next, in verse 9.

9 The prophet which prophesieth of peace, **when the word of the prophet shall come to pass**, *then* shall the prophet be known, that **the LORD hath truly sent him**.

Not yet satisfied, Hananiah next removes the wooden yoke, which Jeremiah is wearing around his neck (to symbolize the coming Babylonian captivity of the Jews and other nations), and breaks it in front of the crowd.

10 ¶ **Then Hananiah the prophet took the yoke from off the prophet Jeremiah's neck, and brake it.**

11 **And Hananiah spake** in the presence of all the people, saying, **Thus saith the LORD; Even so will I break the yoke of Nebuchadnezzar** king of Babylon from the neck of all nations **within the space of two full years**. And the prophet **Jeremiah went his way.**

12 ¶ **Then the word of the LORD came unto Jeremiah** *the prophet,* after that Hananiah the prophet had broken the yoke from off the neck of the prophet Jeremiah, **saying,**

13 **Go and tell Hananiah**, saying, Thus saith the LORD; **Thou hast broken the yokes of wood; but thou shalt make for them** [*in their place*] **yokes of iron** [*in other words, the yokes of wood will be replaced with yokes of iron*].

14 For **thus saith the LORD** of hosts, the God of Israel; **I have put a yoke of iron** [*symbolizing something they cannot get away from*] **upon the neck of all these nations** [*some of whom are mentioned in Jeremiah 27:3*], **that they may serve Nebuchadnezzar** king of Babylon; **and they shall serve him** [*the emphasis is on "shall" as the Lord bears His own witness that this prophecy will come true*]: and I have given him the beasts of the field also.

15 ¶ **Then said the prophet Jeremiah unto Hananiah** the [*false*] prophet, Hear now, Hananiah; **The LORD hath not sent thee** [*you are not a true prophet*]; but **thou makest this people to trust in a lie**.

16 **Therefore** thus saith the LORD; Behold, I will cast thee from off the face of the earth: **this year thou shalt die**, because thou hast taught rebellion against the LORD.

17 **So Hananiah the [*false*] prophet died the same year in the seventh month**.

JEREMIAH 29

Background
This chapter contains the words of a letter (see verse 1) that Jeremiah sent to the captives who had already been taken to Babylon (see note following Jeremiah 27:18 in this study guide), attempting to counteract the words of false prophets among the Jews there. He tells them not to fight against their captivity, rather to build homes, plant gardens, marry, raise families, support the Babylonians, pray for the Babylonians, and, in short, to prepare for many years in Babylon. The following quote sets the stage for understanding this chapter:

"As in Jerusalem, so too in Babylon the predictions of the false prophets fostered a lively hope that the domination of Nebuchadnezzar would not last long, and that the return of the exiles to their fatherland would soon come about. The spirit of discontent thus excited must have exercised an injurious influence on the fortunes of the captives, and could not fail to frustrate the aim which the chastisement inflicted by God was designed to work out, namely, the moral advancement of the people. Therefore Jeremiah makes use of an opportunity furnished by an embassy (ambassador) sent by King Zedekiah to Babel, to address a letter to the exiles, exhorting them to yield with submission to the lot God had assigned to them. He counsels them to prepare, by establishing their households there, for a long sojourn in Babel (Babylon), and to seek the welfare of that country as the necessary condition of their own. They must not let themselves be deceived by the false prophets' idle promises of a speedy return, since God will not bring them back and fulfil His glorious promises till after seventy years have passed (verses 4–14)" (C. F. Keil and F. Delitzsch, *Commentary on the Old Testament*, 8:1:408–9).

1 NOW **these** *are* **the words of the letter that Jeremiah the prophet sent from Jerusalem** unto the residue of the elders which were carried away captives, and to the priests, and to the prophets, and **to all the people whom Nebuchadnezzar had carried away captive from Jerusalem to Babylon** [*in the first wave or two of captives already taken to Babylon*];

Verse 1, above, will continue after a rather long parentheses (verse 2) and then yet another implied parentheses (verse 3). The last word of verse 3 continues, in effect, the substance of verse 1.

Verse 2, next, points out the common practice of first taking captives who were highly educated and capable of learning new languages and customs, skilled craftsmen, and so forth, in the initial waves of conquering a foreign country. This usually included those of the royal family, leaving a puppet king behind. In other words, they first carried off into captivity those who could make a significant contribution to the Babylonian economy.

2 (After that Jeconiah the king, and the queen, and the eunuchs, the princes of Judah and Jerusalem, and the carpenters, and the smiths, were departed from Jerusalem;)

3 By the hand of Elasah the son of Shaphan, and Gemariah the son of Hilkiah, (whom Zedekiah king of Judah sent unto Babylon to Nebuchadnezzar king of Babylon) **saying,**

4 **Thus saith the LORD** of hosts, the God of Israel, **unto all that are carried away captives**, whom I have caused to be carried away **from Jerusalem unto Babylon;**

5 **Build ye houses** [*prepare for many years (seventy years—see verse 10) in Babylonian captivity*], and dwell *in them;* and **plant gardens**, and eat the fruit of them;

6 **Take ye wives**, and **beget sons and daughters**; and **take wives for your sons**, and **give your daughters to husbands**, that they may bear sons and daughters; **that ye may be increased there** [*in Babylon*], and not diminished [*so that you do not die out as a people in captivity*].

7 And **seek the peace of the city** [*do things that contribute to the well-being of Babylon*] whither I have caused you to be carried away captives, and pray unto the LORD for it: **for in the peace thereof shall ye have peace** [*if the Babylonians have peace, you will have peace*].

Next, Jeremiah warns the captives not to listen to the false doctrines and messages of false prophets among them. By the way, there were also true prophets among the captives, such as Daniel (see Daniel 1:1–6) and Ezekiel (see Ezekiel 1:1–3).

8 ¶ For thus saith the LORD of hosts, the God of Israel; **Let not your** [*false*] **prophets and your diviners** [*soothsayers, fortune tellers, and the like*], **that** *be* **in the midst of you, deceive you,** neither hearken to your dreams which ye cause to be dreamed [*perhaps meaning don't give credibility to dreams which you dream in which you see yourselves free and back in Jerusalem*].

9 **For they** [*the false prophets among you*] **prophesy falsely unto you in my name: I have not sent them,** saith the LORD.

10 ¶ For thus saith the LORD, That **after seventy years** be accomplished **at Babylon I will visit** [*bless you*] **you,** and perform my good word toward you, **in causing you to return to this place** [*Jerusalem*].

Verses 11–14, next, contain very tender and encouraging words of prophecy to the Jews who find themselves in Babylonian captivity at this time. They describe what will happen to the Jews after the seventy years in captivity.

11 For **I know the thoughts that I think toward you,** saith the LORD, **thoughts of peace, and not of evil,** to give you an expected end [*freedom in Jerusalem again*].

12 **Then shall ye call upon me,** and ye shall go and pray unto me, **and I will hearken unto you.**

13 **And ye shall seek me, and find** *me,* **when ye shall search for me with all your heart.**

14 **And I will be found of you** [*and I will be available for you to find*], saith the LORD: and I will turn away your captivity, and **I will gather you** from all the nations, and from all the places whither I have driven you, saith the LORD; and **I will bring you again into the place** [*Jerusalem and Judah*] whence I caused you to be carried away captive.

The prophets referred to in verse 15, next, are false prophets. Jeremiah counsels the captives about such deceivers and warns them not to follow them. Verses 15–19 prophetically inform the captives what is yet to happen to those Jews who are still at home in Jerusalem and Judah.

15 ¶ **Because ye have said** [*claimed*], **The LORD hath raised us up prophets in Babylon** [*who are preaching lies to them, telling them that they will soon rejoin their friends and relatives back in Jerusalem*];

16 *Know* **that thus saith the LORD of** [*concerning*] **the king** that sitteth upon the throne of David [*the puppet king in Jerusalem*], **and of** [*about*] **all the people that dwelleth in this**

city, *and* of [*about*] **your brethren that are not gone forth with you into captivity;**

17 Thus saith the LORD of hosts; Behold, **I will send upon them the sword**, the **famine**, and the **pestilence**, and will make them like vile figs [*that one throws away*], that cannot be eaten, they are so evil.

18 And **I will persecute them with the sword**, with the **famine**, and with the **pestilence**, and will deliver them to be **removed** [*scattered*] **to all the kingdoms of the earth**, to be a curse, and an astonishment, and an hissing, and a reproach [*to be disparaged and spoken of with contempt*], **among all the nations whither I have driven them:**

Verse 19, next, makes it sound like the Lord rises up early (which might falsely imply that, as a glorified, resurrected being, He still needs sleep). The JST straightens this out for us.

19 **Because they have not hearkened to my words**, saith the LORD, which I sent unto them by my servants the prophets, **rising up early and sending** *them;* but ye would not hear, saith the LORD.

JST Jeremiah 29:19
19 Because they have not hearkened to my words, saith the Lord, which I sent unto them by my servants the prophets, **commanding them to rise early,**

and sending them; but ye would not hear, saith the Lord.

Next, Jeremiah warns specifically of two false prophets among the captives, one by the name of Ahab and one by the name of Zedekiah (both in verse 21).

20 ¶ **Hear** ye therefore the word of the LORD, **all ye of the captivity** [*all of you in Babylonian captivity*], whom I have sent from Jerusalem to Babylon:

21 **Thus saith the LORD** of hosts, the God of Israel [*in other words, Jehovah, the premortal Jesus Christ*], **of** [*about*] **Ahab** the son of Kolaiah, **and of** [*about*] **Zedekiah** the son of Maaseiah, **which prophesy a lie unto you in my name**; Behold, **I will deliver them into the hand of Nebuchadrezzar** [*usually spelled "Nebuchadnezzar"*] king of Babylon; and **he shall slay them before your eyes**;

Not only will these two false prophets among the Jews in Babylon be killed by the King of Babylon, but they will become the brunt of a saying which will become a popular way to wish death upon enemies.

22 **And of them** [*from what happens to them*] **shall be taken up a curse** [*a saying*] **by all the captivity of Judah which** *are* **in Babylon** [*among all the captive Jews in Babylon*], saying, **The LORD make thee like Zedekiah and like**

Ahab, whom the king of Babylon roasted in the fire;

23 **Because they** [*Ahab and Zedekiah*] **have committed villany** [*vile deeds—see footnote 23a in your Bible*] in Israel [*among the Lord's people*], and **have committed adultery** with their neighbours' wives, and **have spoken lying words in my name**, which I have not commanded them; even I know, and *am* a witness, saith the LORD.

Beginning with verse 24, next, Jeremiah responds (in his letter) to a man named Shemaiah, a man among the captives in Babylon, who has attempted to stir up trouble for Jeremiah by writing letters against him to people in Jerusalem. One letter, sent to a priest named Zephaniah in Jerusalem (verse 25) asks why he has done nothing to stop Jeremiah from prophesying. Among other things, Shemaiah suggests that Jeremiah be put in prison and in the stocks (verses 26–27).

The Lord has instructed Jeremiah as to what to say to Shemaiah in this letter.

24 ¶ *Thus* **shalt thou also speak to Shemaiah** the Nehelamite, saying,

25 Thus speaketh the LORD of hosts, the God of Israel, saying, **Because thou hast sent letters** in thy name **unto all the people that** *are* **at Jerusalem, and to Zephaniah** the son of Maaseiah **the priest, and to all the priests, saying,**

26 **The LORD hath made thee priest** in the stead of [*in place of*] Jehoiada the priest, **that ye should be officers** in the house of the LORD [*in other words, you are supposed to have authority and be in charge*], **for every man** *that is* **mad, and maketh himself a prophet, that thou shouldest put him in prison, and in the stocks**.

27 Now therefore **why hast thou not reproved Jeremiah** of Anathoth, **which maketh himself a prophet** to you [*who has set himself up as a false prophet*]?

Next, Shemaiah complains to Zephaniah that Jeremiah has prophesied a long period of captivity for the Jews in Babylon, and instructed them to settle down as if permanent there. (This is in stark contrast to the false prophets' prophecies of a brief, no longer than two year period of captivity.)

28 For therefore **he** [*Jeremiah*] **sent unto us** *in* **Babylon, saying, This** *captivity is* **long**: build ye houses, and dwell *in them;* and plant gardens, and eat the fruit of them.

29 And **Zephaniah the priest read this letter in the ears of Jeremiah the prophet**.

30 ¶ **Then came the word of the LORD unto Jeremiah, saying,**

31 **Send to all them of the captivity** [*write to all the Jews in Babylonian captivity*], **saying, Thus saith**

the LORD concerning Shemaiah the Nehelamite; **Because** that **Shemaiah hath prophesied unto you, and I sent him not, and he caused you to trust in a lie** [*his own false prophecies*]:

32 **Therefore** thus saith the LORD; Behold, **I will punish Shemaiah the Nehelamite, and his seed**: he shall not have a man to dwell among this people; neither shall he behold [*live to see*] the good that I will do for my people, saith the LORD; **because he hath taught rebellion against the LORD** [*in other words, none of his posterity will return with the Jews in seventy years (about 537 B.C.—see chronology chart in Bible Dictionary), when Cyrus the Persian decrees that they can return and take the temple treasures back with them to Jerusalem*].

JEREMIAH 30

Background

We will quote from the *Old Testament Student Manual* for background for chapters 30–33.

"The prophet Jeremiah lived through one of the most troubled periods of history in the ancient Near East. He witnessed the fall of a great empire (Assyria) and the rising of another (Babylon). In the midst of this turmoil the kingdom of Judah was ruled by five kings, four of them deplorable. Jeremiah declared God's message for forty years, warning of coming disaster

and appealing in vain to the nation to turn back to God.

"During Manasseh's long reign (687–642 B.C.), which was just before Jeremiah's time, Judah remained Assyria's vassal. This situation brought a resurgence of idolatry, in this case a mixture of belief in the Mesopotamian astrological gods and belief in the Canaanite fertility deities. As has been discussed, a great reformation was conducted by Josiah when the book of the law was discovered in the temple and its contents were made known to the people. Aside from this brief period of reform, Judah became increasingly insensitive to spiritual things during Jeremiah's time.

"The Lord showed Jeremiah a vision of the future that put the calamities he had witnessed into a perspective of hope. Like other prophets of his time (Isaiah, Ezekiel, Hosea, Amos, Micah, and Zechariah), Jeremiah was shown that scattered Israel would one day be gathered, that Judah would return to the lands of her possession, and that eventually all of Israel would become great. These visions and prophecies were recorded by Jeremiah and for centuries have provided hope to a nation of suffering people. They hold a very important place in the latter-day work of restoration" (*Old Testament Student Manual*, page 253).

Remember that "Israel," in an

overall sense, refers to the Lord's covenant people, descendants of Abraham through Jacob (whose name was changed to Israel—see Genesis 32:28). It includes all who will make and keep covenants with the Lord, which will ultimately lead to exaltation in the highest degree of the celestial kingdom.

After Solomon's reign as King of Israel, the kingdom split into two nations, Judah and Israel. The tribes of Judah and Benjamin became known as Judah, and the northern ten tribes became known as Israel. The northern ten tribes became known as the lost ten tribes, after Assyria captured and carried them away, in about 722 B.C. Judah is being carried away into Babylonian captivity in waves, during Jeremiah's lifetime.

One of the great prophecies of the latter days is that Israel will be gathered and that the Lord will once again have a righteous covenant people. Jeremiah prophesied of this great gathering in many places, including these next three chapters.

In verses 1–2, next, Jeremiah is instructed by the Savior to record these prophecies of the future gathering of Judah and Israel.

1 THE word that came to Jeremiah from the LORD, saying,

2 Thus speaketh the LORD God of Israel, saying, **Write thee all the words that I have spoken unto thee in a book**.

3 For, lo, **the days come**, saith the LORD, **that I will bring again** the captivity of [*out of captivity*] **my people Israel and Judah**, saith the LORD: and I will cause them to return **to the land that I gave to their fathers**, and they shall possess it.

We understand verse 3, above, to refer both to the return of the captives after seventy years in Babylon and to the gathering of Israel in the last days (see heading to chapter 30 in your Bible). But the main emphasis in this chapter is on the restoration of the gospel and the gathering of Israel in the last days.

4 ¶ And **these** *are* **the words that the LORD spake concerning Israel and concerning Judah**.

Verses 5–7 seem to set the emotional stage for the latter-day gathering of Israel. They serve as reminders of the extreme agony and distress Israel and Judah have gone through throughout the centuries, because of their rebellion against their God.

5 For thus saith the LORD; **We have heard a voice of trembling, of fear, and not of peace**.

The picture "painted" by Jeremiah's words in verse 6, next, is, in effect, a scene in which strong men are trembling in agony, as if they were in childbirth labor. The message is that Israel and Judah have gone through terrible agony to get their attention and prepare them for redemption.

6 **Ask ye now, and see whether a man doth travail with child** [*have you ever heard of a man having labor pains*]? **Wherefore** [*why then*] **do I see every man with his hands on his loins, as a woman in travail** [*NIV "with his hands on his stomach like a woman in labor"*], **and all faces are turned into paleness?**

7 Alas! for that day *is* great [*the punishments and pains of the past*], so that none *is* like it: it *is* even the time of Jacob's trouble [*Jacob (Israel) has gone through terrible pain*]; **but he shall be saved out of it** [*Israel will be gathered and saved in the last days*].

The major message that now follows is that the gospel of Jesus Christ has power to redeem us out of the worst of conditions and spiritual bondage.

8 For it shall come to pass **in that day** [*in the last days*], saith the LORD of hosts, *that* **I will break his yoke from off thy neck, and will burst thy bonds,** and strangers shall no more serve themselves of him [*Israel will no more be in bondage (including the terrible bondage of sin—see footnote 8a in your Bible)*]:

9 **But they shall serve the LORD their God, and David their king** [*Christ—see heading to this chapter in your Bible*], whom I will raise up unto them.

10 ¶ **Therefore fear thou not**, O my servant Jacob, saith the LORD; neither be dismayed, O Israel: for, lo, **I will save thee** from afar, and thy seed from the land of their captivity; and **Jacob** [*Israel*] **shall return**, and shall be in rest, and be quiet [*live in peace*], and none shall make *him* afraid.

11 **For I** *am* **with thee**, saith the LORD, to save thee: though I make a full end of all nations whither **I have scattered thee, yet will I not make a full end of thee** [*you will not be destroyed completely*]: but I will correct [*discipline*] thee in measure, and will not leave thee altogether unpunished.

Without the help of the JST, verses 12, 13, and 15, next, would be completely negative. Whereas, with the JST, we see that there is still hope for these people.

12 For thus saith the LORD, **Thy bruise** *is* **incurable,** *and* **thy wound** *is* **grievous**.

JST Jeremiah 30:12
12 For thus saith the Lord, **Thy bruise is not incurable, although thy wounds are grievous.**

13 ***There is* none** to plead thy cause, that thou mayest be bound up: **thou hast no healing medicines.**

JST Jeremiah 30:13
13 **Is there none** to plead thy cause, that thou mayest be bound up? **Hast thou no healing medicines?**

14 **All thy lovers** [*false gods, idols*] **have forgotten thee; they seek thee not** [*they are not coming to help you out of trouble*]; for I have wounded thee with the wound of an enemy [*in effect, "I have punished you because you are an enemy of righteousness"*], with the chastisement of a cruel one, for [*because of*] the multitude of thine **iniquity**; *because* thy sins **were** increased [*you just keep getting more wicked*].

JST Jeremiah 30:14
14 **Have all thy lovers forgotten thee, do they not seek thee?** For I have wounded thee with the wound of an enemy, with the chastisement of a cruel one, for the multitude of thine **iniquities**; because thy sins **are** increased.

Next, in verse 15, the Lord again repeats the reason He has had to bring such calamities upon these people.

15 Why criest thou for [*because of*] thine affliction? **thy sorrow *is* incurable** for the multitude of thine iniquity: *because* thy sins **were** increased, I have done these things unto thee.

JST Jeremiah 30:15
15 Why criest thou for thine affliction? **Is thy sorrow incurable?** It was for the multitude of thine iniquities, and because thy sins **are** increased I have done these things unto thee.

16 **Therefore** all they that devour thee shall be devoured [*the wicked who conquer you will themselves be conquered*]; and all thine adversaries, every one of them, shall go into captivity [*for example, the Medes and the Persians eventually conquered the Babylonians*]; and they that spoil thee shall be a spoil [*shall become a prey to their own enemies*], and all that prey upon thee will I give for a prey.

JST Jeremiah 30:16
16 **But** all they that devour thee shall be devoured; and all thine adversaries, every one of them, shall go into captivity; and they that spoil thee shall be a spoil, and all that prey upon thee will I give for a prey.

It is interesting to note that all the foreign kingdoms in ancient times who conquered and persecuted the Jews have ceased to exist, but the Jews themselves still exist as a distinct people today.

Verse 17, next, prophesies that Israel will eventually be restored as the people of the Lord, and that their spiritual wounds will be healed.

17 For **I will restore health unto**

thee, and I will heal thee of thy wounds, saith the LORD; because they called thee an Outcast, *saying,* This *is* Zion, whom no man seeketh after.

In verses 18–22, next, we see a prophecy of the conversion and restoration of Israel in the last days, including the establishment of their own political kingdoms. Remember, "Israel," in this context, is a collective term for all of the Lord's covenant people, including the Jews.

18 ¶ Thus saith the LORD; Behold, **I will bring again** [*restore*] **the captivity of Jacob's tents** [*the things lost during Israel's captivity*], and have mercy on his dwellingplaces; and the city shall be builded upon her own heap [*on the same site*], and the palace shall remain after the manner thereof.

19 And **out of them** [*the devastated cities and ruins*] **shall proceed thanksgiving and the voice of them that make merry**: and I will multiply them, and they shall not be few; **I will also glorify them, and they shall not be small** [*insignificant in world politics and influence*].

20 Their children also shall be as aforetime, and their congregation shall be established before me, and **I will punish all that oppress them**.

21 And **their nobles** [*governors, political leaders*] **shall be of** **themselves, and their governor shall proceed from the midst of them** [*in other words, they will no longer be governed and ruled over by foreigners, rather, will produce their own political leaders*]; and I will cause him to draw near, and **he shall approach unto me**: for who *is* this that engaged his heart to approach unto me? saith the LORD.

22 And **ye shall be my people, and I will be your God**.

Verses 23–24, next, serve as a reminder that the punishments of God will continue to be poured out upon the wicked.

23 Behold, **the whirlwind of the LORD** goeth forth with fury, a continuing whirlwind: it **shall fall with pain upon the head of the wicked**.

24 **The fierce anger of the LORD shall not return** [*will not be pulled back*], until he have done *it,* and until he have performed the intents of his heart: **in the latter days ye shall consider it** [*fully understand it—see footnote 24b in your Bible*].

JEREMIAH 31

Background

This chapter continues with the theme of the gathering and restoration of Israel in the last days—see heading in your Bible.

Remember, the most important eternal aspect of the gathering of Israel is that each of us be gathered spiritually to the gospel of Jesus Christ. The physical gathering of Israel to various places, including stakes of Zion (D&C 109:39) is part of the plan which enables people to be gathered to Christ.

As we study this chapter, we will see the restoration of the gospel in the latter days, the role that Ephraim plays in the latter-day gathering, the renewal of the covenant with Israel, including Judah (verse 31), and the eventual coming of the Millennium (verse 34).

In verse 1, Jeremiah begins with the restoration of the gospel to scattered Israel in the last days.

1 **AT the same time** [*referring to the "latter days," mentioned at the very end of chapter 30*], saith the LORD, **will I be the God of all the families of Israel, and they shall be my people**.

Verse 2, next, speaks of the future as if it has already taken place. This is a common form of prophesying among Old Testament prophets.

2 Thus saith the LORD, **The people which were** left of the sword [*the remnant who survived the destruction and captivity*] **found grace** [*the favor of the Lord*] in the wilderness [*after they had been in apostasy*]; *even* **Israel**, when I went to cause

him to rest [*when I restored the gospel to them*].

3 The LORD hath appeared of old [*in times past*] unto me [*Israel*], *saying,* Yea, I have loved thee with an everlasting love: therefore with lovingkindness have I drawn thee [*nourished and brought you forward*].

4 **Again I will build thee** [*beginning with the Restoration through Joseph Smith*], and **thou shalt be built,** O virgin of Israel [*the Lord's covenant people*]: thou shalt again be adorned with thy tabrets, and shalt go forth in the dances of them that make merry.

5 **Thou shalt yet plant vines upon the mountains of Samaria** [*you will be restored to your lands*]: the planters shall plant, and shall eat *them* as common things.

We will quote from the *Old Testament Student Manual* as background for verses 6–9, next:

"The watchmen mentioned in verse 6 are the righteous prophets of the latter days (see also Ezekiel 3:16–21). In the last dispensation they shall cry to all people to join together in proper worship of the Lord (see D&C 1:1–2). Verse 8 speaks of gathered Israel coming from the north country (see D&C 110:11; 133:26) and from the coasts (ends) of the earth.

"Elder LeGrand Richards said of this gathering: ' "I will bring them . . . a great company shall return thither." This was something the Lord was going to do. Note that Jeremiah does not say that they will return hither, or to the place where this prediction was made, but thither, or to a distant place. He understood that Joseph was to be given a new land in the "utmost bound of the everlasting hills" ' (See Genesis 49:22–26; Deuteronomy 33:13–17.)" (Israel! Do You Know? pp. 177–78).

"Verse 9 refers to Israel returning with weeping. They will weep because they will realize that the sufferings they have endured throughout the centuries came about because they rejected the Lord Jesus Christ, who shall lead them in the last days (see Jeremiah 50:4; Zechariah 12:10)" (Old Testament Student Manual, p. 254–55).

6 For **there shall be a day,** *that* **the watchmen** [*righteous latter-day prophets*] **upon the mount Ephraim shall cry,** Arise ye, and **let us go up to Zion unto the LORD our God**.

7 For thus saith the LORD; Sing with gladness for Jacob [*Israel*], and shout among the chief of the nations: publish ye, praise ye, **and say, O LORD, save thy people, the remnant of Israel**.

8 Behold, **I will bring them from the north country** [*when Israel (the lost ten tribes) were captured in*] *about 722 B.C., the Assyrians took them to the north*], **and gather them from the coasts of the earth,** *and* with them the blind and the lame, the woman with child and her that travaileth with child together: **a great company shall return** thither.

The role of the birthright son in ancient times included the responsibility to take care of the rest of his father's children. We see this role for Ephraim, in verse 9, next.

9 They shall come with weeping, and with supplications will I lead them: I will cause them to walk by the rivers of waters in a straight way, wherein they shall not stumble: for **I am a father to Israel, and Ephraim** *is* **my firstborn** [*has the birthright and thus the first responsibility to shepherd the rest of the tribes to the safety of the gospel*].

The word, "isles," as used in the Old Testament, generally means continents and peoples throughout the earth, other than the Near East.

10 ¶ **Hear the word of the LORD,** O ye nations, and **declare** *it* **in the isles** [*continents*] **afar off** [*preach the gospel throughout the world*], and say, He that scattered Israel will gather him, and keep him, as a shepherd *doth* his flock.

11 For **the LORD hath redeemed Jacob** [*through the Restoration, the Lord will have redeemed Israel*],

and ransomed him from the hand of *him that was* stronger than he [*and rescued him from his enemies*].

Note the beautiful descriptive language of Jeremiah as he describes the blessings of the Restoration and the blessings that come to people who allow the Lord to take care of them

12 Therefore they shall come [*will be gathered*] and **sing** in the height of Zion, and shall **flow together to the goodness of the LORD**, for wheat, and for wine, and for oil, and for the young of the flock and of the herd: **and their soul shall be as a watered garden; and they shall not sorrow any more at all.**

13 **Then shall the virgin** [*the faithful saints of Zion*] **rejoice** in the dance, both young men and old together: **for I will turn their mourning into joy, and will comfort them, and make them rejoice from their sorrow.**

14 **And I will satiate** [*completely satisfy*] **the soul of the priests** [*Church leaders*] **with fatness** [*the very best*], **and my people shall be satisfied** [*filled*] **with my goodness**, saith the LORD.

Next, we see the stage set emotionally for us to truly appreciate what it will mean for Israel to finally be gathered.

15 ¶ Thus saith the LORD; **A voice was heard in Ramah** [*a place*

in southern Israel, associated with Rachel's tomb, where the captives were gathered before being taken to Babylon—see BD, under "Ramah"], **lamentation, *and* bitter weeping; Rahel** [*Rachel, the mother of Joseph, hence the grandmother of Ephraim*] **weeping for her children** refused to be comforted for her children, because they *were* not [*the descendants of Rachel, symbolically representing Israel, were carried away captive, both literally by enemies and figuratively by Satan into spiritual bondage*].

Verses 16–17, next, say, in effect, "Cheer up! Look at the future and see the glorious restoration of the gospel and the gathering of Israel to the Lord in the last days."

16 Thus saith the LORD; **Refrain thy voice from weeping, and thine eyes from tears**: for thy work shall be rewarded, saith the LORD; and **they shall come again from the land of the enemy**.

17 And **there is hope** in thine end, saith the LORD, that **thy children shall come again** to their own border.

Using repetition, Jeremiah again drives home the point that Ephraim (another name for Israel or the northern ten tribes, with headquarters in Samaria before the Assyrians carried them away in 722 B.C.) has mourned his wickedness and apostasy and will repent in the last days.

18 ¶ I [*the Lord*] **have surely heard Ephraim bemoaning himself** *thus;* **Thou hast chastised me**, and I was chastised, as a bullock unaccustomed *to the yoke* [*the "yoke" of bondage settled me down and brought me under control*]: **turn thou me, and I shall be turned** [*please guide me now and I will follow*]; **for thou** *art* **the LORD my God.**

19 Surely after that I was turned, **I repented; and after that I was instructed**, I smote upon *my* thigh [*I mourned because of my past wickedness*]: I was ashamed, yea, even confounded, because I did bear the reproach of my youth [*I had to live with the disgrace of my past wickedness*].

Next, the Lord assures Ephraim (Israel, in this context) that he can indeed repent and be gathered back to the Lord. The Lord will once again take delight in blessing him.

20 *Is* **Ephraim my dear son?** *is* **he a pleasant child** [*can he still be blessed*]? for since I spake against him [*punished him in times past*], **I do earnestly remember him still**: therefore **my bowels** [*My deepest feelings*] **are troubled for him** [*sympathize with him*]; **I will surely have mercy upon him**, saith the LORD.

Next, the Lord encourages Israel to do everything in his power to turn around (from apostasy) and return home to God. Highway

signs are used to symbolize his finding the right direction to return home.

21 Set thee up waymarks [*road-signs*], make thee high heaps [*rocks pointing the direction to return to God*]: **set thine heart toward the highway** [*turn your heart to Me*], *even* the way *which* thou wentest: **turn again** [*turn around from the apostate direction you've been going*], O virgin of Israel, turn again to these thy cities [*return home*].

The "paragraph" mark (backward "P") at the beginning of verse 22 in your Bible (if it is a King James version) signals the change to a new topic. In this case, the Lord, having told them how wonderful it will be for them in the future, now asks Israel how long they are going to continue wandering in sin. Then, speaking of the future again, He tells them that a new experience (for them) will be available at that time, namely, "A woman shall compass a man" (end of verse 22).

22 ¶ **How long wilt thou go about, O thou backsliding** [*apostate*] **daughter?** for the LORD hath created a new thing in the earth, **A woman shall compass a man** [*see note, next*].

The last phrase of verse 22, above, needs explaining. As you know, in the covenant relationship between Israel and the Lord, Israel is often referred to as the "bride" or wife, and the Lord (Jesus

Christ or Jehovah) is referred to symbolically as the "bridegroom" or husband. The tender and intimate relationship between the husband and wife are symbolic of the closeness that should exist between the Lord and His people. We generally think of the Lord nourishing His people, but in the phrase above, the implication is that, in the last days, Israel will nourish the Lord and be tender toward Him. This can remind us that the Savior and our Father in Heaven both have joy when we are righteous.

We will use a quote to further explain this:

"In the verse (Jeremiah 31:22) now before us (the Hebrew word which is translated as 'compass'), signifies to encompass with love and care, to surround lovingly and carefully,—the natural and fitting dealing on the part of the stronger to the weak and those who need assistance. And the new thing that God creates consists in this, that the woman, the weaker nature that needs help, will lovingly and solicitously surround the man, the stronger. Herein is expressed a new relation of Israel to the Lord, a reference to a new covenant which the Lord, ver. 31ff., will conclude with His people, and in which He deals so condescendingly toward them that they can lovingly embrace Him. This is the substance of the Messianic meaning in the words" (Keil and Delitzsch, *Commentary*, 8:2:30).

23 Thus saith the LORD of hosts, the God of Israel; **As yet** [*sometime in the future*] **they shall use this speech** [*phrase; saying*] **in the land of Judah and in the cities thereof**, when I shall bring again their captivity [*NIV "When I bring them back from captivity"*]; **The LORD bless thee, O habitation of justice,** *and* **mountain of holiness** [*in other words, there will be peace and righteousness*] .

24 And there shall dwell in Judah itself, and in all the cities thereof together, husbandmen [*farmers*], and they *that* go forth with flocks.

Again, in verse 25, next, a future time of peace is spoken of prophetically as if it had already come to pass.

25 For I have satiated [*satisfied*] the weary soul, and I have replenished [*renewed*] every sorrowful soul.

26 Upon this I awaked, and beheld; and my sleep was sweet unto me [*this is a sweet dream of the future which will someday be fulfilled*].

In verses 27–28, next, we see yet another form of the prophecy concerning the gathering and restoration of Israel and Judah in the last days.

27 ¶ Behold, **the days come,** saith the LORD, **that I will sow** [*plant*] **the house of Israel and the house of Judah with** the seed of **man, and with** the seed of **beast** [*whereas, in*

the past, Israel and Judah have been killed, reduced in population, and scattered, in the last days they will multiply and prosper].

28 **And it shall come to pass,** *that* **like as I have watched over them, to pluck up,** and to **break down,** and to **throw down,** and to **destroy,** and to **afflict** [*just as I supervised their past punishments*]; **so will I watch over them, to build, and to plant,** saith the LORD.

Verse 29, next, is apparently a Jewish proverb in common use in Jeremiah's day, which says, in effect, that children are negatively affected by the sins of their parents.

29 In those days [*in the last days*] they shall say no more [*the false doctrine will no longer be taught among the Lord's people*], The fathers have eaten a sour grape, and the children's teeth are set on edge [*the children are cursed by the sins of their parents*].

Verse 30, next, says that when the gospel is restored, in the last days, the true doctrine will be taught, namely that we are accountable for our own transgressions, not for the sins of others.

30 But **every one shall die for his own iniquity:** every man that eateth the sour grape, his teeth shall be set on edge.

When you read verse 30, above, did you think of the second Article of Faith? We will quote it here:

Article of Faith 2

2 We believe that men will be punished for their own sins, and not for Adam's transgression.

We learn more about the latter-day gathering of Israel and Judah and the important role of covenants associated with it beginning with verse 31, next.

31 ¶ **Behold, the days come, saith the LORD, that I will make a new covenant with** the house of **Israel, and with** the house of **Judah:**

32 **Not according to** [*not like*] **the covenant that I made with their fathers** [*ancestors—the children of Israel*] **in the day** *that* **I took them by the hand to bring them out of the land of Egypt;** which my covenant they brake, although I was an husband unto them [*even though I took good care of them*], saith the LORD:

The covenant, or law of Moses that the Lord gave the wayward children of Israel, included many laws and details that demanded strict obedience to detail. In verse 33, next, the Lord reveals that in the last days the covenants He will make with His people will require deep conversion and the heartfelt desire to live gospel principles, rather than the step-by-step demands of old.

33 **But this** *shall be* **the covenant that I will make with the house of Israel**; After those days, saith the LORD, **I will put my law in their inward parts, and write it in their hearts**; and will be their God, and they shall be my people.

The peaceful and glorious conditions mentioned in verse 33, above, lead into verse 34, next, which alludes to the Millennium (see footnote 34a in your Bible).

34 And **they shall teach no more every man his neighbour, and every man his brother**, saying, Know the LORD: **for they shall all know me** [*during the Millennium*], from the least of them unto the greatest of them, saith the LORD; for I will forgive their iniquity, and I will remember their sin no more.

Verse 35, next, says, in effect, "Thus saith the Lord, the Creator of heaven and earth."

35 ¶ Thus saith the LORD, which giveth the sun for a light by day, *and* the ordinances [*orbits—see footnote 35c in your Bible*] of the moon and of the stars for a light by night, which divideth the sea when the waves thereof roar; The LORD of hosts *is* his name:

36 **If those ordinances** [*the ordinances contained in the covenant spoken of in verse 33, above*] **depart from before me**, saith the LORD, *then* **the seed of Israel also shall cease from being a nation before me for ever**.

We will quote from the *Old Testament Student Manual* to further explain verse 36, above:

"The Lord, who has worked so long and hard to establish his righteous people, said that if those saving and exalting priesthood ordinances cease to exist, then Israel also will cease to exist—forever. This statement surely indicates the importance of ordinances in the Lord's plan" (*Old Testament Student Manual*, page 256).

37 Thus saith the LORD; **If heaven above can be measured** [*which it cannot be by man*], and the foundations of the earth searched out beneath, **I will also cast off all the seed of Israel** for [*because of*] all that they have done, saith the LORD [*in other words, He will not reject Israel forever but will restore them through the use of covenants in the last days*].

In verses 38–40, next, we see a prophecy that Jerusalem will become an eternal city. It will become one of two cities (Old Jerusalem, in the Holy Land, and New Jerusalem, in Independence, Missouri) during the Millennium that will serve as headquarters for the Savior as He rules and reigns during the one thousand years. You can read a bit about these two cities in Ether 13:3–11.

38 ¶ Behold, **the days come, saith the LORD, that the city** [*Jerusalem*] **shall be built to the LORD** from the tower of Hananeel unto the gate of the corner.

39 And the measuring line shall yet go forth over against it upon the hill Gareb, and shall compass about to Goath.

40 And the whole valley of the dead bodies, and of the ashes, and all the fields unto the brook of Kidron, unto the corner of the horse gate toward the east, *shall be* **holy unto the LORD; it shall not be plucked up, nor thrown down any more for ever**.

JEREMIAH 32

Background

At this point in history, about 588 B.C., wicked King Zedekiah has put Jeremiah in prison. The king is displeased with his prophecies about the impending Babylonian captivity of Jerusalem and the prophecy that the king will also be captured and will be taken to Babylon (verses 2–5). Daniel, along with Shadrach, Meshach, and Abednego (Daniel 3:12) have already been taken captive to Babylon with the first group of Jewish intellectuals and craftsmen in about 606 B.C. Lehi and his family left Jerusalem in 600 B.C. Ezekiel was taken to Babylon with another group of captives in about 598 B.C. He will serve as a prophet to the Jews in captivity

for about twenty-two years, from 592–570 B.C. (see Bible Dictionary under "Ezekiel"). The final wave of Babylonian attacks and resulting captivity will soon take place.

It is the tenth year of the eleven-year reign of Zedekiah (see verse 1 coupled with Jeremiah 52:1), which puts the date of this chapter at about 588 B.C. Zedekiah is now about thirty-one years old, and Jeremiah has been serving as a prophet to the Jews for about thirty years.

As the heading to this chapter in your Bible states, Jeremiah will be instructed by the Lord to purchase some property as a means of symbolizing and prophesying that scattered Israel (including the Jews who are soon to be scattered) will be gathered by the Lord back to their land. The final gathering of Israel in the last days will be accomplished by means of covenants with the Lord, such as baptism and the covenants that follow among the faithful.

In verses 1–5, King Zedekiah has Jeremiah brought to him from prison and asks him why he has been so negative in his prophecies about the king and his kingdom.

1 THE word that came to Jeremiah from the LORD **in the tenth year** [*the tenth year of the reign*] **of Zedekiah** king of Judah, which *was* the eighteenth year of Nebuchadrezzar [*king of Babylon*].

2 For then the king [*Nebuchad-nezzar (another Biblical name for Nebuchadrezzar)*] of Babylon's army besieged Jerusalem: and **Jeremiah** the prophet **was shut up in** the court of the **prison,** which *was* in the king of Judah's house [*this prison was located in the king's palace*].

3 For **Zedekiah** king of Judah **had shut him up** [*put him in prison*], **saying, Wherefore** [*why*] **dost thou prophesy, and say, Thus saith the LORD, Behold, I will give this city** [*Jerusalem*] **into the hand of the king of Babylon**, and he shall take it;

4 **And Zedekiah** king of Judah **shall not escape** out of the hand of the Chaldeans [*another name for Babylonians*], but shall surely be delivered into the hand of the king of Babylon, and shall speak with him mouth to mouth, and his eyes shall behold his eyes;

5 **And he shall lead Zedekiah to Babylon**, and there shall he be until I visit him, saith the LORD: though ye fight with the Chaldeans, ye shall not prosper [*will not win*].

> Next, beginning with verse 6, Jeremiah records that, at this point, the Lord told him to buy some property in Anathoth (Jeremiah's home town, about three miles north of Jerusalem). This purchase was to prophetically symbolize the return of Israel.

6 ¶ **And Jeremiah said, The word of the LORD came unto me, saying,**

7 **Behold, Hanameel** [*Jeremiah's cousin*] the son of Shallum thine uncle **shall come unto thee, saying, Buy thee my field that** *is* **in Ana-thoth**: for the right of redemption *is* thine to buy *it* [*you have the legal right to buy it before anyone else is given the option to purchase it*].

8 **So Hanameel** mine uncle's son **came to me in the court of the prison** according to the word of the LORD, **and said unto me, Buy my field**, I pray thee, that *is* in Ana-thoth, which *is* in the country of Benjamin: **for the right of inheri-tance** *is* **thine, and the redemption** *is* **thine** [*symbolic of the prophetic fact that Israel would someday be redeemed by the Savior*]; buy *it* for thyself. Then I knew that this *was* the word of the LORD.

9 **And I bought the field** of Hana-meel my uncle's son, that *was* in Anathoth, and weighed him the money, *even* seventeen shekels [*NIV about seven ounces*] of silver.

10 **And I subscribed the evidence, and sealed** *it* [*I signed and sealed the deed*], and **took witnesses**, and weighed *him* the money in the bal-ances [*paid the bill*].

11 **So I took the evidence of the purchase**, *both* that which was sealed *according* to the law and custom, and that which was open:

12 **And I gave the evidence of the purchase unto Baruch** [*Jeremiah's personal scribe*] the son of Neriah, the son of Maaseiah, in the sight of Hanameel mine uncle's *son,* and **in the presence of the witnesses** that subscribed the book [*deed—see footnote 12b in your Bible*] of the purchase, **before** [*in the presence of*] **all the Jews that sat in the court of the prison**.

13 ¶ **And I charged Baruch before them, saying,**

14 **Thus saith the LORD** of hosts, the God of Israel; **Take these evidences** [*paper, documents*], this evidence **of the purchase**, both which is sealed, and this evidence which is open; **and put them in an earthen vessel** [*a clay jar*], that they may continue [*be preserved*] many days.

The prophetic symbolism of this transaction is explained in verse 15, next.

15 For thus saith the LORD of hosts, the God of Israel; **Houses and fields and vineyards shall be possessed again in this land** [*Israel, including the Jews, will return to their own lands*].

16 ¶ **Now when I had delivered the evidence of the purchase unto Baruch** the son of Neriah, **I prayed unto the LORD, saying,**

The words of Jeremiah's prayer are given in verses 17–25, next.

17 **Ah Lord GOD!** behold, thou hast made the heaven and the earth by thy great power and stretched out arm, *and* **there is nothing too hard for thee**:

18 **Thou shewest lovingkindness** unto thousands, **and recompensest** the **iniquity** of the fathers into the bosom of their children after them: the Great, the Mighty God, the LORD of hosts, *is* his name,

19 **Great in counsel**, and **mighty in work**: for **thine eyes** *are* **open upon all** the ways of the sons of men: **to give every one according to his ways**, and according to the fruit of his doings [*the law of the harvest*]:

20 Which **hast set signs and wonders in the land of Egypt** [*redeemed Israelites from Egyptian bondage; symbolic of being redeemed from the bondage of sin*], *even* unto this day, and in Israel, and among *other* men; and hast made thee a name, as at this day;

21 And **hast brought forth thy people Israel out of the land of Egypt** with signs, and with wonders [*miracles*], and with a strong hand, and with a stretched out arm, and with great terror;

22 **And hast given them this land** [*Palestine*], which thou didst swear [*covenant, promise*] to their fathers [*ancestors*] to give them, a land flowing with milk and honey [*a land*

of prosperity; symbolic of heaven];

23 **And they came in, and possessed it; but they obeyed not thy voice**, neither walked in thy law; they have done nothing of all that thou commandedst them to do: **therefore thou hast caused all this evil** [*the Babylonian armies*] **to come upon them**:

24 **Behold the mounts** [*the mounds of dirt around Jerusalem, used by the Babylonians in the siege*], **they are come unto the city to take it**; and the city is given into the hand of the Chaldeans [*Babylonians*], that fight against it, because of the sword, and of the famine, and of the pestilence: **and what thou hast spoken** [*the prophecies of Jerusalem's downfall*] **is come to pass**; and, behold, thou seest *it*.

25 **And thou hast said unto me** [*Jeremiah*], O Lord GOD, **Buy thee the field for money, and take witnesses**; for the city is given into the hand of the Chaldeans.

Beginning with verse 26, the Lord answers Jeremiah's prayer.

26 ¶ **Then came the word of the LORD unto Jeremiah, saying**,

27 **Behold, I** *am* **the LORD**, the God of all flesh: **is there any thing too hard for me?**

28 Therefore thus saith the LORD; Behold, **I will give this city** [*Jerusalem*] **into the hand of the Chaldeans**, and into the hand of Nebuchadrezzar king of Babylon, and he shall take it:

29 **And the Chaldeans** [*Babylonians*], **that fight against this city, shall come and set fire on this city**, and burn it with the houses, upon whose roofs they [*the Jews*] have offered incense unto Baal [*idol worship*], and poured out drink offerings unto other gods, to provoke me to anger.

30 **For the children of Israel** [*the northern ten tribes, who were taken captive by Assyria in about 722 B.C.*] **and the children of Judah** [*the Jews*] **have only done evil before me from their youth**: for the children of Israel have only provoked me to anger with the work of their hands [*such as idols*], saith the LORD.

31 **For this city** [*Jerusalem*] **hath been** to me *as* **a provocation of mine anger** and of my fury **from the day that they built it even unto this day**; that I should remove it from before my face,

32 **Because of all the evil of the children of Israel and of the children of Judah**, which they have done to provoke me to anger, they, their kings, their princes, their priests, and their [*false*] prophets, and the men of Judah, and the inhabitants of Jerusalem.

33 And **they have turned unto me**

the back, and not the face [*they have rebelled against the Lord, and gone away from Him*]: though I taught them, rising up early and teaching *them* [*having My prophets teach and warn them constantly*], yet **they have not hearkened to receive instruction**.

34 **But they set their abominations in the house**, which is called by my name, **to defile it** [*they set up idols to worship in the temple in Jerusalem*].

35 **And they built the high places** [*worship sites*] **of Baal**, which *are* in the valley of the son of Hinnom [*south and west of Jerusalem where idol worship included human sacrifices*], **to cause their sons and their daughters to pass through** *the fire* **unto Molech** [*Baal worship included idol worship, sexual immorality, and human sacrifice, including babies*]; which I commanded them not, neither came it into my mind, that they should do this abomination, to cause Judah to sin.

36 ¶ And **now therefore thus saith the LORD, the God of Israel, concerning this city** [*Jerusalem*], **whereof ye say** [*about which Jeremiah has prophesied*], **It shall be delivered into the hand of the king of Babylon** by the sword, and by the famine, and by the pestilence;

Verses 37–41, next, contain the marvelous prophecy of the gathering of Israel in the last days.

37 Behold, **I will gather them out of all countries, whither I have driven them** in mine anger, and in my fury, and in great wrath; and **I will bring them again unto this place, and I will cause them to dwell safely**:

38 **And they shall be my people, and I will be their God**:

39 And **I will give them one heart, and one way** [*they will be united in following the gospel of Jesus Christ*], **that they may fear** [*respect and honor*] **me for ever, for the good of them** [*to their great benefit*], **and of their children after them**:

Next, in verses 40–41, we see the great value of making and keeping covenants with God.

40 And **I will make an everlasting covenant with them**, that I will not turn away from them, to do them good; but I will put my fear in their hearts, **that they shall not depart from me**.

41 Yea, **I will rejoice over them to do them good, and I will plant them in this land assuredly with my whole heart and with my whole soul**.

The return of Israel to the various lands of their inheritance in the last days is symbolic of the return of Israel to the Lord, which, as stated above, is accomplished through making and keeping covenants with Him.

42 For thus saith the LORD; **Like as I have brought all this great evil upon this people, so will I bring upon them all the good that I have promised them**.

The symbolism involved in having Jeremiah purchase land in his hometown is again explained in verses 43–44, next.

43 And **fields shall be bought in this land**, whereof ye say, *It is* desolate without man or beast; it is given into the hand of the Chaldeans.

Next, in verse 44, the Lord again explains the prophetic symbolism of having Jeremiah purchase land, having witnesses and proper documents to close the deal. It is prophesying the fact that the day will come in the future that the Jews will be gathered back to the Holy Land and be again able to buy land.

44 Men shall buy fields for money, and subscribe evidences, and seal *them,* and take witnesses in the land of Benjamin, and in the places about Jerusalem, and in the cities of Judah, and in the cities of the mountains, and in the cities of the valley, and in the cities of the south: **for I will cause their captivity to return** [*in the future, I will cause Israel to be gathered and return*], saith the LORD.

JEREMIAH 33

Background
This chapter continues the prophetic theme of the gathering of Israel, including the Jews, in the last days. The most important aspect of the gathering is the gathering of people to Christ, regardless of what land they live in.

This prophecy was given to Jeremiah while he was in the king's personal prison in the palace.

1 MOREOVER **the word of the LORD came unto Jeremiah the second time, while he was yet shut up in the court of the prison,** saying,

2 **Thus saith the LORD** the maker thereof [*the Creator of the earth*], the LORD that formed it, to establish it; the LORD *is* his name;

3 **Call unto me, and I will answer thee, and shew thee great and mighty things**, which thou knowest not.

4 For thus saith the LORD, the God of Israel, **concerning** the houses of **this city** [*Jerusalem*], **and** concerning **the houses of the kings of Judah**, which are thrown down by the mounts [*the mounds of dirt used in laying siege to a city*], and by the sword;

Next, in verse 5, the Lord tells Jeremiah that any attempts by the Jews to successfully defeat the Babylonian armies who have laid siege to Jerusalem will be unsuccessful because of the wickedness of the people of Judah. In their rebellion against God, they plan to defeat the Babylonians without His help, but in reality, they are coming to fill the trenches dug by the enemy armies around Jerusalem with their own dead bodies.

5 **They** [*the people of Judah and Jerusalem*] **come to fight with the Chaldeans** [*Babylonians*], **but** *it is* **to fill them with the dead bodies of men**, whom I have slain in mine anger and in my fury, and for [*because of*] all whose wickedness I have hid my face from this city.

Next, beginning with verse 6, the Lord speaks of the restoration of the gospel and the gathering of Israel, including the Jews in the last days. You have likely noticed that when Old Testament prophets speak and prophesy, they often jump directly from their day to the future without particularly announcing that they are doing so. We have an example of this in these verses.

6 Behold, **I will bring it health and cure, and I will cure them**, and will reveal unto them the abundance of peace and truth [*found in the true gospel of Jesus Christ*].

7 And **I will cause the captivity of Judah and the captivity of Israel to return** [*I will restore Judah and Israel*], and will build them, as at the first.

8 And **I will cleanse them from all their iniquity**, whereby they have sinned against me; and **I will pardon all their iniquities**, whereby they have sinned, and whereby they have transgressed against me.

9 ¶ **And it** [*Israel, the Lord's covenant people*] **shall be to me a name of joy**, a praise and **an honour before all the nations of the earth, which shall hear all the good that I do unto them**: and they shall fear and tremble [*have respect and admiration for the Lord*] for all the goodness and for all the prosperity that I procure unto it.

10 **Thus saith the LORD; Again there shall be heard in this place, which ye say** [*which Jeremiah has prophesied under the direction of the Lord*] *shall be* **desolate** without man and without beast, *even* in the cities of Judah, and in the streets of Jerusalem, that are desolate, without man, and without inhabitant, and without beast,

11 **The voice of joy, and the voice of gladness**, the voice of the bridegroom, and the voice of the bride, the voice of them that shall say, Praise the LORD of hosts: for the LORD *is* good; for his mercy *endureth* for ever: *and* of them that shall bring the sacrifice of praise into the house of the LORD. **For I will cause to return the captivity of the land, as at the first, saith the LORD.**

12 Thus saith the LORD of hosts; **Again in this place**, which is desolate without man and without beast, and in all the cities thereof, **shall be an habitation of shepherds causing *their* flocks to lie down** [*once again, the Holy Land will be inhabited in righteousness by the Lord's covenant people*].

13 In the cities of the mountains, in the cities of the vale, and in the cities of the south, and **in the land of Benjamin, and in the places about Jerusalem, and in the cities of Judah**, shall the flocks pass again under the hands of him that telleth *them,* saith the LORD.

14 Behold, **the days come**, saith the LORD, **that I will perform that good thing which I have promised unto the house of Israel and to the house of Judah**.

Verses 15–16, next, remind us again that the source of the peace and prosperity spoken of above is the Savior.

15 ¶ **In those days, and at that time, will I cause the Branch of righteousness** [*Jesus Christ—see heading to this chapter in your Bible*] **to grow up unto David**; and **he shall execute judgment and righteousness in the land** [*in the earth—see footnote 15d in your Bible*].

16 **In those days shall Judah be saved, and Jerusalem shall dwell safely**: and this *is the name* wherewith she shall be called, The LORD our righteousness.

We will quote from the *Old Testament Student Manual* for additional clarification of verses 15–16, above:

"'The Branch of righteousness to grow up unto David' who will 'execute judgment and righteousness in the land' (verse 15) is Jesus Christ (see Isaiah 11:1; Jeremiah 23:5–6). When this millennial event occurs, the Jews will dwell safely in Jerusalem.

"The last part of verse 16 is not a particularly good translation since it implies that Jerusalem herself shall be called 'the Lord our righteousness.' According to Adam Clarke it should read: 'And this one who shall call to her is the Lord our Justification,' that is, Jesus Christ himself, the Branch of David (*The Holy Bible . . . with a Commentary and Critical Notes*, 4:344)" (*Old Testament Student Manual*, page 257).

17 ¶ For thus saith the LORD; **David shall never want** [*lack*] **a man to sit upon the throne of the house of Israel** [*when this time comes, there will be no lack of leadership for Israel*];

18 **Neither shall the priests the Levites want** [*lack*] **a man** before me to offer burnt offerings, and to kindle meat offerings, and **to do sacrifice continually** [*there will be no lack of authorized priesthood*

holders to carry on the work of salvation among the covenant people of the Lord].

19 ¶ And the word of the LORD came unto Jeremiah, saying,

Next, in verses 20–22, the Lord says, in effect, that just as sure as day and night come and go, His promise to restore and redeem Israel someday in the future will be fulfilled.

20 Thus saith the LORD; If ye can break my covenant of the day, and my covenant of the night [*if you can stop the coming of day and night*], and that there should not be day and night in their season;

21 *Then* may also my covenant [*given in verses 17–18, above*] be broken with David my servant, that he should not have a son to reign upon his throne; and with the Levites the priests, my ministers.

22 As the host of heaven cannot be numbered, neither the sand of the sea measured: so will I multiply the seed of David [*faithful members of the Lord's covenant people*] my servant, and the Levites that minister unto me [*innumerable hosts of Israel will yet be converted and gathered to the Father through Christ—compare with D&C 76:67*].

23 Moreover [*in addition*] the word of the LORD came to Jeremiah, saying,

24 Considerest thou not [*don't pay any attention to*] what this people [*the apostate Jews*] have spoken, saying, The two families [*Israel and Judah*] which the LORD hath chosen, he hath even cast them off? thus they have despised my people, that they should be no more a nation before them.

In verses 25–26, next, the Lord says, yet again, in effect, that just as sure as He is the Creator, He will keep His promise to restore Israel and Judah when the proper time arrives. He uses the opposite to emphasize the positive.

25 Thus saith the LORD; If my covenant *be* not with day and night, *and if* I have not appointed the ordinances of heaven and earth [*if I have not created the heaven and earth*];

26 Then will I cast away the seed of Jacob [*Israel*], and David [*symbolic of Judah*] my servant, *so that* I will not take *any* of his seed *to be* rulers over the seed of Abraham, Isaac, and Jacob: for I will cause their captivity to return [*I will cause them to return from captivity*], and have mercy on them.

JEREMIAH 34

Background

In this chapter, Jeremiah foretells the captivity of Zedekiah, king of Jerusalem. As you have no doubt noticed thus far in your study of

Jeremiah, the prophecy of the destruction of Jerusalem and the scattering and subsequent gathering of the Jews is often repeated in Jeremiah's writings.

In chapter 32, verses 4–5, we saw the prophecy that Zedekiah would be captured and taken to Babylon. Here, in chapter 34, we see it again. Chapter 52, verses 1–11, will tell of the fulfillment of this prophecy including the fact that Zedekiah was forced to watch as his sons were killed, then his eyes were put out and he was taken prisoner to Babylon.

It is a bit interesting, from an academic standpoint, to note that here in verse 1, "Nebuchadnezzar" is spelled in the way that we normally think of it (not that many people worry a whole lot about how to spell it), rather than "Nebuchadrezzar," as was the case earlier in Jeremiah (example: 24:1).

1 **THE word which came unto Jeremiah from the LORD, when Nebuchadnezzar king of Babylon**, and all his army, and all the kingdoms of the earth of his dominion [*every nation under Nebuchadnezzar's subjection*], and all the people, **fought against Jerusalem, and against all the cities thereof, saying,**

2 Thus saith the LORD, the God of Israel; **Go and speak to Zedekiah king of Judah, and tell him, Thus saith the LORD**; Behold, **I will give this city** [*Jerusalem*] **into the hand of the king of Babylon, and he shall burn it with fire**:

3 **And thou shalt not escape** out of his hand, but shalt surely be taken, and delivered into his hand; and thine eyes shall behold the eyes of the king of Babylon, and he shall speak with thee mouth to mouth, **and thou shalt go to Babylon**.

4 Yet hear the word of the LORD, O Zedekiah king of Judah; Thus saith the LORD of thee, **Thou shalt not die by the sword**:

5 *But* **thou shalt die in peace: and with the burnings of thy fathers** [*people will light funeral fires in honor of you, like they did for previous kings of Judah*], the former kings which were before thee, so shall they burn *odours* for thee; **and they will lament thee**, *saying,* Ah lord [*in effect, hail to the king*]! for I have pronounced the word [*I, the Lord, have said it*], saith the LORD.

6 **Then Jeremiah the prophet spake all these words unto Zedekiah** king of Judah in Jerusalem,

7 **When the king of Babylon's army fought against Jerusalem, and against all the cities of Judah that were left**, against Lachish, and against Azekah: for these defenced cities remained of the cities of Judah.

The deceptiveness and dishonesty of King Zedekiah and his corrupt people is illustrated in verses 8–11, next. It is helpful to remember that the possession of slaves, including servants who had been put in bondage for a period of time to pay off personal or family debts, was a common part of the culture in this society at the time.

It appears that Zedekiah, for whatever reason, had proclaimed that all Hebrews who were in bondage to other Hebrews should be set free. After the people had carried out the king's orders, they simply turned around and put the freed Jews back into bondage.

8 ¶ *This is* the word that came unto Jeremiah from the LORD, after that the king Zedekiah had made a covenant with all the people which *were* at Jerusalem, to proclaim liberty unto them;

9 That every man should let his manservant, and every man his maidservant, *being* an Hebrew or an Hebrewess, go free; that none should serve himself of them, *to wit* [*namely; for example*], of a Jew his brother.

10 Now when all the princes, and all the people, which had entered into the covenant, heard that every one should let his manservant, and every one his maidservant, go free, that none should serve themselves of them any more, then they obeyed, and let *them* go.

11 But afterward they turned, and caused the servants and the handmaids, whom they had let go free, to return, and brought them into subjection for servants and for handmaids.

Next, Jeremiah is told by the Lord to tell these Jews that they are hypocrites.

12 ¶ Therefore the word of the LORD came to Jeremiah from the LORD, saying,

13 Thus saith the LORD, the God of Israel; I made a covenant with your fathers in the day that I brought them forth out of the land of Egypt, out of the house of bondmen [*when I set them free from Egyptian bondage*], saying,

14 At the end of seven years let ye go every man his brother an Hebrew, which hath been sold unto thee; and when he hath served thee six years, thou shalt let him go free from thee: but your fathers [*ancestors*] hearkened not unto me, neither inclined their ear [*refused to listen to Me*].

15 And ye were now turned [*had reversed your position on holding slaves*], and had done right in my sight, in proclaiming liberty every man to his neighbour; and ye had made a covenant before me in the house which is called by my name [*in the temple at Jerusalem*]:

16 **But ye turned and polluted my name** [*violated your covenant*], and caused every man his servant, and every man his handmaid, whom ye had set at liberty at their pleasure, to return, **and brought them into subjection**, to be unto you for servants and for handmaids.

Verse 17, next, contains a very impactful message.

<u>Major Message</u>
When we set ourselves "free" from covenants we have made with the Lord, He is obligated by the law of justice to set us "free" from His blessings and protection.

17 **Therefore** thus saith the LORD; **Ye have not hearkened unto** [*obeyed*] **me**, in proclaiming liberty, every one to his brother, and every man to his neighbour: **behold, I proclaim a liberty for you**, saith the LORD, **to the sword**, to the **pestilence**, and to the **famine**; and I will make you to be **removed** [*scattered*] **into all the kingdoms of the earth**.

18 **And I will give the men that have transgressed my covenant**, which have not performed the words of the covenant which they had made before me, when they cut the calf in twain, and passed between the parts thereof [*a reference to a type of ritual associated with making covenants in the culture of the Jews at the time—compare with Genesis 15:8–10, 17*],

19 The princes of Judah, and the princes of Jerusalem, the eunuchs, and the priests, and all the people of the land, which passed between the parts of the calf [*who made a covenant and did not keep it—see note at end of verse 18, above*];

20 **I will even give them into the hand of their enemies**, and into the hand of them that seek their life: and their dead bodies shall be for meat [*food*] unto the fowls of the heaven, and to the beasts of the earth.

21 **And Zedekiah king of Judah and his princes will I give into the hand of their enemies**, and into the hand of them that seek their life, and into the hand of **the king of Babylon's army**, which are gone up from you [*who have temporarily gone away from you to do battle with an army which has come up from Egypt—see Jeremiah 37:5–10*].

22 **Behold, I will** command, saith the LORD, and **cause them to return** [*after temporarily leaving to defeat the Egyptians*] **to this city** [*Jerusalem*]; **and they shall fight against it, and take it, and burn it** with fire: and I will make the cities of Judah a desolation without an inhabitant.

JEREMIAH 35

<u>Background</u>
According to verse 1, the date of

this chapter would be somewhere between 609 B.C. and 598 B.C. (see dates for Jehoiakim's reign on the chronology chart at the back of your Bible).

Some Bible scholars believe that the Rechabites, spoken of here, were descendants of Jethro, father-in-law to Moses. They are mentioned in 2 Kings 2:15, and were also known as Kenites (1 Chronicles 2:55). It is believed that they came into the Holy Land along with the children of Israel. They existed at various times in both the Northern Kingdom (Israel) and the Southern Kingdom (Judah).

The ancestors of these Rechabites had made a covenant long ago not to drink wine or other strong drink, and they were still faithful to that covenant, as shown in this chapter. The Lord holds them up as an example of people who keep their promises (as opposed to the Jews at this time in history), and, as you will see in this chapter, they are blessed because of this integrity.

1 **THE word which came unto Jeremiah** from the LORD **in the days of Jehoiakim** the son of Josiah **king of Judah** [*from 609–598 B.C.*], **saying,**

2 **Go unto** the house of **the Rechabites, and speak unto them, and bring them into the house of the LORD**, into one of the chambers, **and give them wine to drink**.

3 **Then I took** Jaazaniah the son of Jeremiah, the son of Habaziniah, and his brethren, and all his sons, and **the whole house of the Rechabites**;

4 **And I brought them into the house of the LORD** [*the temple in Jerusalem*], into the chamber of the sons of Hanan, the son of Igdaliah, a man of God, which *was* by the chamber of the princes, which *was* above the chamber of Maaseiah the son of Shallum, the keeper of the door:

Next, Jeremiah puts these Rechabites to the test, as instructed by the Lord, to see if they will keep their covenant not to drink wine or strong drink.

5 **And I set before the sons** [*descendants*] **of the house of the Rechabites pots full of wine, and cups, and I said unto them, Drink ye wine**.

6 **But they said, We will drink no wine**: for Jonadab the son of Rechab **our father** [*ancestor*] **commanded us, saying, Ye shall drink no wine**, *neither* ye, nor your sons for ever:

7 Neither shall ye build house [*they had also covenanted to live in tents*], nor sow seed, nor plant vineyard, nor have *any*: but all your days ye shall dwell in tents; that ye may live many days in the land where ye *be* strangers.

8 **Thus have we obeyed the voice of Jonadab the son of Rechab our father** in all that he hath charged us, **to drink no wine all our days, we, our wives, our sons, nor our daughters;**

9 Nor to build houses for us to dwell in: neither have we vineyard, nor field, nor seed:

10 **But we have dwelt in tents, and have obeyed, and done according to all that Jonadab our father commanded us**.

Next, in verse 11, these Rechabites explain why they are currently living in the city of Jerusalem instead of in their tents elsewhere.

11 **But** it came to pass, **when Nebuchadrezzar king of Babylon came** up into the land [*in earlier waves of siege and attack*], that **we said, Come, and let us go to Jerusalem** for fear of the army of the Chaldeans [*Babylonians*], and for fear of the army of the Syrians: **so we dwell at Jerusalem**.

12 ¶ **Then came the word of the LORD unto Jeremiah, saying,**

13 Thus saith the LORD of hosts, the God of Israel; **Go and tell the men of Judah and the inhabitants of Jerusalem, Will ye not receive instruction to hearken to my words? saith the LORD.** [*In other words, can't you be like the Rechabites and keep your word?*]

14 **The words of Jonadab** the son of Rechab, that he commanded his sons not to drink wine, **are performed**; for **unto this day they drink none, but obey their father's commandment**: notwithstanding I have spoken unto you, rising early and speaking [*having My prophets teach and preach to you from early each day—see verse 15*]; **but ye hearkened not unto me**.

Next, in verse 15, the Lord reminds the wicked people of Judah that He has sent many prophets (see 1 Nephi 1:4) to invite them to repent.

A very important message, repeated yet again by the Lord at this point in Jeremiah's teaching, is that in spite of their gross and repeated wickedness, these people are still invited to repent. They can still successfully return to the Lord. This is a most comforting testimony of the power of the Atonement of Jesus Christ to cleanse and heal all of us, if we will.

15 **I have sent also unto you all my** servants the **prophets**, rising up early [*and they have risen up early*] and **sending them, saying, Return ye now every man from his evil way, and amend your doings**, and go not after other gods [*idols*] to serve them, and ye shall dwell in the land which I have given to you and to your fathers: **but ye have not inclined your ear, nor hearkened unto me**.

16 **Because the sons of Jonadab** the son of Rechab [*the Rechabites*] **have performed the command- ment of their father**, which he commanded them; **but this people** [*Judah*] **hath not hearkened unto me:**

17 **Therefore thus saith the LORD** God of hosts, the God of Israel; Behold, **I will bring upon Judah and upon all the inhabitants of Jerusalem all the evil that I have pronounced against them**: because I have spoken unto them, but they have not heard; and I have called unto them, but they have not answered.

18 ¶ **And Jeremiah said unto** the house of **the Rechabites, Thus saith the LORD** of hosts, the God of Israel; **Because ye have obeyed the commandment of Jonadab** your father, and kept all his pre- cepts, and done according unto all that he hath commanded you:

19 **Therefore** thus saith the LORD of hosts, the God of Israel; **Jonadab the son of Rechab shall not want a man to stand before me for ever** [*in other words, the Rechabites will be protected and preserved*].

JEREMIAH 36

Background
Baruch, Jeremiah's faithful scribe, had painstakingly written down the prophecies of Jeremiah so far, in order to have a written record of

the words of the Lord given through him. After Baruch had read them in the temple at Jerusalem, King Jehoiakim ordered the writings of Jeremiah to be burned. He reaps the reward of his tyranny.

Afterward, Jeremiah dictates the prophecies again, and adds many additional revelations and teach- ings. This could remind us of the destruction by mobs of the original compilation of revelations through the Prophet Joseph Smith, known as the Book of Commandments, published in 1833. As the revela- tions were assembled again for pub- lication, many more were added and it was named the Doctrine and Covenants, published in 1835. It can also remind us of the loss of the 116 manuscript pages by Martin Harris, which were replaced by the transla- tion of the small plates of Nephi, which contained more spiritual matters (see D&C 10:30, 38–45).

As we proceed, we will remind you again that the chapters in Jer- emiah are not necessarily compiled in chronological order.

1 AND it came to pass **in the fourth year of Jehoiakim** [*about 605 B.C.*] the son of Josiah king of Judah, *that* **this word came unto Jeremiah from the LORD, saying,**

2 **Take thee a roll of a book** [*NIV a scroll*]**, and write therein all the words that I have spoken unto thee against Israel, and against Judah,**

and against all the nations, from the day I spake unto thee, from the days of Josiah, even unto this day [*over the last twenty-three years, since the time you were called (in about 628 B.C.) up to the present time (about 605 B.C.)*].

3 **It may be that the house of Judah** [*the Jews*] **will hear all the evil** [*the punishments*] **which I purpose to do unto them; that they may return every man from his evil way** [*repent*]**; that I may forgive their iniquity and their sin**.

4 **Then Jeremiah called Baruch** [*Jeremiah's scribe*] the son of Neriah: **and Baruch wrote from the mouth of Jeremiah** [*as Jeremiah dictated*] **all the words of the LORD**, which he had spoken unto him, upon a roll of a book.

5 **And Jeremiah commanded Baruch, saying, I** *am* **shut up** [*I am under arrest—see footnote 5a in your Bible*]**; I cannot go into the house of the LORD** [*the temple in Jerusalem*]**:**

6 **Therefore go thou, and read in the roll** [*scroll*]**, which thou hast** written from my mouth, **the words of the LORD in the ears of the people in the LORD's house** upon the fasting day [*a special day set aside for fasting and reading the scriptures together—see verse 9; also see Nehemiah 9:1–3*]: and **also thou shalt read them in the ears of all Judah that come out of their**

cities [*who gather to the Jerusalem Temple from surrounding cities*].

7 **It may be they will present their supplication before the LORD** [*ask the Lord for forgiveness*]**, and** will **return** [*repent*] every one from his evil way: for great *is* the anger and the fury that the LORD hath pronounced against this people.

8 **And Baruch** the son of Neriah **did according to all that Jeremiah the prophet commanded him**, reading in the book the words of the LORD in the LORD's house.

9 And it came to pass **in the fifth year** [*about 604 B.C.*] of Jehoiakim the son of Josiah king of Judah, in the ninth month, *that* **they proclaimed a fast** before the LORD **to all the people in Jerusalem, and to all the people** that came from the cities **of Judah** unto Jerusalem.

10 **Then read Baruch in the book the words of Jeremiah in the house of the LORD**, in the chamber of Gemariah the son of Shaphan the scribe, in the higher court, **at the entry of the new gate of the LORD's house, in the ears of all the people**.

11 ¶ **When Michaiah** the son of Gemariah, the son of Shaphan, **had heard** out of the book all the words of the LORD,

12 **Then he went down into the king's house** [*to the palace*], into

the scribe's chamber: **and, lo, all the princes** [*leaders of the Jews*] **sat there**, *even* Elishama the scribe, and Delaiah the son of Shemaiah, and Elnathan the son of Achbor, and Gemariah the son of Shaphan, and Zedekiah the son of Hananiah, and all the princes.

13 Then Michaiah declared unto them all the words that he had heard, when Baruch read the book in the ears of the people.

Next, in verses 14–15, the princes (usually means "government leaders") send for Baruch and ask him to come to them and read Jeremiah's words to them.

14 Therefore all the princes sent Jehudi the son of Nethaniah, the son of Shelemiah, the son of Cushi, **unto Baruch, saying, Take in thine hand the roll** [*scroll*] **wherein thou hast read in the ears of the people, and come**. So Baruch the son of Neriah took the roll in his hand, and came unto them.

15 And they said unto him, Sit down now, and read it in our ears. So Baruch read *it* in their ears.

16 Now it came to pass, **when they had heard all the words, they were afraid** both one and other, **and said unto Baruch, We will surely tell the king of all these words**.

17 **And they asked Baruch**, saying, Tell us now, **How didst thou write all these words at his mouth** [*how did you end up writing all this; did he dictate it to you*]?

18 Then **Baruch answered them, He pronounced all these words unto me with his mouth** [*he dictated them to me*], **and I wrote *them* with ink in the book** [*scroll*].

19 **Then said the princes** unto Baruch, **Go, hide thee, thou and Jeremiah**; and let no man know where ye be.

20 ¶ **And they went in to the king** into the court, but they laid up the roll [*put the scroll*] in the chamber of Elishama the scribe, **and told all the words in the ears of the king**.

21 **So the king sent Jehudi to fetch the roll**: and he took it out of Elishama the scribe's chamber. **And Jehudi read it in the ears of the king**, and in the ears of all the princes which stood beside the king.

22 Now **the king sat in the winterhouse** [*the winter apartment*] in the ninth month: **and *there was a fire* on the hearth** [*in the fireplace*] burning before him.

Next, in verses 23–25, we see that the king became angry after hearing just three or four pages of the scroll, and cut it up with a knife and threw it into the fire, despite the objections from some of his men.

23 And it came to pass, *that* **when

Jehudi had read three or four leaves, he [*the king*] cut it with the penknife, and cast *it* into the fire that *was* on the hearth, until all the roll was consumed in the fire that *was* on the hearth.

24 Yet they were not afraid, nor rent their garments, *neither* the king, nor any of his servants that heard all these words [*they were not afraid of the prophecies of Jeremiah*].

25 Nevertheless Elnathan and Delaiah and Gemariah had made intercession to [*had tried to intervene with*] the king that he would not burn the roll: but he would not hear them.

Next, in verse 26, the king commands that Baruch and Jeremiah be arrested, but the Lord hides them. It will be interesting someday to get the rest of this story.

26 But the king commanded Jerahmeel the son of Hammelech, and Seraiah the son of Azriel, and Shelemiah the son of Abdeel, to take Baruch the scribe and Jeremiah the prophet: but the LORD hid them.

Next, in verses 27–32, the Lord commands Jeremiah to dictate the same words to Baruch to write again plus add many more words from the Lord.

27 ¶ Then the word of the LORD came to Jeremiah, after that the king had burned the roll, and the words which Baruch wrote at the mouth of Jeremiah, saying,

28 Take thee again another roll, and write in it all the former words that were in the first roll, which Jehoiakim the king of Judah hath burned.

29 And thou shalt say to Jehoiakim king of Judah, Thus saith the LORD; Thou hast burned this roll, saying, Why hast thou written therein, saying, The king of Babylon shall certainly come and destroy this land, and shall cause to cease from thence man and beast?

30 Therefore thus saith the LORD of Jehoiakim king of Judah; He shall have none to sit upon the throne of David [*he shall have no posterity to take his place on the throne when he dies*]: and his dead body shall be cast out in the day to the heat, and in the night to the frost [*he will be despised and won't even get a burial*].

31 And I will punish him and his seed and his servants for their iniquity; and I will bring upon them, and upon the inhabitants of Jerusalem, and upon the men of Judah, all the evil that I have pronounced against them; but they hearkened not.

32 ¶ Then took Jeremiah another roll, and gave it to Baruch the scribe, the son of Neriah; who wrote therein from the mouth

of Jeremiah all the words of the book which Jehoiakim king of Judah had burned in the fire: and there were added besides unto them many like words.

JEREMIAH 37

Background
This chapter begins at the start of Zedekiah's wicked reign over the kingdom of Judah, about 598 B.C. He is twenty-one years old (see 52:1) and will rule as king for eleven years.

The Babylonians have already begun the process of defeating the cities of Judah and Jerusalem. Daniel and others have already been taken captive to Babylon. Lehi and his family fled from the Jerusalem area in 600 B.C. and are likely still in the wilderness, journeying toward the ocean where Nephi will be commanded to build a ship.

Egyptian armies are coming up from Egypt to engage the Babylonian armies in battle, which will cause Nebuchadnezzar, king of Babylon to pull his armies away from Jerusalem temporarily in order to engage and defeat the Egyptians.

As we begin the chapter, we are given a brief description of King Zedekiah and his people.

1 AND **king Zedekiah** the son of Josiah **reigned instead of** [*in the place of*] **Coniah** the son of

Jehoiakim, whom Nebuchadrezzar king of Babylon made king in the land of Judah.

2 **But neither he, nor his servants, nor the people of the land, did hearken unto the words of the LORD**, which he spake by the prophet Jeremiah.

Next, wicked King Zedekiah sends word to Jeremiah requesting him to pray for him and his people. The king has not yet arrested Jeremiah and put him in prison.

3 **And Zedekiah the king sent** Jehucal the son of Shelemiah and Zephaniah the son of Maaseiah the priest **to the prophet Jeremiah, saying, Pray now unto the LORD our God for us**.

4 **Now Jeremiah came in and went out among the people** [*he was still free to come and go as he pleased*]: **for they had not put him into prison**.

At this point in history, the Babylonian armies had already laid siege to Jerusalem. As you can see in verse 5, next, Egyptian armies had been sent up from Egypt by Pharaoh to engage the Babylonians in battle. It will prove to be merely a temporary distraction for Nebuchadnezzar's powerful Babylonian forces.

5 **Then Pharaoh's army was come forth out of Egypt: and when**

the Chaldeans [*Babylonians*] that besieged Jerusalem **heard** tidings of them, **they departed from Jerusalem**.

The prophecy that Jeremiah now gives King Zedekiah is not well received by him and his people.

6 ¶ **Then came the word of the LORD unto the prophet Jeremiah, saying,**

7 Thus saith the LORD, the God of Israel; **Thus shall ye say to the king** of Judah [*Zedekiah*], that sent you unto me to enquire of me; **Behold, Pharaoh's army, which is come forth to help you, shall return to Egypt into their own land**.

8 **And the Chaldeans shall come again, and fight against this city** [*Jerusalem*], and take it, and burn it with fire.

Remember that false prophets among the Jews at this time have repeatedly prophesied that the King of Babylon and his armies would not destroy Jerusalem—see verse 19. This made Jeremiah look bad as he prophesied the opposite.

9 Thus saith the LORD; **Deceive not yourselves, saying, The Chaldeans shall surely depart from us: for they shall not depart**.

As you can see by what the Lord says in verse 10, next, the Jews

do not have any chance at all of defeating the Babylonians, when they focus again on the siege of Jerusalem after coming back from defeating the Egyptians.

10 **For though** [*even if*] **ye had smitten the whole army of the Chaldeans** [*the Babylonians*] that fight against you, **and there remained** *but* **wounded men among them,** *yet* **should they rise up** every man in his tent, **and burn this city with fire**.

Next, beginning with verse 11, we are told what happened to Jeremiah during the temporary lull in the siege while the Chaldeans (Babylonian army) left to deal with the Egyptians.

11 ¶ And it came to pass, **that when the army of the Chaldeans was broken up from Jerusalem for fear of Pharaoh's army,**

12 Then **Jeremiah went** forth out of Jerusalem **to go into the land of Benjamin** [*in other words, as Jeremiah started to leave Jerusalem*], to separate himself thence in the midst of the people.

13 And **when he was in the gate of Benjamin** [*in other words, just as he was leaving Jerusalem*], **a captain** of the ward [*an officer in the king's army*] *was* there, whose name *was* Irijah, the son of Shelemiah, the son of Hananiah; and he **took** [*arrested*] **Jeremiah the prophet, saying** [*accusing him,*

saying], **Thou fallest away to the Chaldeans** [*you are deserting to the Babylonians*].

14 **Then said Jeremiah,** *It is* **false; I fall not away to the Chaldeans**. But he [*the officer*] hearkened not to him: **so Irijah took Jeremiah, and brought him to the princes** [*the leaders of the Jews*].

15 Wherefore **the princes were wroth with Jeremiah, and smote him, and put him in prison** in the house of Jonathan the scribe: for they had made that the prison.

16 ¶ **When Jeremiah was entered into the dungeon**, and into the cabins, **and Jeremiah had remained there many days**;

> Next, King Zedekiah secretly sends for Jeremiah and asks what the Lord has to say. He doesn't want anyone to know that he is asking such a question.

17 **Then Zedekiah the king sent, and took him out** [*of the dungeon*]: **and** the king **asked him secretly** in his house, and said, **Is there** *any* **word from the LORD?** And **Jeremiah said, There is**: for, said he, **thou shalt be delivered into the hand of the king of Babylon**.

18 **Moreover** Jeremiah said unto king Zedekiah, **What have I offended against thee, or against thy servants, or against this people, that ye have put me in prison?**

19 **Where** *are* **now your** [*false*] **prophets** which prophesied unto you, saying, The king of Babylon shall not come against you, nor against this land?

20 **Therefore hear now**, I pray thee, O my lord the king: **let my supplication**, I pray thee, **be accepted before thee; that thou cause me not to return to the house of Jonathan the scribe, lest I die there**.

> In response to Jeremiah's urgent request (verse 20, above) not to go back to the terrible conditions in the dungeon, Zedekiah has him put in the palace prison. As you can see, in verse 21, next, conditions of famine were already getting severe because of the Babylonian siege of Jerusalem.

21 **Then Zedekiah the king commanded that they should commit Jeremiah into the court of the prison** [*a prison in the palace*], **and that they should give him daily a piece of bread** out of the bakers' street, **until all the bread in the city were spent**. Thus Jeremiah remained in the court of the prison.

JEREMIAH 38

Background

This chapter continues the account of Jeremiah's imprisonment, which started in chapter 37. Our hearts go out to him as he is put in a miserable dungeon, where he sinks in the mud. A kindly Ethiopian, in the service of the king, is gentle with Jeremiah as he pulls him out of the mire, giving the prophet rags to put under his shoulders to pad the ropes used to pull him out so that they won't cut him (verses 11–13). It is apparently a dungeon that is accessed only by a hole in the ceiling. Prisoners are dropped in and must be hauled out with ropes.

As we begin reading this chapter, we soon discover that some influential government leaders are angry at what Jeremiah has prophesied concerning the destruction of Jerusalem by the Babylonians. They feel that his prophecies are demoralizing the Jewish soldiers assigned to protect Jerusalem and do battle against the Babylonians. They are particularly angry about Jeremiah's counsel from the Lord to them that they should surrender the city to Nebuchadnezzar's forces—see Background to chapter 27 in this study guide. See also verse 2 here in chapter 38.

1 **THEN Shephatiah** the son of Mattan, **and Gedaliah** the son of Pashur, **and Jucal** the son of Shelemiah, **and Pashur** the son of Malchiah, **heard the words that Jeremiah had spoken unto all the people, saying,**

2 **Thus saith the LORD, He that remaineth in this city shall die by the sword, by the famine, and by the pestilence: but he that goeth forth** [*surrenders*] **to the Chaldeans shall live**; for he shall have his life for a prey, and shall live.

3 Thus saith the LORD, **This city shall surely be given into the hand of the king of Babylon's army, which shall take it**.

4 **Therefore the princes** [*government leaders, rulers—see footnote 4a in your Bible*] **said unto the king, We beseech thee, let this man** [*Jeremiah*] **be put to death**: for thus he weakeneth the hands of the men of war [*soldiers and defenders*] that remain in this city, and the hands of all the people, in speaking such words unto them: **for this man seeketh not the welfare of this people, but the hurt** [*Jeremiah is trying to undermine, and hurt our people*].

Next, in verse 5, we see the cowardly nature of King Zedekiah as he meekly claims he can do nothing to stop these men if they want to harm Jeremiah.

5 Then Zedekiah the king said, **Behold, he** *is* **in your hand: for the king** *is* **not** *he that* **can do** *any* **thing against you**.

6 **Then took they Jeremiah, and cast him into the dungeon of Malchiah** the son of Hammelech, that *was* in the court of the prison: **and they let down Jeremiah with cords** [*ropes*]. **And in the dungeon** *there was* **no water, but mire: so Jeremiah sunk in the mire**.

7 ¶ **Now when Ebed-melech** the Ethiopian, one of the eunuchs which was in the king's house [*one of the king's servants*], **heard that they had put Jeremiah in the dungeon**; the king then sitting in the gate of Benjamin [*the king was conducting business in an area set aside for that purpose in a city gate*];

8 **Ebed-melech** went forth out of the king's house, and **spake to the king, saying,**

9 **My lord the king, these men have done evil in all that they have done to Jeremiah the prophet**, whom they have cast into the dungeon; **and he is like to die for hunger in the place where he is**: for *there is* no more bread in the city [*the famine as a result of the Babylonian siege was getting very severe*].

10 **Then the king commanded Ebed-melech** the Ethiopian, saying, Take from hence thirty men with thee, and **take up Jeremiah the prophet out of the dungeon, before he die.**

11 **So Ebed-melech took the men with him**, and went into the house of the king under the treasury, **and took** thence old cast clouts [*threadbare, worn out clothes*] **and old rotten rags, and let them down by cords into the dungeon to Jeremiah.**

12 **And** Ebed-melech the Ethiopian **said unto Jeremiah, Put now** *these* **old cast clouts** [*discarded clothes*] **and rotten rags under thine armholes** [*armpits*] **under the cords** [*to pad the ropes*]. **And Jeremiah did so.**

13 **So they drew up Jeremiah with cords, and took him up out of the dungeon**: and Jeremiah remained in the court of the prison [*stayed in another prison in the palace*].

Beginning with verse 14, next, we watch as Zedekiah again calls for Jeremiah to be brought from prison in order to speak with him. He asks, in effect, that Jeremiah tell him exactly what the Lord has told him about the fate of Jerusalem and her king, and to withhold no information. You will see that this makes Jeremiah a bit nervous.

14 ¶ **Then Zedekiah the king sent, and took Jeremiah the prophet unto him** into the third entry that *is* in the house of the LORD: **and the king said unto Jeremiah, I will ask thee a thing; hide nothing from me.**

15 **Then Jeremiah said** unto Zedekiah, **If I declare** *it* **unto thee, wilt thou not surely put me to death?** and if I give thee counsel, wilt thou not hearken unto me [*and if I give you advice, isn't it true that you won't listen to me*]?

16 **So Zedekiah the king sware** [*promised*] **secretly unto Jeremiah**, saying, *As* the LORD liveth

[*the strongest oath in Jewish culture of that day*], that made us this soul [*who gave us life*], **I will not put thee to death, neither will I give thee into the hand of these men that seek thy life**.

17 **Then said Jeremiah unto Zedekiah**, Thus saith the LORD, the God of hosts, the God of Israel; **If thou wilt assuredly go forth** [*surrender*] **unto the king of Babylon's princes** [*army commanders*], **then thy soul shall live, and this city shall not be burned** with fire; **and thou shalt live, and thine house** [*your wives and children also—see verse 23*]:

18 **But if thou wilt not go forth to the king of Babylon's princes**, then shall this city be given into the hand of the Chaldeans, and they shall burn it with fire, and thou shalt not escape out of their hand.

19 **And Zedekiah** the king **said unto Jeremiah, I am afraid of the Jews that are fallen to the Chaldeans** [*who have already deserted to the Babylonians—see footnote 19a in your Bible*], **lest they deliver me into their hand** [*lest the Babylonians turn me over to them*], **and they mock** [*abuse, mistreat*] **me**.

20 **But Jeremiah said, They shall not deliver thee** [*hand you over to the Jews who have surrendered*]. Obey, I beseech thee, the voice of the LORD, which I speak unto thee:

so it shall be well unto thee, and thy soul shall live.

21 **But if thou refuse to go forth** [*surrender*]**, this** *is* **the word that the LORD** hath shewed me:

In order to understand verse 22, next, it is helpful to know that one of the worst insults in Jewish culture of the day was to be mocked in public by women. Jeremiah warns Zedekiah that this is exactly what will happen to him if he does not follow the Lord's counsel and surrender to the invading army.

22 And, **behold, all the women that are left in the king of Judah's house** [*in other words, in the palace*] *shall be* **brought forth to the king of Babylon's princes** [*generals and leaders*], **and those** *women* **shall say** [*mock you, saying*], **Thy friends** [*German Bible: your trusted advisers*] **have set thee on** [*have misled you; i.e., you are gullible*], **and have prevailed against thee** [*have overruled you, the king*]: **thy feet are sunk in the mire** [*they have led you into a trap*], *and* **they are turned away back** [*your friends have deserted you*].

23 So they **shall bring out all thy wives and thy children to the Chaldeans** [*this indeed happened; and all of his sons (except Mulek) were killed before his eyes—see 52:10*]: and **thou shalt not escape** out of their hand, **but shalt be taken by the hand of the king**

of Babylon: and **thou shalt cause this city to be burned with fire** [*it will be your fault that Jerusalem is burned*].

Next, King Zedekiah tells Jeremiah that under penalty of death he is not to tell anyone about their secret conversation.

24 ¶ Then said Zedekiah unto Jeremiah, **Let no man know of these words, and thou shalt not die**.

25 **But if the princes hear that I have talked with thee, and they come unto thee**, and say unto thee, Declare unto us now what thou hast said unto the king, hide it not from us, and we will not put thee to death; also what the king said unto thee:

26 **Then thou shalt say** unto them, I presented my supplication before the king, that he would not cause me to return to Jonathan's house [*which had been made into a prison—see 37:15*], to die there.

27 **Then came all the princes unto Jeremiah, and asked him**: and he told them according to all these words that the king had commanded. So they left off speaking with him; for the matter was not perceived [*they did not find out what Jeremiah and Zedekiah had discussed*].

Verse 28, next, informs us that Jeremiah was kept in the royal palace prison until Jerusalem was captured.

28 **So Jeremiah abode in the court of the prison until the day that Jerusalem was taken**: and he was *there* when Jerusalem was taken.

JEREMIAH 39

Background
This chapter is an account of the fall of Jerusalem, about 587 B.C. (see "Capture of Jerusalem" on the chronology chart in the Bible Dictionary at the back of your LDS Bible).

1 **IN the ninth year of Zedekiah** king of Judah, in the tenth month, **came Nebuchadrezzar king of Babylon and all his army against Jerusalem, and they besieged it** [*laid siege to it*].

2 *And* **in the eleventh year of Zedekiah, in the fourth month, the ninth** *day* **of the month, the city was broken up** [*the Babylonian soldiers broke through the city wall*].

3 **And all the princes** [*military leaders*] **of the king of Babylon came in**, and sat in the middle gate, *even* Nergal-sharezer, Samgar-nebo, Sarsechim, Rab-saris, Nergal-sharezer, Rab-mag, with all the residue of the princes [*other military leaders*] of the king of Babylon.

Next we are told that King Zedekiah and some of his people made a futile attempt to escape and were captured near Jericho.

4 ¶ And it came to pass, *that* **when Zedekiah the king of Judah saw them**, and all the men of war, then **they fled, and went forth out of the city by night**, by the way of the king's garden, by the gate betwixt the two walls: and he went out the way of the plain.

5 **But the Chaldeans' army pursued after them, and overtook Zedekiah in the plains of Jericho**: **and** when they had taken him, they **brought him up to Nebuchadnezzar king of Babylon** to Riblah [*in northern Syria*] in the land of Hamath, where he gave judgment upon him [*where he sentenced him*].

6 **Then the king of Babylon slew the sons of Zedekiah in Riblah before his eyes**: also the king of Babylon slew all the nobles of Judah.

We know from the Book of Mormon that one of Zedekiah's sons, Mulek, escaped, and was brought by the Lord to America. We will include two references from the Book of Mormon here:

Helaman 6:10
10 Now the land south was called Lehi and the land north was called Mulek, which was after the son of Zedekiah; for **the Lord did bring Mulek into the land north**, and Lehi into the land south.

Helaman 8:21
21 And now will you dispute that Jerusalem was destroyed? **Will ye say that the sons of Zedekiah were not slain, all except it were Mulek?** Yea, and do ye not behold that the seed of Zedekiah are with us, and they were driven out of the land of Jerusalem? But behold, this is not all—

7 Moreover **he put out Zedekiah's eyes, and bound him with chains, to carry him to Babylon**.

8 ¶ **And the Chaldeans burned the king's house** [*the palace in Jerusalem*], **and the houses of the people, with fire, and brake down the walls of Jerusalem**.

Some groups of Jewish prisoners had already been taken to Babylon in earlier waves of the Babylonian conquest. Included in those groups of prisoners were Daniel and Ezekiel. Next, in verses 9–10, we see that many of the remaining Jews were taken to Babylon. However, many of the poor were left in the land of Judah and given land to farm.

9 **Then Nebuzar-adan** the captain of the guard [*NIV commander of the imperial guard*] **carried away captive into Babylon the remnant** of the people that remained in the city, and those that fell away, that fell to him [*who had deserted to the Babylonians—see footnote 9a in your Bible*], with the rest of the people that remained.

10 **But Nebuzar-adan** the captain

of the guard **left of the poor** of the people, which had nothing, **in the land of Judah, and gave them vineyards and fields** at the same time.

Next, in verses 11–14, we see that King Nebuchadnezzar commanded that Jeremiah be set free from the prison he was in and be treated well.

11 ¶ **Now Nebuchadrezzar** king of Babylon **gave charge concerning Jeremiah** to Nebuzar-adan the captain of the guard, saying,

12 **Take him, and look well to him, and do him no harm; but do unto him even as he shall say unto thee**.

13 So Nebuzar-adan the captain of the guard sent, and Nebushasban, Rab-saris, and Nergal-sharezer, Rab-mag, and all the king of Babylon's princes;

14 Even **they sent, and took Jeremiah out of the court of the prison**, and committed him unto Gedaliah the son of Ahikam the son of Shaphan, **that he should carry him home**: so he dwelt among the people.

Next, in verses 15–18, we find that before Jeremiah was set free, he had prophesied concerning the kind Ethiopian servant who threw him rags with which to pad his armpits with when he was pulled from the dungeon— see Jeremiah 38:7–13.

15 ¶ **Now the word of the LORD came unto Jeremiah, while he was shut up in the court of the prison, saying**,

16 **Go and speak to Ebed-melech the Ethiopian**, saying, Thus saith the LORD of hosts, the God of Israel; **Behold, I will bring my words upon this city for evil** [*all that has been prophesied concerning the destruction of Jerusalem will take place, because of wickedness*], and not for good; and they shall be *accomplished* in that day before thee.

17 **But I will deliver thee** [*the kind Ethiopian servant*] **in that day, saith the LORD: and thou shalt not be given into the hand of the men of whom thou *art* afraid**.

18 For **I will surely deliver thee, and thou shalt not fall by the sword, but thy life shall be for a prey unto thee** [*your life will be preserved*]: **because thou hast put thy trust in me, saith the LORD**.

JEREMIAH 40

Background

After the fall of Jerusalem to the Babylonians, in about 587 B.C., King Nebuchadnezzar's soldiers captured King Zedekiah, as detailed in chapter 39, verses 4–7. He then appointed a Jew named Gedaliah to serve as the governor over the remaining Jews who were left behind in Judah. It was Gedaliah's father, Ahikam, who had saved Jeremiah's life about twenty-two years earlier (see Jeremiah 26:24).

Jeremiah had been taken to Ramah, about five miles north of Jerusalem, in chains, with the other prisoners, but was set free by order of King Nebuchadnezzar of Babylon to Nebuzar-adan, his captain of the guard (verse 1). (By the way, there were two towns called Ramah that were significant in Old Testament times. One was about twenty miles northwest of Jerusalem, and the other, mentioned here in verse 1, was about five miles north of Jerusalem.) After having been set free at Ramah, Jeremiah was allowed to choose whether to accompany the Jews being taken to Babylon or remain in Judah. In either case, he was to be treated well, by order of the king of Babylon. He stayed in Judah.

1 **THE word that came to Jeremiah from the LORD**, **after** that **Nebuzar-adan** the captain of the guard **had let him go** [*set him free*] **from Ramah**, when he had taken him being bound in chains among all that were carried away captive of Jerusalem and Judah, which were carried [*which were about to be carried*] away captive unto Babylon.

2 **And the captain of the guard took Jeremiah, and said** unto him, The LORD thy God hath pronounced this evil upon this place.

3 Now the LORD hath brought *it,* and done according as he hath said: because ye have sinned against the LORD, and have not obeyed his voice, therefore this thing is come upon you.

4 And now, **behold, I loose thee this day from the chains** which *were* upon thine hand. **If it seem good unto thee to come with me into Babylon, come**; and I will look well unto thee: **but if it seem ill unto thee to come with me** into Babylon, forbear [*don't come*]: **behold, all the land *is* before thee: whither it seemeth good and convenient for thee to go, thither go** [*you may live wherever you desire in Judah*].

5 Now while he [*Jeremiah*] was not yet gone back [*before Jeremiah turned to go back*], he [*Nebuzaradan*] *said,* **Go back** also **to Gedaliah** the son of Ahikam [*who had saved Jeremiah's life about twenty-two years ago*] the son of Shaphan, **whom the king of Babylon hath made governor** over the cities of Judah, **and dwell with him among the people: or go wheresoever it seemeth convenient unto thee to go**. So the captain of the guard gave him victuals [*a food allowance—see footnote 5b in your Bible*] and a reward, and let him go.

6 **Then went Jeremiah unto Gedaliah** the son of Ahikam to Mizpah; and dwelt with him among the people that were left in the land.

Next, in verses 7–11, we see that many Jews who had fled to open country to escape the Babylonians, or to neighboring nations, came back when things settled down and Gedaliah had been made governor.

7 ¶ **Now when all the captains of the forces** [*Jewish army*] **which** *were* **in the fields** [*who had fled to open country*], *even* they **and their men, heard that the king of Babylon had made Gedaliah** the son of Ahikam **governor** in the land, and had committed unto him [*had put him in charge of*] men, and women, and children, and of the poor of the land, of them that were not carried away captive to Babylon;

8 **Then they came to Gedaliah to Mizpah** [*about ten miles north of Jerusalem*], even Ishmael the son of Nethaniah, and Johanan and Jonathan the sons of Kareah, and Seraiah the son of Tanhumeth, and the sons of Ephai the Netophathite, and Jezaniah the son of a Maachathite, **they and their men**.

Next, Governor Gedaliah assures these men that they will be safe if they submit to the Babylonian rule.

9 **And Gedaliah** the son of Ahikam the son of Shaphan **sware unto them** and to their men, saying, **Fear not to serve the Chaldeans** [*the Babylonians*]: **dwell in the land, and serve the king of Babylon, and it shall be well with you.**

10 **As for me, behold, I will dwell at Mizpah to serve the Chaldeans**, which will come unto us: **but ye, gather ye wine, and summer fruits, and oil**, and put *them* in your vessels, **and dwell in your cities that ye have taken** [*in other words, settle down to farming in the cities you have occupied*].

11 **Likewise when all the Jews** [*other Jews who had fled to neighboring countries*] that *were* **in Moab**, and **among the Ammonites**, and **in Edom, and** that *were* **in all the countries, heard that the king of Babylon had left a remnant of Judah, and that he had set over them Gedaliah** the son of Ahikam the son of Shaphan;

12 Even **all the Jews returned** out of all places whither they were driven, and came to the land of Judah, to Gedaliah, unto Mizpah, **and gathered wine and summer fruits very much** [*and gathered an abundant harvest*].

Next, Governor Gedaliah is warned about a plot by the Ammonite king to assassinate him. The Ammonite nation was located east of the Jordan River, north of Jerusalem.

13 ¶ Moreover **Johanan** the son of Kareah, **and all the captains** of the forces that *were* in the fields, **came to Gedaliah to Mizpah,**

14 **And said** unto him, **Dost thou certainly know that Baalis the**

king of the Ammonites hath sent Ishmael the son of Nethaniah to slay thee? But Gedaliah the son of Ahikam **believed them not**.

15 **Then Johanan** the son of Kareah **spake to Gedaliah** in Mizpah **secretly, saying, Let me go, I pray thee, and I will slay Ishmael** the son of Nethaniah, and no man shall know *it:* **wherefore should he slay thee** [*why should he be allowed to assassinate you*], that all the Jews which are gathered unto thee should be scattered, and the remnant in Judah perish?

16 **But Gedaliah** the son of Ahikam **said** unto Johanan the son of Kareah, **Thou shalt not do this thing: for thou speakest falsely of Ishmael** [*you are falsely accusing Ishmael*].

JEREMIAH 41

Background
The assassination plot discussed in chapter 40 is carried out in this chapter. Jeremiah's friend, Gedaliah, who has been appointed governor of the remaining Jews in the land of Judah, by the king of Babylon, is murdered. As you found out near the end of chapter 40, Gedaliah was warned by friends about Ishmael's plot, but refused to believe that he would do such a thing to him.

As verse 1 indicates, Ishmael was a member of the Jewish royal family.

He plotted with other former government leaders of the Jews to go visit Gedaliah at his headquarters at Mizpah, about ten miles north of Jerusalem, and kill him.

1 NOW it came to pass in the seventh month, *that* **Ishmael** the son of Nethaniah the son of Elishama, **of the seed royal, and the princes of the king** [*who was of royal blood and who had been one of King Zedekiah's officers in his government*], even **ten men with him**, **came unto Gedaliah** the son of Ahikam to Mizpah; **and** there **they did eat bread together in Mizpah**.

2 **Then** arose **Ishmael** the son of Nethaniah, **and the ten men that were with him,** and smote **Gedaliah** the son of Ahikam the son of Shaphan with the sword, **and slew him**, whom the king of Babylon had made governor over the land.

Next, in verse 3, we see that Ishmael and his men not only killed Governor Gedaliah and the Jews who were with him, but they also killed the Babylonian soldiers there, so that it took a couple of days before anyone found out about the assassination and slaughter.

3 **Ishmael also slew all the Jews that were with** him, *even* with **Gedaliah**, at Mizpah, **and the Chaldeans** that were found there, *and* **the men of war** [*NIV as well as the Babylonian soldiers who were there*].

Apparently, Gedaliah's stronghold was sufficiently isolated from the rest of Mizpah that no one immediately noticed the slaughter.

4 And it came to pass **the second day** after he had slain Gedaliah, and **no man knew** *it,*

5 That **there came certain from Shechem, from Shiloh, and from Samaria** [*cities in the Holy Land*], **even fourscore men** [*eighty men*], having their beards shaven, and their clothes rent, and having cut themselves [*physical signs in that culture that they had made a vow, in this case to bring offerings to the temple no matter what*], **with offerings and incense** in their hand, **to bring** *them* **to the house of the LORD** [*on their way to the temple in Jerusalem*].

Next, Ishmael and his henchmen set up an ambush for these Jews who were going to Jerusalem.

6 **And Ishmael** the son of Nethaniah **went forth from Mizpah to meet them, weeping all along** as he went: and it came to pass, **as he met them, he said** unto them, **Come to Gedaliah the son of Ahikam**.

7 **And** it was *so,* **when they came into the midst of the city**, that **Ishmael** the son of Nethaniah **slew them**, *and cast them* into the midst of the pit, **he, and the men that** *were* **with him**.

Next, ten of the men who were ambushed persuade Ishmael not to kill them, in return for supplies of food.

8 But **ten men** were found among them that **said unto Ishmael, Slay us not: for we have treasures in the field, of wheat, and of barley, and of oil, and of honey**. So he forbare, and slew them not among their brethren.

9 Now the pit wherein Ishmael had cast all the dead bodies of the men, whom he had slain because of Gedaliah, *was* it which Asa the king had made for fear of Baasha king of Israel: *and* Ishmael the son of Nethaniah filled it with *them that were* slain.

10 **Then Ishmael carried away captive all the residue** [*the rest*] **of the people that** *were* **in Mizpah**, *even* [*including*] **the king's daughters, and all the people that remained in Mizpah**, whom Nebuzar-adan the captain of the guard had committed to Gedaliah the son of Ahikam: and **Ishmael the son of Nethaniah carried them away captive, and departed to go** [*intending to go*] **over to the Ammonites** [*an area east of the Jordan River and north of Jerusalem*].

11 ¶ **But when Johanan** the son of Kareah, **and all the captains of the forces that** *were* **with him, heard of all the evil that Ishmael** the son of Nethaniah **had done,**

12 Then **they took all the men, and went to fight with Ishmael** the son of Nethaniah, and found him by the great waters that *are* in Gibeon [*some pools of water, a bit northwest of Jerusalem*].

Imagine the relief of the prisoners taken by Ishmael and his accomplices when they saw Johanan and the Jewish soldiers that were with him coming to rescue them!

13 Now it came to pass, *that* **when all the people which** *were* **with Ishmael saw Johanan** the son of Kareah, **and all the captains of the forces that** *were* **with him, then they were glad.**

14 **So all the people that Ishmael had carried away captive** from Mizpah **cast about** [*turned around*] **and returned**, and went unto Johanan the son of Kareah.

15 **But Ishmael** the son of Nethaniah **escaped from Johanan with eight men, and went to the Ammonites**.

Next, we see that Johanan and his men and the people with them were afraid of retaliation from the Babylonians, and so they decided to go to Egypt for safety.

16 **Then took Johanan** the son of Kareah, **and all the captains** of the forces that *were* with him, **all the remnant of the people whom he had recovered** [*rescued*] from

Ishmael the son of Nethaniah, from Mizpah, after *that* he had slain Gedaliah the son of Ahikam, *even* mighty men of war, and the women, and the children, and the eunuchs, whom he had brought again from Gibeon:

17 **And they departed, and dwelt** in the habitation of Chimham, which is **by Beth-lehem, to go to enter into Egypt**,

18 Because of the Chaldeans: **for they were afraid** of them, **because Ishmael** the son of Nethaniah **had slain Gedaliah** the son of Ahikam, **whom the king of Babylon made governor in the land**.

JEREMIAH 42

Background
This chapter is a continuation of the account in chapters 40–41. At the end of chapter 41, you saw Johanan and his soldiers, along with the Jews they had rescued from Ishmael, gather near Bethlehem, preparing to attempt an escape to Egypt.

They decided to go visit Jeremiah and ask for counsel from the Lord concerning their plans. Let's see what happens.

1 **THEN** all **the captains** of the forces [*the military officers*], **and Johanan** the son of Kareah, and Jezaniah the son of Hoshaiah, **and all the people** [*in Johanan's group*] from the least even unto the

greatest, **came near** [*went and found Jeremiah*],

2 **And said unto Jeremiah** the prophet, Let, we beseech thee, our supplication be accepted before thee, and **pray for us unto the LORD thy God**, *even* **for all this remnant**; (for we are left *but* a few of many, as thine eyes do behold us [*we are a small enough group that you can see all of us before your eyes*]:)

3 **That the LORD thy God may shew us** the way wherein we may walk, and **the thing that we may do**.

4 **Then Jeremiah** the prophet **said** unto them, I have heard *you;* behold, **I will pray unto the LORD** your God according to your words; **and** it shall come to pass, *that* **whatsoever thing the LORD shall answer you, I will declare** *it* **unto you; I will keep nothing back** from you.

Next, these refugees promise faithfully that they will follow the Lord's counsel exactly, no matter what He says.

5 **Then they said to Jeremiah**, The LORD be a true and faithful witness between us, **if we do not even according to all things** for the which the LORD thy God shall send thee to us.

6 **Whether** *it be* **good, or whether** *it be* **evil, we will obey the voice of the LORD** our God, to whom we send thee; that it may be well with us, when we obey the voice of the LORD our God.

7 ¶ And it came to pass **after ten days, that the word of the LORD came unto Jeremiah**.

8 **Then called he Johanan** the son of Kareah, **and all the captains** of the forces which *were* with him, **and all the people** from the least even to the greatest,

9 **And said unto them, Thus saith the LORD**, the God of Israel, unto whom ye sent me to present your supplication before him;

Next, Jeremiah gives these men the answer from the Lord per their request (in verses 1 and 2). We will need the JST to clarify correct doctrine regarding the last phrase of verse 10.

By the way, some have wondered why JST changes such as the one following verse 10 are not found in the footnotes in our LDS English edition of the Bible or at the back of it. The answer is that there was not enough room in our Bible to include them all. I use *Joseph Smith's "New Translation" of the Bible*, printed by Herald Publishing House, Independence, Missouri, 1970, which contains all of the Prophet's changes to the Bible as the source for these additional JST changes. It has been shown by LDS scholars to be reliable and true to the Prophet's original work on the Bible. Most LDS bookstores either carry books that have all of the JST changes to the Bible or can get it for you if you ask them to.

10 **If ye will still abide in this land** [*if you will stay here in Judah*], **then will I build you, and not pull** *you* **down, and I will plant you, and not pluck** *you* **up** [*in other words, you will prosper if you stay in Judah in subjection to the Babylonians*]: for I repent me of the evil that I have done unto you.

JST Jeremiah 42:10

10 If you will still abide in this land, then will I build you, and not pull down; I will plant you, and not pluck up; **and I will turn away the evil that I have done unto you.**

11 **Be not afraid of the king of Babylon**, of whom ye are afraid; be not afraid of him, saith the LORD: **for I** *am* **with you to save you, and to deliver you from his hand**.

12 **And I will shew mercies unto you, that he may have mercy upon you**, and cause you to return to your own land.

13 ¶ **But if ye say, We will not dwell in this land, neither obey the voice of the LORD** your God,

14 **Saying, No; but we will go into the land of Egypt, where we shall** see no war, nor hear the sound of the trumpet [*the signal to battle for armies*], nor have hunger of bread; and there will we dwell:

15 And now therefore hear the word of the LORD, ye remnant of Judah; **Thus saith the LORD** of hosts, the God of Israel; **If ye** wholly set your faces to **enter into Egypt, and go to sojourn** [*remain*] **there;**

16 **Then it shall come to pass,** *that* **the sword**, which ye feared, shall overtake you there in the land of Egypt, **and the famine**, whereof ye were afraid, **shall follow close after you there in Egypt; and there ye shall die**.

17 So shall it be with all the men that set their faces to go into Egypt to sojourn there; **they shall die by the sword,** by the **famine,** and by the **pestilence** [*disease, plagues, disasters, and so forth*]: and **none of them shall remain or escape** from the evil that I will bring upon them.

18 For **thus saith the LORD** of hosts, the God of Israel; **As mine anger and my fury hath been poured forth upon the inhabitants of Jerusalem; so shall my fury be poured forth upon you, when ye shall enter into Egypt: and ye shall be an execration** [*people will curse and swear at you*], **and an astonishment** [*horror*], **and a curse, and a reproach** [*people will look down on you*]; **and ye shall see this place no more** [*you will never*

come back to Jerusalem and the land of Judah].

19 ¶ **The LORD hath said** concerning you, O ye remnant of Judah [*fragment of the Jews*]; **Go ye not into Egypt**: know certainly that I have admonished you this day [*consider yourselves fairly warned*].

Next, Jeremiah warns these people, who were not being honest with themselves when they asked Jeremiah to get the word of the Lord to them, that they have made a fatal mistake by planning to ignore the Lord's counsel.

20 **For ye dissembled in your hearts** [*you were not sincere in your request for counsel from the Lord*], **when ye sent me unto the LORD** your God, saying, Pray for us unto the LORD our God; and according unto all that the LORD our God shall say, so declare unto us, and we will do *it.*

21 **And** *now* **I have this day declared** *it* **to you; but ye have not obeyed the voice of the LORD** your God, nor any *thing* for the which he hath sent me unto you.

22 **Now therefore know certainly that ye shall die by the sword, by the famine, and by the pestilence, in the place whither ye desire to go** [*Egypt*] *and* **to sojourn** [*live*].

JEREMIAH 43

Background

This chapter is a continuation of the tense situation described at the end of chapter 42. In the end, Jeremiah and his faithful scribe, Baruch, will be kidnapped and taken by these rebels to Egypt.

1 AND it came to pass, *that* **when Jeremiah had made an end of speaking unto all the people all the words of the LORD** their God [*as recorded in chapter 42*], for which the LORD their God had sent him to them, *even* all these words,

2 **Then spake Azariah** the son of Hoshaiah, **and Johanan** the son of Kareah, **and all the proud men**, saying unto **Jeremiah, Thou speakest falsely** [*you are lying*]: the LORD our God hath not sent thee to say, Go not into Egypt to sojourn there:

Next, these rebellious men claim that Jeremiah's faithful scribe, Baruch, has prejudiced him against them and induced Jeremiah to give them a false revelation which will lead to their deaths or captivity.

3 **But Baruch** the son of Neriah **setteth thee on against us**, for to deliver us into the hand of the Chaldeans [*Babylonians*], that they might put us to death, and carry us away captives into Babylon.

4 **So Johanan** the son of Kareah, **and all the captains of the forces, and all the people, obeyed not the voice of the LORD**, to dwell in the land of Judah.

Next, we see that these rebels not only reject Jeremiah's words, but they kidnap Jeremiah and Baruch, and take them to Egypt with them.

5 **But Johanan** the son of Kareah, **and all the captains** of the forces, **took all the remnant of Judah**, that were returned from all nations, whither they had been driven, to dwell in the land of Judah;

6 *Even* men, and women, and children, and the king's daughters, and **every person that Nebuzar-adan the captain of the guard had left with Gedaliah** [*the Jewish governor who was assassinated by Jewish rebels led by Ishmael—see chapter 41*] the son of Ahikam the son of Shaphan, **and Jeremiah the prophet, and Baruch** the son of Neriah.

7 **So they came into the land of Egypt**: for they obeyed not the voice of the LORD: thus came they *even* **to Tahpanhes** [*in Egypt, in the land of Goshen, where Joseph, his brothers, father, and their families settled anciently*].

Next, the Lord uses drama as He has Jeremiah prophesy that the Babylonians will attack and overcome Egypt.

8 ¶ **Then came the word of the LORD unto Jeremiah in Tahpanhes, saying,**

9 **Take great stones in thine hand, and hide them** in the clay in the brickkiln, which *is* **at the entry of Pharaoh's house in Tahpanhes, in the sight of the men of Judah**;

10 **And say unto them, Thus saith the LORD** of hosts, the God of Israel; Behold, **I will send** and take **Nebuchadrezzar the king of Babylon**, my servant [*the tool of the Lord to "hammer" Egypt*], **and will set his throne upon these stones** that I have hid; **and he shall spread his royal pavilion over them**.

11 **And when he cometh, he shall smite the land of Egypt**, *and deliver* such *as are* for death to death; and such *as are* for captivity to captivity; and such *as are* for the sword to the sword.

12 And **I will kindle a fire in the houses of the gods of Egypt; and he shall burn them, and carry them away captives**: and he shall array himself with the land of Egypt, as a shepherd putteth on his garment; and he shall go forth from thence in peace.

13 **He shall break also the images of Beth-shemesh, that** *is* **in the land of Egypt; and the houses of the gods of the Egyptians shall he burn with fire.**

JEREMIAH 44

Background

Jeremiah and Baruch, his scribe, have now been taken captive into Egypt by a group of Jewish rebels, who believe they will find peace and safety from the Babylonians in Egypt. They won't. They have rebelled against the clear counsel of the Lord to them to stay in Judah (chapters 42–43). Jeremiah will prophesy that the group will all be destroyed, except for a small remnant.

1 **THE word that came to Jeremiah concerning all the Jews which dwell in the land of Egypt**, which dwell at Migdol [*in northern Egypt*], and at Tahpanhes [*in the eastern part of the Nile Delta*], and at Noph [*Memphis, capital of ancient Egypt, not far south of modern Cairo*], and in the country of Pathros [*upper Egypt*], saying,

2 **Thus saith the LORD** of hosts, the God of Israel; **Ye have seen all the evil that I have brought upon Jerusalem, and upon all the cities of Judah**; and, behold, this day they *are* a desolation, and no man dwelleth therein,

3 **Because of their wickedness** which they have committed to provoke me to anger, **in that they went to burn incense,** *and* **to serve other gods** [*worshiping false gods, including idol worship*], whom they knew not, *neither* they, ye, nor your fathers.

The JST helps us with verse 4, next.

4 Howbeit **I sent unto you all my servants the prophets**, rising early and sending *them,* **saying, Oh, do not this abominable thing that I hate**.

JST Jeremiah 44:4

4 Howbeit I sent unto you all my servants the prophets, **commanding them to rise early**, and sending them, saying, Oh, do not this abominable thing that I hate.

5 **But they hearkened not**, nor inclined their ear to turn from their wickedness, to burn no incense unto other gods.

6 **Wherefore my fury and mine anger** [*the law of justice*] **was poured forth, and was kindled in the cities of Judah and in the streets of Jerusalem**; and they are wasted *and* desolate, as at this day.

Next, having reviewed the recent destruction of the Jews in the land of Judah, the Lord asks this rebellious colony of Jews in Egypt why they can't learn a lesson from what happened to their fellow Jews in the Holy Land. In effect, He asks them why they would want to get themselves likewise cut off from mortality.

7 **Therefore now thus saith the LORD**, the God of hosts, the God of Israel; **Wherefore** [*why*] **commit**

ye *this* great evil against your souls [*against yourselves*], to cut off from you man and woman, child and suckling, out of Judah, to leave you none to remain;

8 In that ye provoke me unto wrath with the works of your hands, burning incense unto [*worshiping*] other gods in the land of Egypt, whither ye be gone to dwell, that ye might cut yourselves off, and that ye might be a curse and a reproach among all the nations of the earth?

Sometimes we tend to think mainly in terms of wicked men when it comes to the destruction of nations. However, as shown in verse 9, next, wicked women likewise play a major role in the downfall of nations. In fact, as described in Isaiah 3:16–26, when Satan succeeds in luring women as well as men into the paths of sin and evil, a nation and people are doomed. They are "ripe in iniquity."

9 Have ye forgotten the wickedness of your fathers [*ancestors*], and the wickedness of the kings of Judah, and the wickedness of their wives, and your own wickedness, and the wickedness of your wives, which they have committed in the land of Judah, and in the streets of Jerusalem?

10 They are not humbled *even* unto this day, neither have they feared, nor walked in my law, nor in my statutes, that I set before you and before your fathers [*those who were not slaughtered by the Babylonians still have not repented*].

11 ¶ Therefore thus saith the LORD of hosts, the God of Israel; Behold, I will set my face against you for evil [*because of wickedness*], and to cut off all Judah.

12 And I will take the remnant of Judah [*the group of rebel Jews*], that have set their faces to go into the land of Egypt to sojourn there, and they shall all be consumed, *and* fall in the land of Egypt; they shall *even* be consumed by the sword *and* by the famine: they shall die, from the least even unto the greatest, by the sword and by the famine: and they shall be an execration [*people will curse you and swear at you*], *and* an astonishment [*horror*] , and a curse, and a reproach [*people will look down on you*].

13 For I will punish them that dwell in the land of Egypt, as I have punished Jerusalem, by the sword, by the famine, and by the pestilence:

14 So that none of the remnant of Judah, which are gone into the land of Egypt to sojourn there, shall escape or remain, that they should return into the land of Judah, to the which they have a desire to return to dwell there: for none shall return but such as shall escape

[*there will be a few Jews who will survive*].

Next, these rebellious people blatantly reject the word of the Lord, knowing full well that they are guilty as stated. We see that the women were just as wicked as their husbands.

15 ¶ **Then all the men which knew that their wives had burned incense unto other gods, and all the women** that stood by, a great multitude, **even all the people** [*the Jews in this group*] that dwelt in the land of Egypt, in Pathros [*upper Egypt*], **answered Jeremiah, saying,**

16 *As for* the word that thou hast spoken unto us in the name of the LORD, **we will not hearken unto thee**.

Next, these rebels proudly boast that they will go on doing what they have been doing.

17 **But we will certainly do whatsoever thing goeth forth out of our own mouth** [*we will do whatever we want*]**, to burn incense unto the queen of heaven** [*a heathen female god*], and to pour out drink offerings unto her, **as we have done, we, and our fathers, our kings, and our princes, in the cities of Judah, and in the streets of Jerusalem**: for *then* had we plenty of victuals [*food*], and were well, and saw no evil [*in other words, we prospered under the false gods we were worshiping in the land of Judah*].

18 **But since we left off to burn incense to the queen of heaven** [*when we quit worshiping that female god*], and to pour out drink offerings unto her, **we have wanted** [*lacked*] **all** *things,* and have been consumed by the sword and by the famine.

19 **And when we** [*the women in the group are speaking now*] **burned incense to the queen of heaven**, and poured out drink offerings unto her, **did we make her cakes to worship her, and pour out drink offerings unto her, without our men?**

20 ¶ **Then Jeremiah said unto all the people**, to the men, and to the women, and to all the people which had given him *that* answer, saying,

21 **The incense that ye burned in the cities of Judah** [*as you worshiped your idols*], and in the streets of Jerusalem, ye, and your fathers, your kings, and your princes, and the people of the land, did not the LORD remember them, and came it *not* into his mind?

22 **So that the LORD could no longer bear, because of the evil of your doings,** *and* **because of the abominations which ye have committed**; therefore **is your land** [*Judah, including Jerusalem*] **a desolation**, and an astonishment, and a curse, without an inhabitant, as at this day.

23 **Because ye have burned incense** [*worshiped idols*], **and because ye have sinned against the LORD**, and have not obeyed the voice of the LORD, nor walked in his law, nor in his statutes, nor in his testimonies; **therefore this evil is happened unto you**, as at this day.

24 **Moreover Jeremiah said unto all the people, and to all the women**, Hear the word of the LORD, all Judah that *are* in the land of Egypt:

25 **Thus saith the LORD** of hosts, the God of Israel, saying; **Ye and your wives have both spoken with your mouths, and fulfilled with your hand, saying, We will surely perform our vows that we have vowed, to burn incense to the queen of heaven**, and to pour out drink offerings unto her: ye will surely accomplish your vows, and surely perform your vows.

26 **Therefore hear ye the word of the LORD, all Judah that** [*all of you Jews who*] **dwell in the land of Egypt**; Behold, I have sworn by my great name, saith the LORD, that **my name shall no more be named in the mouth of any man of Judah in all the land of Egypt, saying, The Lord GOD liveth** [*in other words, apostasy will be complete among the Jews who fled to Egypt at this time*].

27 **Behold, I will watch over them for evil, and not for good** [*punishments instead of blessings will come upon them*]: and all the men of Judah that *are* in the land of Egypt shall be consumed by the sword and by the famine, until there be an end of them.

28 **Yet a small number that escape the sword shall return out of the land of Egypt into the land of Judah, and all the remnant of Judah**, that are gone into the land of Egypt to sojourn there, **shall know whose words shall stand, mine, or theirs** [*in other words, these proud and haughty people will find out who is right, them or God*].

Verses 29–30, next, contain the last words of Jeremiah that we are aware of. It is a prophecy foretelling the death of Pharaoh in Egypt. He was killed during a rebellion in his own kingdom about 570 B.C.

29 ¶ **And this** *shall be* **a sign unto you, saith the LORD, that I will punish you in this place**, that ye may know that my words shall surely stand against you for evil:

30 Thus saith the LORD; Behold, **I will give Pharaoh-hophra king of Egypt into the hand of his enemies**, and into the hand of them that seek his life; as I gave Zedekiah king of Judah into the hand of Nebuchadrezzar king of Babylon, his enemy, and that sought his life.

NOTE

The remaining chapters in the Book of Jeremiah, except for chapter 52, are a compilation of prophecies given by Jeremiah. They appear to be added by someone as a sort of appendix to the main book, chapters 1–44. They are not given in chronological order and consist of chapter 45, which is a promise to Baruch, Jeremiah's faithful scribe; chapters 46–51, which are prophecies against several surrounding wicked nations; and chapter 52, a review of the conquest of Jerusalem and Judah by King Nebuchadnezzar in about 587 B.C. in which Zedekiah was taken captive.

JEREMIAH 45

Background

Baruch served faithfully as Jeremiah's scribe throughout his ministry. The last we hear of him is in Egypt, where he continued to serve with Jeremiah. The prophecy and blessing for him, given in this chapter, was given about 605 B.C.

1 **THE word that Jeremiah the prophet spake unto Baruch** the son of Neriah, when he had written these words in a book at the mouth of Jeremiah, in the fourth year of Jehoiakim the son of Josiah king of Judah, saying,

2 **Thus saith the LORD, the God of Israel, unto thee, O Baruch**;

In verse 3, next, we are given to understand that it was a rough

life for Baruch, as he faithfully remained loyal to Jeremiah through thick and thin.

3 **Thou** [*Baruch*] **didst say, Woe is me now!** for **the LORD hath added grief to my sorrow** [*it has been one thing after another*]; **I fainted in my sighing** [*I am constantly worn out and groaning under my burdens*], and **I find no rest**.

4 ¶ **Thus shalt thou** [*Jeremiah*] **say unto him** [*Baruch*], The LORD saith thus; Behold, *that* which I have built will I break down, and that which I have planted I will pluck up, even this whole land.

5 And **seekest thou great things for thyself? seek** *them* **not** [*don't set your heart on great things of the world*]: for, behold, I will bring evil upon all flesh [*mortality has its share of troubles*], saith the LORD: **but thy life will I give unto thee for a prey** [*your life will be preserved*] **in all places whither thou goest**.

JEREMIAH 46

Background

This chapter is a prophecy against Egypt, foretelling that the Egyptian army will be conquered by Babylon. It also contains a prophecy about the scattering and gathering of Israel (verses 27–28). As mentioned in the note before Jeremiah, chapter 45 in this study guide, this chapter is not in chronological sequence.

Verses 1–26 foretell the Babylonian conquest of Egypt in about 605 B.C. The Egyptian army had marched as far north as Carchemish (on the border between modern-day Turkey and Syria), and, as explained in verse 2, Pharaoh-necho (the king or Pharaoh of Egypt at the time) was defeated there by the Babylonians.

Jeremiah is a master at using lively language to describe his visions. For example, you will feel the Egyptians' optimistic rallying call to prepare for battle (verses 3–4) and then the sudden devastation among them as they realize defeat (verse 5).

1 **THE word of the LORD** which came to Jeremiah the prophet **against the Gentiles**;

2 **Against Egypt**, against the army of Pharaoh-necho king of Egypt, **which was by the river Euphrates in Carchemish, which Nebuchadrezzar king of Babylon smote** in the fourth year of Jehoiakim the son of Josiah king of Judah.

A vivid, prophetic description of the battle is seen in the next verses.

3 **Order ye the buckler and shield, and draw near to battle**.

4 **Harness the horses**; and get up, ye horsemen, and stand forth with *your* helmets; furbish the spears, *and* **put on the brigandines** [*armor*].

5 **Wherefore** [*why*] **have I seen them dismayed** *and* **turned away back** [*why are they retreating*]? and their mighty ones are beaten down, and are fled apace, and look not back: *for* fear *was* round about, saith the LORD.

6 Let not the swift flee away, nor the mighty man escape; **they shall stumble, and fall toward the north by the river Euphrates**.

7 [*Question*] **Who** *is* **this** *that* **cometh up as a flood**, whose waters are moved as the rivers [*what nation is behind this flood of soldiers*]?

8 [*Answer*] **Egypt** riseth up like a flood, and *his* waters are moved like the rivers; **and he saith, I will go up,** *and* **will cover the earth; I will destroy the city and the inhabitants thereof** [*Egypt plans to conquer the whole known world*].

Verse 9, next, shows us that the Egyptians had allies with them as they went north to "conquer the world."

9 Come up, ye horses; and rage, ye chariots; and **let the mighty men come forth**; the **Ethiopians** and the **Libyans**, that handle the shield; and the **Lydians**, that handle *and* bend the bow.

10 For this *is* the day of the Lord GOD of hosts, a day of vengeance, that he may avenge him of his adversaries: and **the sword shall**

devour, and it shall be satiate and made drunk with their blood: **for the Lord GOD of hosts hath a sacrifice in the north country by the river Euphrates** [*Egypt will become a sacrifice to the Babylonians, along the Euphrates River*].

11 Go up into Gilead, and take balm, O virgin, the daughter of Egypt: **in vain shalt thou use many medicines** [*try different strategies to win the battle*]; *for* **thou shalt not be cured** [*you will be defeated, no matter what*].

Next, Jeremiah prophetically describes the shame to be felt by the Egyptians when their mighty army is defeated.

12 **The nations have heard of thy shame**, and thy cry hath filled the land: for the mighty man hath stumbled against the mighty, *and* they are fallen both together.

13 ¶ **The word that the LORD spake to Jeremiah** the prophet, **how Nebuchadrezzar king of Babylon should come** *and* **smite the land of Egypt**.

Several Egyptian cities are mentioned in verses 14–15, next, as Jeremiah describes the future destruction in Egypt by the Babylonians under King Nebuchadnezzar.

14 Declare ye in Egypt, and publish in **Migdol**, and publish in **Noph** and in **Tahpanhes**: say ye, Stand fast, and prepare thee; for **the sword shall devour round about thee**.

15 **Why are thy valiant** *men* **swept away?** they stood not, **because the LORD did drive them**.

16 **He made many to fall**, yea, one fell upon another: and they said, Arise, and let us go again to our own people, and to the land of our nativity, from the oppressing sword.

17 **They did cry there, Pharaoh king of Egypt** *is but* **a noise** [*does not have any power against the Babylonians*]; he hath passed the time appointed.

18 *As* **I live, saith the King** [*Jehovah*], whose name *is* the LORD of hosts, **Surely as Tabor** [*Mt. Tabor, just southwest of the Sea of Galilee*] *is* **among the mountains, and as Carmel by the sea** [*Mt. Carmel, by the Mediterranean Sea*], *so* **shall he come**.

19 **O thou daughter dwelling in Egypt** [*O you inhabitants of Egypt*], furnish thyself to go into captivity [*prepare yourselves for captivity*]: for Noph [*the capital of ancient Egypt, not far south of modern-day Cairo*] shall be waste and desolate without an inhabitant.

20 **Egypt** *is like* **a very fair heifer** [*a vulnerable young cow, that has not yet had a calf*], *but* **destruction cometh**; it cometh **out of the north**

[*the direction from which the Babylonian army will come*].

21 Also **her hired men** [*the trained soldiers who intend to protect Egypt*] *are* **in the midst of her like fatted bullocks** [*ready to be sacrificed*]; **for they also are turned back,** *and* **are fled away together** [*will be forced to retreat and flee*]: they did not stand [*they will not stand their ground*], because the day of their calamity was come upon them, *and* the time of their visitation [*punishment for wickedness*].

22 **The voice thereof shall go like a serpent** [*they will be like a hissing snake as it retreats from danger*]; for **they** [*the Babylonians*] **shall march with an army, and come against her** [*Egypt*] **with axes, as hewers of wood** [*the Babylonians will chop down the Egyptians like an army of lumberjacks chopping down a forest*].

23 **They shall cut down her forest,** saith the LORD, **though it cannot be searched** [*even though the "forest" of Egyptians seems very dense*]; **because they** [*the Babylonian armies*] **are more than the grasshoppers, and** *are* **innumerable**.

24 The daughter of [*people of*] **Egypt shall be confounded** [*confused; stopped*]; **she shall be delivered into the hand of the people of the north** [*the Babylonians*].

25 **The LORD** of hosts, the God of Israel, **saith**; Behold, **I will punish the multitude of No** [*Thebes, the capital city of upper Egypt*], **and Pharaoh, and Egypt, with their gods**, and their kings; even Pharaoh, and *all* them that trust in him [*the Egyptians considered their Pharaoh to be a god and worshiped him as such*]:

26 **And I will deliver them into the hand of those that seek their lives** [*in other words, their enemies*], and **into the hand of Nebuchadrezzar king of Babylon**, and into the hand of his servants: and afterward it shall be inhabited, as in the days of old, saith the LORD.

The last two verses are a prophecy about the scattering and gathering of Israel.

27 ¶ **But fear not** thou, O my servant [*the Lord's covenant people*] **Jacob** [*Israel*], and **be not dismayed** [*discouraged*], O **Israel** [*Jacob*]: for, behold, **I will save thee from afar off** [*I will gather you from far away*], and thy seed from the land of their captivity; and **Jacob shall return**, and **be in rest** and at ease, and **none shall make** *him* **afraid** [*this will be fulfilled in the last days and into the Millennium*].

28 **Fear thou not, O** Jacob my servant, saith the LORD: for **I** *am* **with thee**; for **I will make a full end of all the nations** [*when the Millennium comes—see D&C 87:6*]

whither I have driven thee: **but I will not make a full end of thee, but correct** [*discipline*] **thee in measure** [*appropriately*]**; yet will I not leave thee wholly unpunished** [*you still need some correction and discipline in order to fill your role as the Lord's covenant people*].

JEREMIAH 47

Background

This chapter is a prophecy against the Philistines, a wicked nation at the time, located to the west of Jerusalem, down on the coast of the Mediterranean Sea.

1 **THE word of the LORD that came to Jeremiah** the prophet **against the Philistines**, before that Pharaoh smote Gaza.

2 Thus saith the LORD; **Behold, waters rise up out of the north, and shall be an overflowing flood** [*in other words, a "flood" of enemy soldiers is coming from the north, a reference to the army of Babylon*], **and shall overflow the land** [*you will be flooded, overrun with Babylonians*]**, and all that is therein; the city, and them that dwell therein: then the men shall cry, and all the inhabitants of the land shall howl**.

Next, Jeremiah describes the sounds of war and battle, which will be heard when the Babylonians attack the Philistines.

3 At the noise of the **stamping of the hoofs of his strong** *horses,* at the **rushing of** his **chariots,** *and at* the **rumbling of** his **wheels**, the fathers shall not look back to *their* children for feebleness of hands [*NIV Fathers will not turn to help their children; their hands will hang limp*];

4 **Because of the day that cometh to spoil all the Philistines,** *and* to cut off from Tyrus and Zidon every helper [*ally*] that remaineth: for **the LORD will spoil** [*will cause the defeat of*] **the Philistines**, the remnant of the country of Caphtor.

5 **Baldness** [*humiliation, captivity—conquering nations often shaved their captives bald, for purposes of humiliation and identification*] **is come upon Gaza; Ashkelon** [*Gaza and Ashkelon were cities in southern Philistia*] **is cut off** *with* the remnant of their valley: **how long wilt thou cut thyself** [*how long will you keep bringing destruction upon yourselves through wicked living*]?

With great dramatic skill, Jeremiah poses a question in verse 6 and then gives the answer in verse 7. The "sword of the Lord" could be considered to be the law of justice, which cannot be sheathed until the unrepentant wicked are punished by justice. You may wish to read Alma 42 for a refresher course on the laws of mercy and justice.

6 **O thou sword of the LORD, how long** *will it be* **ere thou be quiet?**

put up thyself into thy scabbard, rest, and be still.

7 **How can it be quiet, seeing the LORD hath given it a charge against Ashkelon** [*a charge or mission against the Philistines*], **and against the sea shore** [*the Philistines, many of whom lived along the coast of the Mediterranean Sea*]? **there hath he appointed it** [*the sword of justice still has work to do there*].

JEREMIAH 48

Background

This chapter contains a prophecy of destruction against Moab. You might wish to read Isaiah, chapters 15–16, as well as Ezekiel 25:8–11, for similar prophecies against this nation. Moab was a country immediately east of the Dead Sea. In fact, as recorded in the Book of Ruth, Naomi had been living in Moab because of the famine in the Holy Land (see Ruth 1:1–2) and returned to Bethlehem to live when the famine was over. Her daughter-in-law, Ruth, came with her.

The citizens of Moab were known for their materialism and contempt for Jehovah, the God of Israel. They were engulfed in idol worship, with its associated sexual immorality and debauchery.

The Babylonians conquered the land of Moab and took many of its people into captivity. The country never regained its status as an independent nation. The last verse of this chapter contains a message of hope for the people of that area and seems to say that they will receive the gospel of Jesus Christ in the last days.

As is often the case, Jeremiah specifies many cities and landmarks in Moab as he prophesies about it. Remember, Jeremiah is speaking of the future as if it had already taken place. He will use many words and phrases, along with much repetition to get his message across.

1 **AGAINST Moab thus saith the LORD** of hosts, the God of Israel; Woe unto Nebo [*a mountainous area in northern Moab, east of the Jordan River*]! for **it is spoiled** [*ruined*]: Kiriathaim [*a city in central Moab*] is **confounded** *and* taken: Misgab is confounded and **dismayed**.

2 *There shall be* **no more praise of Moab** [*Moab will cease to exist as a nation*]: in Heshbon [*a city to the northeast of Mt. Nebo, which originally was part of the country of Moab but eventually belonged to the Amorites and then to the Israelite tribes of Reuben and Gad*] they have devised evil against it; come, and **let us cut it off from** *being* **a nation**. Also **thou shalt be cut down**, O Madmen; **the sword shall pursue thee**.

3 A voice of **crying** *shall be* from

Horonaim, **spoiling** and **great destruction**.

4 **Moab is destroyed**; her little ones have caused a cry to be heard.

5 For in the going up of Luhith **continual weeping** shall go up; for in the going down of Horonaim the enemies have heard a cry of **destruction**.

6 **Flee, save your lives**, and be like the heath [*juniper tree—see Jeremiah 17:6, footnote a in your Bible*] in the wilderness.

Next, in verse 7, we see that materialism was a major cause of Moab's destruction. The worship of false gods was likewise a major cause of their demise.

7 ¶ For **because thou hast trusted in thy works and in thy treasures, thou shalt also be taken**: and **Chemosh** [*the god of the Moabites; Solomon introduced the worship of Chemosh at Jerusalem—see 1 Kings 11:7*] **shall go forth into captivity** *with* **his priests and his princes together** [*in other words, Chemosh, your false god, with all his false priests and servants will not protect you from destruction*].

8 And **the spoiler shall come upon every city**, and no city shall escape: the valley also shall perish, and the plain shall be destroyed, as the LORD hath spoken.

9 **Give wings unto Moab, that it may flee and get away** [*in order to escape this destruction, you would have to sprout wings and fly away*]: for the cities thereof shall be desolate, without any to dwell therein.

10 **Cursed** *be* **he that doeth the work of the LORD deceitfully** [*with hypocrisy*], and cursed *be* he that keepeth back his sword from blood.

Next, in effect, Jeremiah says that Moab has had it so good for so long that they are not able to face reality or change their thinking and attitudes.

11 ¶ **Moab hath been at ease from his youth,** and he hath settled on his lees [*has relaxed his guard against danger—see footnote 11a in your Bible*], and hath not been emptied from vessel to vessel, neither hath he gone into captivity: **therefore his taste** [*for wickedness*] **remained in him, and his scent is not changed**.

12 **Therefore, behold, the days come, saith the LORD, that I will send unto him wanderers** [*enemies*], **that** **shall cause him to wander, and shall empty his vessels** [*enemies will tip you over and empty you out—compare with footnote 12a in your Bible*]**, and break their bottles**.

13 And **Moab shall be ashamed of Chemosh** [*embarrassed, put to shame, by the inability of Chemosh, their false god, to save them*]**, as**

the house of Israel [*the northern ten tribes*] **was ashamed of Beth-el** [*a formerly sacred site selected by Jeroboam for setting up golden calf worship in place of worshiping God—see 1 Kings 12:28–29*] **their confidence** [*in which the Israelites had trusted*].

14 ¶ **How say ye, We** *are* **mighty and strong men for the war** [*how can you say you are powerful and strong and can defend yourselves just fine*]?

15 **Moab is** [*will be*] **spoiled**, and gone up *out of* her cities, and his chosen young men are gone down to the slaughter, **saith the King** [*the true God*], whose name *is* the LORD of hosts.

16 **The calamity of Moab** *is* **near** to come, and **his affliction hasteth fast** [*is rapidly approaching*].

17 All ye that are about him, **bemoan him**; and all ye that know his name, **say, How is the strong staff broken,** *and* **the beautiful rod** [*be startled at what will happen to a once-strong nation*]!

18 **Thou daughter that dost inhabit Dibon** [*you people of Dibon—a town in central Moab*], **come down from** *thy* **glory, and sit in thirst**; for the spoiler of Moab [*the coming Babylonian armies; they would be at least one fulfillment of this prophecy*] shall come upon thee, *and* he shall destroy thy strong holds.

19 **O inhabitant of Aroer** [*a town south of Dibon, in central Moab*], stand by the way, and espy [*watch*]; ask him that fleeth, and her that escapeth, *and* **say, What is done** [*prepare to ask what is going on*]?

20 **Moab is confounded** [*brought to a halt*]; for it is **broken down: howl and cry**; tell ye it in Arnon [*a river that formed the border between the Moabites and the Amorites to the north*], that Moab is spoiled,

21 And **judgment is come** upon the plain country; upon Holon, and upon Jahazah, and upon Mephaath,

22 And upon Dibon, and upon Nebo, and upon Beth-diblathaim,

23 And upon Kiriathaim, and upon Beth-gamul, and upon Beth-meon,

24 And upon Kerioth, and upon Bozrah, and **upon all the cities of the land of Moab**, far or near.

25 **The horn** [*power*] **of Moab is cut off**, and **his arm** [*power*] **is broken**, saith the LORD.

26 ¶ **Make ye him drunken** [*in your mind's eye, picture him drunk*]: for he magnified *himself* [*exhibited pride*] against the LORD: **Moab** also **shall wallow in his vomit**, and he also shall be in derision [*will be mocked by others*].

27 **For was not Israel a derision unto thee** [*didn't you make fun of*

Israel, the Lord's people, and claim that their God, Jehovah, was not as powerful as your god, therefore you rebelled against Israel—see 2 Kings 3:5]? was he found among thieves? for since thou spakest of him [every time you ridiculed Israel], thou skippedst for joy.

Jeremiah is a master at using imagery with which the people were familiar to illustrate his message. As he continues this rather lively and frightening prophecy of coming doom to Moab, he warns the inhabitants of that country to get out while they can.

28 O ye that dwell in Moab, **leave the cities**, and **dwell in the rock** [*hide among the boulders*], and **be like the dove** *that* **maketh her nest in the sides of the hole's mouth** [*find caves to live in*].

Next, in verse 29, we are reminded that the Moabites were afflicted by the sin of pride, just as is the case with many today.

29 **We have heard the pride of Moab**, (he is exceeding proud) his **loftiness**, and his **arrogancy**, and his **pride**, and the **haughtiness of** his **heart**.

30 **I know his wrath** [*anger at righteousness*], saith the LORD; **but** *it shall* not *be* so [*but it will not do him any good*]; **his lies shall not so effect** *it* [*his false beliefs and boasts against Jehovah will not turn back his destruction*].

31 **Therefore will I howl for Moab**, and **I will cry out for all Moab**; *mine heart* **shall mourn** for the men of Kir-heres.

32 O vine of Sibmah, **I will weep for thee** with the weeping of Jazer [*an Amorite town east of the Jordan River, which was conquered by the Israelites as they entered the promised land*]: thy plants are gone over the sea, they reach *even* to the sea of Jazer: the spoiler [*enemy*] is fallen upon thy summer fruits and upon thy vintage.

33 And **joy and gladness is taken** from the plentiful field, and **from the land of Moab**; and I have caused wine to fail [*become nonexistent*] from the winepresses: none shall tread with shouting; *their* shouting *shall be* no shouting.

Next, in verse 34, Jeremiah uses specific geography in Moab to illustrate the prophetic message that Moab will be devastated from north to south and east to west, in other words, completely.

34 From the cry of Heshbon [*in the far northeast of Moab*] *even* unto Elealeh [*a bit farther northeast*], *and even* unto Jahaz [*in the northeast*], have they uttered their voice, from Zoar [*in the far southwest*] *even* unto Horonaim [*in south central Moab*], *as* an heifer of three years old [*symbolic of being in the prime of life; in other words, prosperous and haughty Moab will be destroyed in the prime of life*]:

for **the waters also of Nimrim** [*a major source of water in far west central Moab*] **shall be desolate**.

35 **Moreover I will cause to cease in Moab**, saith the LORD, **him that offereth in the high places** [*locations used for idol worship*], **and him that burneth incense to his gods** [*idol worshipers will be destroyed*].

36 **Therefore mine heart shall sound for Moab like pipes** [*like sad music played on a flute*], and mine heart shall sound like pipes for the men of Kir-heres [*Kir-hareseth, the capital city, located in south central Moab*]: because **the riches** *that* **he hath gotten are perished**.

Verse 37, next, describes symbolically as well as literally the fate of captives and slaves.

37 For every head *shall be* **bald**, and every **beard clipped**: upon all the hands *shall be* **cuttings** [*perhaps a reference to having marks cut into their hands which identify them as prisoners*], and upon the loins **sackcloth**.

38 *There shall be* **lamentation** generally [*everywhere*] upon all the housetops of Moab, and in the streets thereof: for I have broken Moab like a vessel wherein *is* no pleasure [*NIV: like a jar that no one wants*], saith the LORD.

39 **They shall howl**, *saying,* How

is it broken down! how hath Moab turned the back with shame! so shall Moab be a derision and a dismaying [*a topic of gossip and a source of horror*] to all them about him.

40 For thus saith **the LORD**; Behold, he **shall fly as an eagle, and shall spread his wings over Moab** [*destruction is coming to Moab*].

41 Kerioth is taken, and the strong holds are surprised, and **the mighty men's hearts in Moab at that day shall be as the heart of a woman in her pangs** [*in labor*].

42 And **Moab shall be destroyed** from *being* a people [*as a nation*], **because he hath magnified** *himself* **against the LORD**.

43 **Fear, and the pit, and the snare,** *shall be* **upon thee**, O inhabitant of Moab, saith the LORD.

Note how Jeremiah emphasizes that the wicked in Moab cannot escape from the Lord, in verse 44, next. The imagery is that of a hunted animal, running away in fear, who escapes from one trap only to be caught in another.

44 **He that fleeth from the fear shall fall into the pit; and he that getteth up out of the pit shall be taken in the snare**: for I will bring upon it, *even* upon Moab, the year of their visitation [*when the time for punishment is right*], saith the LORD.

Remember, as mentioned previously, Jeremiah is speaking prophetically of the future as if it has already taken place. This is illustrated in the first phrase of verse 45, next.

45 They that fled stood under the shadow of Heshbon because of the force [*those who try to flee from Moab will be helpless*]: but a fire shall come forth out of Heshbon, and **a flame** from the midst of Sihon, and **shall devour** the corner of **Moab**, and the crown of the head of the tumultuous ones [*the noisy boasters*].

46 **Woe be unto thee, O Moab! the people of Chemosh perisheth** [*the people who worship Chemosh will perish*]: for **thy sons are taken captives, and thy daughters captives**.

As mentioned in the background to this chapter in this study guide, verse 47, next, is the one bright spot in this message of doom to Moab. It is a reminder that all people will be given a completely fair chance, before final Judgment Day, to understand and then accept or reject the gospel of Jesus Christ. The great missionary work in the last days, the marvelous missionary work now being done in spirit prison, and the temple work done during the Millennium, will afford this opportunity to everyone. No one will be missed.

47 ¶ **Yet will I bring again the captivity of Moab** [*the people of Moab will have their opportunity to come unto Christ*] **in the latter days**, saith the LORD. Thus far *is* the judgment of Moab.

JEREMIAH 49

Background
This chapter contains prophecies of judgment and destruction directed at several different nations and peoples, the Ammonites (verses 1–6), Edom (verses 7–22), Damascus (verses 23–27), Kedar and Hazor (verses 28–33), and Elam (verses 34–39). Many Bible scholars believe that this set of prophecies was given after the downfall of Jerusalem.

All people have a certain degree of accountability to choose right and avoid wrong. Every person in the nations to whom this chapter was directed had the light of Christ (see John 1:9), which is a conscience and much more, a constant influence persuading each person born on earth to choose right and avoid wrong. Without this understanding, we might think it not fair for such stinging prophecies of doom and punishment to be directed at them. With this understanding, the reality of accountability for all people beyond age eight looms large.

Thus, one of the major messages we can derive from each of these prophecies directed at heathen nations is the fact that all people should do right and treat each other well. They have the conscience necessary to do so and are accountable to God when they go against it. We will take just another moment before we start this chapter and read a quote from the Bible Dictionary describing the light of Christ. We will add **bold** for teaching purposes.

Bible Dictionary: Light of Christ

"**The light of Christ is** just what the words imply: **enlightenment, knowledge, and an uplifting, ennobling, persevering influence that comes upon mankind because of Jesus Christ**. For instance, Christ is 'the true light that lighteth every man that cometh into the world' (D&C 93:2; John 1:9) . . . 'the light that quickeneth' man's understanding (see D&C 88:6–13, 41). In this manner, the light of Christ is related to man's conscience and tells him right from wrong (cf. Moro. 7:12–19)."

Keeping in mind that because of the light of Christ all people are accountable for their actions to a much higher degree than their actions might indicate, we will now proceed with this chapter. The prophecy against the Ammonites is given in verses 1–6. They lived east of Jerusalem, several miles east of the Jordan River. This area was originally given to the tribe of Gad when the children of Israel entered the Holy Land. However, the Ammonites (descendants of Lot) maintained a strong presence and at the time of Jeremiah's

prophecy here, they were essentially their own nation.

1 **CONCERNING the Ammonites**, thus saith the LORD; Hath Israel no sons? hath he no heir? why *then* doth their king inherit Gad, and his people dwell in his cities?

2 Therefore, behold, the days come, saith the LORD, that **I will cause an alarm of war to be heard in Rabbah** [*the capital city*] **of the Ammonites**; and it shall be a desolate heap [*it will be destroyed*], and her daughters [*her people*] shall be burned with fire: then shall Israel be heir unto them that were his heirs, saith the LORD.

3 Howl, O Heshbon, for Ai is **spoiled**: cry, ye daughters of Rabbah, gird you [*dress yourselves*] with **sackcloth** [*a sign of mourning in their culture*]; **lament**, and run to and fro by the hedges; for **their king shall go into captivity,** *and* **his priests and his princes** together.

4 Wherefore gloriest thou in the valleys, thy flowing valley, O **backsliding daughter** [*apostate people*]? that trusted in her treasures [*materialism*], *saying,* Who shall come unto me [*who could possibly defeat us*]?

5 Behold, **I will bring a fear upon thee, saith the Lord** GOD of hosts, from all those that be about thee [*from surrounding nations*]; and ye

shall be driven out every man right forth; and none shall gather up him that wandereth.

Verse 6, next, is the Lord's promise that the Ammonites would return again to their land. One probable fulfillment of this promise was when Cyrus the Persian, who defeated Babylon in about 538 B.C., decreed that these people could return to their homeland. That decree also applied to the Jews who were allowed to return to Jerusalem.

6 And **afterward I will bring again the captivity of** [*I will overturn the captivity of*] **the children of Ammon**, saith the LORD.

7 ¶ **Concerning Edom** [*a mountainous country south of the Dead Sea where the descendants of Esau settled*], thus saith the LORD of hosts; *Is* **wisdom no more** in Teman [*doesn't anyone in Edom have common sense any more*]? **is counsel perished** from the prudent? is their **wisdom vanished**?

8 Flee ye, turn back, dwell deep, O inhabitants of Dedan; for I will bring the **calamity** of Esau upon him, the time *that* I will visit [*punish*] him.

Next, a comparison is made between harvesting, where there are always a few grapes left, and the complete destruction of Edom (Esau).

9 **If grapegatherers come to thee,** **would they not leave** *some* **gleaning grapes?** if thieves by night, they will destroy till they have enough [*they don't take everything*].

10 **But I have made Esau bare** [*I will completely destroy Edom as a nation*], I have uncovered his secret places [*his hiding places*], and he shall not be able to hide himself: his seed is spoiled, and his brethren, and his neighbours, and **he** *is* **not**.

11 Leave thy fatherless children, I will preserve *them* alive; and let thy widows trust in me [*the Lord will take care of the orphans and widows*].

12 For thus saith the LORD; Behold, **they whose judgment** *was* **not to drink of the cup** [*those who thought to avoid punishment*] **have assuredly drunken** [*have been punished*]; and *art* thou he *that* shall altogether go unpunished? **thou shalt not go unpunished**, but thou shalt surely drink *of it* [*the bitter cup of paying for their wickedness*].

13 For I have sworn by myself, saith the LORD, that **Bozrah** [*a city in Edom, about eighty miles south of modern-day Amman in Jordan*] **shall become a desolation**, a **reproach**, a **waste**, and a **curse**; and all the cities thereof shall be perpetual wastes;

14 I have heard a rumour from the LORD, and an ambassador is sent

unto the heathen, *saying,* Gather ye together, and come against her, and rise up to the battle.

15 For, lo, **I will make thee small among the heathen, *and* despised among men**.

16 Thy terribleness [*your fierceness*] hath deceived thee [*has given you a false sense of security*], *and* **the pride of thine heart**, O thou that dwellest in the clefts of the rock, that holdest the height of the hill: **though thou shouldest make thy nest as high as the eagle, I will bring thee down** from thence, saith the LORD.

17 Also **Edom shall be a desolation** [*NIV: will become an object of horror*]: every one that goeth by it shall be astonished [*appalled, shocked*], and shall hiss at [*gossip, deride*] all the plagues thereof.

18 **As in the overthrow of Sodom and Gomorrah** and the neighbour *cities* thereof, saith the LORD, **no man shall abide there**, neither shall a son of man dwell in it.

19 **Behold, he** [*the Lord*] **shall come up like a lion** from the swelling [*the thickets of the floodplain*] of Jordan **against the habitation of the strong** [*against Edom*]: but I [*the Lord*] will suddenly make him run away from her [*the inhabitants of Edom will be driven out of their land in an instant*]: and who *is* a chosen *man, that* I may appoint

over her? for who *is* like me? and who will appoint me the time? and who *is* that shepherd that will stand before me [*in other words, who would dare try to prevent the Lord from carrying out this prophecy*]?

20 **Therefore hear the counsel of the LORD**, that he hath taken **against Edom**; and his purposes, that he hath purposed against the inhabitants of Teman [*part of Edom*]: Surely the least of the flock shall draw them out: **surely he shall make their habitations desolate** with them.

21 The earth is moved at the noise of their fall, at the cry the noise thereof was heard in the Red sea [*in effect, the whole earth will be startled by what happens to once-proud Edom*].

22 **Behold, he** [*the Lord; could also refer to Nebuchadnezzar and his Babylonian armies*] **shall come up and fly as the eagle, and spread his wings over Bozrah** [*a large city in Edom*]: and at that day shall the heart of the mighty men of Edom be as the heart of a woman in her pangs [*in labor; in other words, desperate for relief from the pain*].

23 ¶ **Concerning Damascus** [*Syria*]. Hamath [*a city in Syria*] is **confounded,** and Arpad: for they have heard **evil tidings**: they are **fainthearted**; *there is* **sorrow** on the sea; it cannot be quiet.

24 Damascus is waxed **feeble** [*has grown weak*], *and* turneth herself to flee, and **fear** hath seized on *her:* **anguish** and **sorrows** have taken her, as a woman in travail [*in labor*].

25 How is **the city of praise not left**, the city of my joy!

26 Therefore **her young men shall fall** in her streets, and **all the men of war shall be cut off** in that day, saith the LORD of hosts.

27 And **I will kindle a fire in the wall of Damascus**, and it shall consume the palaces of Ben-hadad.

28 ¶ **Concerning Kedar** [*Arabia*], **and** concerning the kingdoms of **Hazor** [*in Arabia; this is not the city by the same name in Palestine*], which **Nebuchadrezzar king of Babylon shall smite**, thus saith the LORD; Arise ye, go up to Kedar, and **spoil** [*ruin*] the men of the east.

29 Their tents and their flocks shall they take away: they shall take to themselves their curtains, and all their vessels, and their camels; and they shall cry unto them, **Fear *is* on every side**.

30 ¶ **Flee**, get you far off, **dwell deep** [*hide in deep caves*], O ye inhabitants of Hazor, saith the LORD; **for Nebuchadrezzar king of Babylon hath taken counsel against you, and hath conceived a purpose against you**.

Verse 31, next, appears to be symbolic instruction to Nebuchadnezzar, king of Babylon, to attack the Arabians, who are wealthy and at ease, living in tents rather than in cities with walls and gates.

31 **Arise, get you** [*Nebuchadnezzar*] **up unto the wealthy nation** [*the inhabitants of Arabia*], that dwelleth without care, saith the LORD, which have neither gates nor bars, *which* dwell alone.

32 And **their camels shall be a booty** [*will provide wealth for the Babylonian conquerors*], and the multitude of their cattle a spoil [*more wealth for you*]: and I will scatter into all winds them *that are* in the utmost corners; and I will bring their **calamity from all sides** thereof, saith the LORD.

33 And Hazor shall be a dwelling for dragons [*jackals, wild dogs; symbolically representing lonely and desolate ruins inhabited by wild animals that avoid areas inhabited by humans*], *and* a desolation [*in ruins*] for ever: there shall no man abide there, nor *any* son of man dwell in it.

34 ¶ **The word of the LORD** that came to Jeremiah the prophet **against Elam** [*located east of Babylon, in what is southwest Iran today*] in the beginning of the reign of Zedekiah king of Judah [*about 598 B.C.*], saying,

35 Thus saith the LORD of hosts; Behold, **I will break the bow of Elam** [*I will disarm them*], the chief of their might.

36 And **upon Elam will I bring the four winds** [*destruction*] from the four quarters of heaven, **and will scatter them** toward all those winds; and **there shall be no nation whither the outcasts of Elam shall not come** [*they will be scattered into all the world*].

37 For I will cause Elam to be **dismayed** before their enemies, and before them that seek their life: and **I will bring evil** [*calamity, disaster—see footnote 37a in your Bible*] **upon them,** *even* **my fierce anger,** saith the LORD; and I will send **the sword** after them, till I have consumed them:

38 And **I will** set my throne in Elam, and will **destroy** from thence **the king and the princes**, saith the LORD.

39 ¶ But it shall come to pass **in the latter days**, *that* **I will bring again the captivity of Elam** [*I will restore them and they will have an opportunity to be converted and set free from the captivity of sin*], saith the LORD.

We will quote from the *Old Testament Student Manual* regarding the phrase "I will bring again the captivity of Elam," in verse 39, above:

"Verse 39 speaks of the Lord's bringing again the captivity of Elam in the latter days. Again, it is supposed that this passage means their conversion, as with the Moabites" (*Old testament Student Manual*, page 258).

JEREMIAH 50

Background

From Jeremiah 50:1 through 51:58, we have a prophecy against Babylon. Interspersed within this prophecy is a prophecy about the scattering and gathering of Israel.

Keep in mind that "Babylon" is often used in the scriptures as well as in the teachings of modern prophets and Apostles to mean both the literal ancient city of Babylon, and also extreme wickedness, the kingdom of the devil, and so forth.

Literally, Babylon was a huge city, whose walls were fifty-six miles in length, 335 feet high, and 85 feet wide (see Bible Dictionary under "Babylon"). It was a center of military power and wickedness and seemed invincible.

Symbolically, Babylon represents Satan's kingdom, with all its worldly wickedness. It, too, can seem invincible, but it is not. Just as ancient Babylon was defeated suddenly by Cyrus the Persian, in about 538 B.C., so also will Satan's kingdom be defeated suddenly at the Second Coming. He will be let loose again at the end of the Millennium for "a little season" (D&C 88:111) and will ultimately be defeated completely and, with his evil followers, "be cast away into their own place" forever (D&C 88:112–15).

In this chapter you will see many examples of the kind of repetition used by Jeremiah, Isaiah, and others of the Old Testament prophets to drive home a point. The prophet makes a statement and then says it again, then again, then again, and again, using a bit different wording or using different examples to illustrate the message. We will point out much of this "manner of prophesying among the Jews (2 Nephi 25:1) as we go along. Be aware that the terms "Babylonians" and "Chaldeans" are used interchangeably by Jeremiah. Technically, the Chaldeans lived in the southeast portion of Babylon.

1 **THE word that the LORD spake against Babylon** *and* against the land of the Chaldeans [*Babylonians*] **by Jeremiah the prophet**.

As you have no doubt noticed, one of Jeremiah's favorite techniques in prophesying is to speak of the future as if it has already taken place. Here, he uses this approach to prophesying as he foretells the future downfall and destruction of Babylon.

2 **Declare ye** [*spread the news*] among the nations, and publish, and set up a standard; publish, *and* conceal not: say, **Babylon is taken**, **Bel** [*the chief god of Babylon*] **is**

confounded [*is powerless to stop it*], **Merodach** [*the name of a Babylonian god, perhaps another name for Bel*] **is broken in pieces**; her idols are confounded, **her images are broken in pieces**.

3 For **out of the north there cometh up a nation against her**, which shall make her land desolate, and none shall dwell therein: they shall remove, they shall depart, both man and beast.

Verses 4–8, next, contain a prophecy about the gathering of Israel and Judah.

4 ¶ **In those days**, and in that time, saith the LORD, the children of **Israel** shall come, they **and** the children of **Judah** together, going and weeping: they **shall** go, and **seek the LORD their God**.

5 **They shall ask the way to Zion** with their faces thitherward [*with intense, internal desire to come to Zion*], **saying, Come, and let us join ourselves to the LORD in a perpetual covenant** *that* shall not be forgotten.

6 **My people hath been lost sheep: their shepherds** [*their false prophets and false priests, teachers, political leaders and so forth*] **have caused them to go astray, they have turned them away** *on* **the mountains** [*have used idol worship carried out in high places in the mountains to turn them away*

from Jehovah]: they have gone from mountain to hill [*from idol to idol, shrine to shrine*], they have forgotten their restingplace.

7 **All that found them have devoured them** [*they have been easy prey to their enemies*]: **and their adversaries** [*enemies*] **said, We offend not** [*we are not doing anything wrong in brutalizing Israel and Judah*]**, because they have sinned against the LORD**, the habitation of justice, even the LORD, the hope of their fathers.

The message in verse 8, next, seems to be to get out of Babylon before it is conquered (verse 9). Symbolically, we must flee Babylon, Satan's kingdom, before we are destroyed with it.

8 **Remove** [*flee*] **out of the midst of Babylon**, and go forth out of the land of the Chaldeans [*a repetition of the first phrase*], **and be as the he goats before the flocks** [*lead the way as they flee*].

9 ¶ **For, lo, I will raise and cause to come up against Babylon an assembly** [*alliance*] **of great nations** from the north country: and they shall set themselves in array against her; from thence **she shall be taken**: their arrows *shall be* as of a mighty expert man; none shall return in vain.

The alliance of nations, spoken of in verse 9, above, is described in the following quote:

"The army of Cyrus was composed of Medes, Persians, Armenians, Caducians, Sacae, &c. Though all these did not come from the north; yet they were arranged under the Medes, who did come from the north, in reference to Babylon" (*Clarke's Commentary*, 4:383).

10 **And Chaldea shall be a spoil** [*Babylon will be left in ruins*]: **all that spoil her shall be satisfied**, saith the LORD.

11 **Because ye were glad, because ye rejoiced, O ye destroyers of mine heritage**, because ye are grown fat as the heifer at grass, and bellow as bulls;

12 **Your mother shall be sore confounded; she that bare you shall be ashamed**: behold, the hindermost of the nations *shall be* a wilderness, a dry land, and a desert.

In verse 13, next, Jeremiah prophesies that the ruins of Babylon will never be inhabited again nor built upon. Such is still the case today.

13 **Because of the wrath of the LORD it shall not be inhabited, but it shall be wholly desolate**: every one that goeth by Babylon shall be astonished, and hiss at all her plagues.

14 **Put yourselves in array** [*lay siege*] **against Babylon round about**: all ye that bend the bow,

shoot at her, **spare no arrows: for she hath sinned against the LORD**.

15 **Shout against her round about**: she hath given her hand: **her foundations are fallen, her walls are thrown down**: for it *is* the vengeance of the LORD: **take vengeance upon her; as she hath done, do unto her**.

16 **Cut off the sower** [*farmer*] from Babylon, **and him that handleth the sickle in the time of harvest**: for fear of the oppressing sword they shall turn every one to his people, and **they shall flee every one to his own land** [*foreigners who have been living in Babylon because of the available protection and prosperity will flee away*].

Verses 17–20 contain another prophecy about the scattering and gathering of Israel.

Do you find it interesting that the prophecies about Babylon and those about Israel are going along simultaneously, interwoven with each other? Could it be that there is symbolism here, pointing out that the kingdom of Satan will exist at the same time as the kingdom of God, throughout the earth's history? "It must needs be that there is an opposition in all things" (2 Nephi 2:11) is a principle illustrated effectively here.

17 ¶ **Israel** [*referring here to both the lost ten tribes and the kingdom of Judah*] **is** a **scattered** sheep; the lions have driven *him* away: **first the king of Assyria hath devoured him** [*the northern ten tribes*]; **and last this Nebuchadrezzar king of Babylon hath broken his** [*Judah's*] **bones**.

18 **Therefore thus saith the LORD** of hosts, the God of Israel; Behold, **I will punish the king of Babylon and his land, as I have punished the king of Assyria** [*both kings can be symbolic of Satan*].

The gathering and restoration of Israel is prophesied in verse 19, next.

19 And **I will bring Israel again to his habitation**, and he shall feed on Carmel and Bashan, and his soul shall be satisfied upon mount Ephraim and Gilead.

The doctrine of repentance and forgiveness is taught in verse 20, next. Being gathered unto Christ is the ultimate meaning of the "gathering of Israel."

20 **In those days, and in that time**, saith the LORD, **the iniquity of Israel shall be sought for** [*looked for*], **and *there shall be* none**; and the sins of Judah, and they shall not be found: **for I will pardon them whom I reserve** [*the Lord will forgive the righteous remnant of Israel whom He spares*].

This prophecy returns once again to the destruction of Babylon.

21 ¶ **Go up against the land of Merathaim** [*"double rebellion;" apparently a symbolical name for Babylon*], *even* against it, **and against the inhabitants of Pekod** [*a place in Babylonia, perhaps meaning "punishment"*]: **waste and utterly destroy after them**, saith the LORD, and do according to all that I have commanded thee.

22 **A sound of battle** *is* **in the land, and of great destruction.**

23 **How is the hammer** [*Babylon*] **of the whole earth cut asunder and broken** [*how incredible it is that the "hammer" that pounded all other nations is now broken*]! **how is Babylon become a desolation among the nations!**

24 **I have laid a snare for thee, and thou art also taken, O Babylon,** and thou wast not aware [*it caught you by surprise*]: **thou art found, and also caught, because thou hast striven against the LORD.**

25 **The LORD hath opened his armoury, and hath brought forth the weapons of his indignation:** for this *is* the work of the Lord GOD of hosts **in the land of the Chaldeans.**

26 **Come against her** from the utmost border, **open her storehouses**: cast her up as heaps [*throw her in piles, like grain*], and **destroy her utterly: let nothing of her be left**.

27 Slay all her bullocks [*young bulls*]; let them go down to the slaughter: woe unto them! for **their day is come, the time of their visitation** [*punishment*].

28 The voice of them that flee and escape out of the land of Babylon, to **declare in Zion the vengeance of the LORD our God**, the vengeance of his temple.

In verse 29, next, we see at least two doctrines. One is that the unrepentant wicked will not escape the punishments of God. Another is that pride is the root cause of all sin.

29 **Call together the archers against Babylon**: all ye that bend the bow, camp against it round about; **let none thereof escape: recompense her according to her work**; according to all that she hath done, do unto her: **for she hath been proud against the LORD, against the Holy One of Israel**.

30 **Therefore shall her young men fall in the streets, and all her men of war shall be cut off** in that day, saith the LORD.

31 **Behold, I** *am* **against thee, O thou most proud**, saith the Lord GOD of hosts: for thy day is come, the time *that* I will visit [*punish*] thee.

32 And **the most proud shall stumble and fall**, and none shall

raise him up: and I will kindle a fire in his cities, and it shall devour all round about him.

One of the major messages found in verses 33–34, next, is that the Savior has the power to redeem us from the bondage of sin. Satan does not want to let anyone escape from him, but he cannot prevent the Savior from setting us free if we repent.

33 ¶ Thus saith the LORD of hosts; **The children of Israel** [*the northern ten tribes who became the "lost ten tribes"*] **and the children of Judah** [*the Jews*] *were* **oppressed** together: and all that took them captives held them fast; they refused to let them go.

34 **Their Redeemer** *is* **strong**; the LORD of hosts [*Jehovah, Jesus Christ*] *is* his name: **he shall throughly plead their cause, that he may give rest to the land** [*symbolic of the righteous*], **and disquiet the inhabitants of Babylon** [*while at the same time being a source of unrest for the wicked*].

Now, back again to the punishment of the wicked in Babylon.

35 ¶ **A sword** *is* **upon the Chaldeans**, saith the LORD, and **upon the inhabitants of Babylon**, and upon her princes, and upon her wise *men*.

36 A sword *is* upon the **liars** [*NIV false prophets*]; and they shall dote

[*will become viewed as fools*]: a sword *is* upon her mighty men; and **they shall be dismayed**.

In Old Testament symbolism, horses and chariots are used to symbolize military might.

37 **A sword** [*destruction*] *is* **upon their horses, and upon their chariots**, and **upon all the mingled people** [*foreigners*] that *are* in the midst of her [*outsiders who have chosen to live in Babylon*]; and they shall become as women [*a phrase meaning "weak" in the culture of the day*]: **a sword** *is* **upon her treasures; and they shall be robbed**.

38 **A drought** *is* **upon her** waters; and they shall be dried up: **for it** *is* **the land of graven images**, and they are mad upon *their* idols.

Whenever Jeremiah wants us to get the idea that a city will be destroyed completely and abandoned, he paints a picture with words depicting the ruins with lonely creatures and wild animals that live away from humans.

39 Therefore **the wild beasts of the desert with the wild beasts of the islands shall dwell** *there* [*in the ruins of Babylon*]**, and the owls shall dwell therein: and it shall be no more inhabited for ever**; neither shall it be dwelt in from generation to generation.

40 **As God overthrew Sodom and Gomorrah and the neighbour**

cities thereof, saith the LORD; *so shall no man abide there*, neither shall any son of man dwell therein.

The prophecy again reminds us how the ancient wicked nation of Babylon was to be destroyed.

41 Behold, **a people shall come from the north, and a great nation, and many kings** [*a great alliance against Babylon*] shall be raised up from the coasts of the earth.

42 They shall hold the bow and the lance: **they** *are* **cruel, and will not shew mercy**: their voice shall roar like the sea, and **they shall ride upon horses**, *every one* put in array, like a man **to the battle, against thee, O daughter** [*inhabitants*] **of Babylon**.

43 **The king of Babylon hath heard** the report of them, **and his hands waxed feeble: anguish took hold of him**, *and* pangs as of a woman in travail [*labor; in other words, he can't get out of it now*].

44 **Behold, he** [*the Lord, ultimately; can also refer to the alliance of nations who will conquer Babylon*] **shall come up like a lion** from the swelling of Jordan [*from the thickets on the Jordan River floodplain*] **unto the habitation of the strong** [*to Babylon*]: but I will make them suddenly run away from her: and who *is* a chosen *man, that* I may appoint over her? for who *is* like me? and who will appoint me the time? **and who** *is* **that shepherd that will stand before me** [*in other words, whom could Babylon call upon to successfully protect her from the wrath of the Lord*]?

45 **Therefore hear ye the counsel** [*the plan*] **of the LORD**, that he hath taken **against Babylon**; and his purposes, that he hath purposed against the land of the Chaldeans: Surely the least of the flock shall draw them out: **surely he shall make** *their* **habitation desolate** with them.

46 At the noise of the taking of Babylon the earth is moved, and the cry is heard among the nations [*when Babylon falls, it will startle those who have enjoyed living in it*].

JEREMIAH 51

Background
This chapter is a continuation of the prophecy about the downfall of Babylon, contained in chapter 50. The material in chapters 50–51 was written down in the days of Zedekiah, king of Judah, and sent to Babylon (see verses 59–64). You may wish to read Revelation, chapters 17–18, which prophesy the fall of Babylon, along with this chapter of Jeremiah.

As explained in the background notes for chapter 50, "Babylon" can have dual meaning: (1) the literal ancient city of Babylon, and (2) wickedness; Satan's kingdom. Also keep in mind that "Israel" can mean the literal descendants of Abraham, Isaac, and Jacob (whose name was changed to Israel—see Genesis 32:28), but can also mean any who choose to accept the gospel, be baptized, and keep the commandments. Those who desire to be part of the Lord's covenant people, Israel, are commanded to flee from Babylon (verse 6).

As in other prophecies of Jeremiah, this one will make much use of symbolism and repetition. It will deal with events all the way from the literal fall of ancient Babylon (also referred to as Chaldea) to the fall of Satan's kingdom at the time of the Second Coming of the Savior.

Each time you see the word "Babylon" in this prophecy, you may wish to think of a major message as being that the Lord has power over Satan and thus will ultimately destroy his kingdom and cast him out into his "own place" (D&C 88:114). Another major message is that we must flee Babylon, in other words, wickedness, in order to be on the Lord's side when Babylon is a thing of the past.

Yet a third message to keep in mind comes from the fact that not all people who choose to live in "Babylon" know anything about the true gospel and thus have no chance at all to live it. One of the truths of

the gospel is that the Lord is completely fair. Thus, before the day of final judgment, everyone, whether in this life, the postmortal spirit world mission field, or during the Millennium, will have a completely fair chance to hear, understand, accept, or reject the pure gospel of Jesus Christ.

Also, keep in mind that since everyone born into this world has the Light of Christ (John 1:9), everyone over age eight has a degree of accountability, and so those who choose to live the lifestyle found in "Babylon," despite the pricks of conscience that accompany such choices (especially initially), can rightly be taken down with the fall of Babylon. God will be the final judge as to gospel opportunities that still remain for them after their demise with the destruction of Satan's kingdom.

We will now proceed with the Lord's great prophecy through His humble prophet, Jeremiah, concerning the guaranteed fall of Babylon.

1 **THUS saith the LORD; Behold, I will raise up against Babylon**, and against them that dwell in the midst of them that rise up against me, **a destroying wind** [*the "east wind" which is symbolic of destruction*];

2 **And will send unto Babylon fanners** [*foreign enemies*], **that shall fan her** [*scatter her—see footnote*

2a in your Bible], and shall empty her land: for in the day of trouble they shall be against her round about.

3 **Against** *him that* **bendeth** [*strings his bow in preparation to defend Babylon*] **let the archer** [*in the foreign armies*] **bend his bow** [*prepare for battle*], and against *him that* lifteth himself up in his brigandine [*canvas or leather body armor, sometimes with metal strips in it*]: and **spare ye not her** [*Babylon's*] **young men; destroy ye utterly all her host**.

4 Thus **the slain shall fall in the land of the Chaldeans** [*Babylon*], and *they that are* thrust through in her streets.

Next, in verses 5–6, we see that the Lord will yet gather Israel and that they will be gathered to Him as they flee from the ways of Babylon.

5 **For Israel** *hath* **not** *been* **forsaken, nor Judah of his God**, of the LORD of hosts; though their land was filled with sin [*even though they were once involved in wickedness*] against the Holy One of Israel.

6 **Flee out of the midst of Babylon, and deliver every man his soul** [*and thus save your souls*]: **be not cut off in her iniquity**; for this *is* the time of the LORD's vengeance; **he will render unto her a recompence** [*those in Babylon will face*

God's punishments as they take the consequences of their sins].

The symbolism of the "golden cup" mentioned in verse 7, next, is likely the same as that found in the Book of Revelation, chapter 17. If so, it represents having one's "cup" or life full of gross wickedness. We will quote from Revelation and then go on to verse 7, here, in Jeremiah.

Revelation 17:4
4 And the woman [*symbolic of Babylon; Satan's kingdom*] was arrayed in purple and scarlet colour, and decked with gold and precious stones and pearls, **having a golden cup in her hand full of abominations and filthiness** of her fornication [*wickedness; breaking of God's laws and commandments; counterfeits of the true gospel*]:

7 **Babylon** *hath been* **a golden cup** in the LORD's hand [*allowed by the Lord to exist during the mortal years of the earth's existence—compare with 2 Nephi 2:11, which says "for it must needs be, that there is an opposition in all things*], **that made all the earth drunken: the nations have drunken of her wine** [*have participated in her wickedness*]; **therefore the nations are mad** [*out of their mind with wickedness*].

8 **Babylon is suddenly fallen** and destroyed: howl for her; take balm for her pain, if so be she may be healed.

9 **We would have healed Babylon** [*if she had repented*], **but she is not healed**: forsake her, and let us go every one into his own country: for her judgment reacheth unto heaven, and is lifted up *even* to the skies.

We will include a quote that verifies the interpretation of the first part of verse 9, above:

"God would have healed them, as he would all his children, before their destruction, but sometimes, like Babylon, they resist turning to the Lord and therefore are not healed" (*Old Testament Student Manual*, page 258).

Verse 10, next, depicts those who do repent, flee Babylon, and become part of righteous Israel.

10 **The LORD hath brought forth our righteousness** [*in effect, the Atonement of Christ has enabled us to become righteous*]: come, and let us declare in Zion the work of the LORD our God [*let's spread the word of God*].

Next, Jeremiah specifically prophesies that the Medes (an empire located east of Babylon, led by Cyrus the Persian) will defeat ancient Babylon. They did, in about 538 B.C.

As you will notice, one aspect of "the manner of prophesying among the Jews," spoken of by Nephi (2 Nephi 25:1), is nicely illustrated here. Rather than simply saying that the Medes will prepare for war against Babylon, as most in our modern culture prefer and do, the "manner of prophesying" used by ancient prophets consisted of elaborate and detailed descriptions, conjuring up pictures in the minds and imaginations of the readers of a variety of activities associated with preparing for war against Babylon. In effect, Jeremiah paints dramatic pictures in our minds and involves our emotions as he tells us what will happen.

11 **Make bright the arrows; gather the shields** [*prepare for battle*]: the LORD hath raised up the spirit of the kings of **the Medes**: for his device *is* **against Babylon, to destroy it**; because it *is* the vengeance of the LORD, the vengeance of his temple.

12 Set up the standard upon [*lift up a banner against*] the walls of Babylon, make the watch strong [*strengthen the guard*], set up the watchmen, **prepare the ambushes**: for the LORD hath both devised and done that which he spake **against the inhabitants of Babylon**.

13 **O thou that dwellest upon many waters** [*symbolic of Satan's kingdom—see 1 Nephi 14:11, Revelation 17:1, D&C 61 heading*], abundant in treasures, **thine end is come**, *and* the measure of thy covetousness.

14 **The LORD** of hosts **hath sworn by himself** [*has covenanted in His*

own name; *the strongest oath or promise available in ancient Jewish culture*], **saying, Surely I will fill thee with men**, as with caterpillers [*enemy armies will break into your city; they will be everywhere, like an invasion of caterpillars*]; **and they shall lift up a shout against thee**.

Next, in verses 15–16, Jeremiah testifies that Jehovah, the Creator of earth and heaven, has the power to carry out this prophecy against Babylon.

15 **He** [*the Lord*] **hath made the earth by his power**, he hath established the world by his wisdom, and hath stretched out the heaven by his understanding.

16 **When he uttereth** *his* **voice** [*when He commands*], *there is* a multitude of waters in the heavens; and he causeth the vapours to ascend from the ends of the earth: he maketh lightnings with rain, and bringeth forth the wind out of his treasures [*in other words, all things obeyed His voice as He created the earth*].

Having reminded the people of the power of Jehovah, Jeremiah now points out that idols and other false gods have absolutely no power, in verses 17–18, next.

17 **Every man is brutish by** *his* **knowledge** [*every idol worshiper is like a brute animal, completely without common sense and doesn't*

know what he is doing]; **every founder** [*blacksmith who pours molten metal to form graven images*] **is confounded** by the graven image: for **his molten image** *is* **falsehood, and** *there is* **no breath in them**.

18 **They** *are* **vanity, the work of errors**: in the time of their visitation they shall perish [*when idol worshipers are destroyed, their powerless idols will perish with them*].

19 **The portion of Jacob** [*the benefit available to Israel from the true God*] *is* **not like them** [*is not like that from idols to their worshipers*]; **for he** [*the Lord*] *is* **the former** [*creator*] **of all things**: and *Israel is* **the rod** [*power*] **of his inheritance** [*Israel is the covenant people of the Lord through whom the power of salvation is taken to the whole earth—see Abraham 2:9–11*]: the LORD of hosts *is* his name.

In verses 20–23, next, we see that Israel, the Lord's covenant people, are the tool in the hand of the Lord through which the Church and kingdom of God will be taken to the whole earth (see Daniel 2:34, 44–45). The true gospel of Jesus Christ has the power to cut through falsehood and error and defeat Satan's power and grasp upon the wicked, if they choose to repent.

20 **Thou** [*Israel*] *art* **my** [*the Lord's*] **battle axe** *and* **weapons of war: for with thee will I break in pieces**

the nations, and with thee will I destroy kingdoms;

Remember that horses and chariots were used symbolically in Jeremiah's day to represent military might. You might think of verse 21, next, as referring to Satan's armies, the host of wicked mortals who follow his lead in their lives.

21 **And with thee will I break in pieces** the **horse** and his **rider**; and with thee will I break in pieces the **chariot** and his **rider** [*in other words, the enemy armies, or armies of the wicked*];

22 **With thee also will I break in pieces man and woman**; and with thee will I break in pieces **old and young**; and with thee will I break in pieces the young man and the maid [*in other words, all who oppose righteousness*];

23 **I will also break in pieces with thee** [*Israel*] **the shepherd** [*the false prophet and other misguided leaders*] **and his flock** [*followers*]; and with thee will I break in pieces the husbandman [*farmer*] and his yoke of oxen; and with thee will I break in pieces captains and rulers [*military and political leaders*].

One very important aspect of the message in verses 20–23, above, is the fact that goodness and righteousness will ultimately triumph over evil on earth.

24 **And I will render** [*pay back*] **unto Babylon and to all the inhabitants of Chaldea** [*another term for Babylon*] **all their evil** that they have done in Zion in your sight, saith the LORD.

The "destroying mountain" in verses 25–26, next, seems to be a reference to Babylon, both literally the ancient city and also, symbolically Satan's kingdom. See Revelation 8:8

25 Behold, **I** *am* **against thee, O destroying mountain** [*Babylon*], saith the LORD, **which destroyest all the earth**: and **I will stretch out mine hand upon thee, and roll thee down from the rocks, and will make thee a burnt mountain** [*compare with Revelation 8:8*].

26 And they shall not take of thee a stone for a corner, nor a stone for foundations; but **thou shalt be desolate for ever, saith the LORD** [*Babylon is still ruins today, and Satan and his evil followers will be cast into outer darkness, at the end of the Millennium—see D&C 88:114*].

The next several verses continue to repeat much that has been said in the previous verses. As already pointed out, this type of repetition is typical in Jeremiah's culture. In some verses, he speaks prophetically of the future as though it had already happened.

27 Set ye up a standard in the land, blow the trumpet among the nations, **prepare the nations against her** [*Babylon*], call together against her the kingdoms of Ararat, Minni, and Ashchenaz; appoint a captain against her; cause the horses to come up as the rough caterpillers.

28 **Prepare against her the nations with the kings of the Medes**, the captains thereof, and all the rulers thereof, and all the land of his dominion.

29 And the land shall tremble and sorrow: for **every purpose of the LORD shall be performed against Babylon, to make the land of Babylon a desolation without an inhabitant**.

30 **The mighty men of Babylon have forborn to fight** [*have stopped fighting*], they **have remained in** *their* **holds: their might hath failed**; they became as women: **they** [*Babylon's enemies*] **have burned her dwellingplaces; her bars are broken**.

31 **One post** [*messenger*] **shall run to meet another**, and one messenger to meet another, **to shew the king of Babylon that his city is taken at** *one* **end** [*captured completely—see footnote 31d in your Bible*],

32 And that **the passages** [*NIV river crossings*] **are stopped, and the reeds** [*marshlands*] **they have burned with fire**, and **the men of war are affrighted** [*Babylon's soldiers are terrified*].

33 For **thus saith the LORD** of hosts, the God of Israel; **The daughter of Babylon** [*in other words, Babylon*] *is* **like a threshingfloor,** *it is* **time to thresh her**: yet a little while, and the time of her harvest shall come.

Symbolically, verses 34–35, next, have Israel saying that he has been beaten around badly by Satan's kingdom for thousands of years, and now (in the last days and at the Second Coming of Christ), all of Babylon's wickedness will catch up with her.

34 Nebuchadrezzar the king of **Babylon hath devoured me** [*Israel, Judah*], he hath **crushed me**, he hath **made me an empty vessel**, he hath **swallowed me up like a dragon**, he hath **filled his belly with my delicates**, he hath **cast me out**.

35 **The violence done to me and to my flesh** *be* **upon Babylon**, shall the inhabitant of Zion say; and my blood upon the inhabitants of Chaldea, shall Jerusalem say.

In verses 36–37, next, Jeremiah teaches us that it is the power of the Lord through which we are redeemed from Satan and the forces of evil.

36 **Therefore thus saith the LORD; Behold, I will plead thy**

cause [*through the Atonement—see D&C 45:3–5*], and take vengeance for thee; and I will dry up her sea, and make her springs dry [*I will destroy Babylon*].

37 And **Babylon shall become heaps** [*ruins*], a dwellingplace for dragons [*jackals*], an astonishment [*an object of surprise and horror*], and an hissing [*scorn*], without an inhabitant.

Next, beginning with verse 38, Jeremiah prophetically depicts Babylon at its prime, when its inhabitants are feeling powerful and invincible in their wickedness.

38 **They shall roar together like lions: they shall yell as lions' whelps** [*cubs*].

39 In their heat I will make their feasts, and I will make them drunken, that they may rejoice [*they will keep right on partying and living riotously*], and sleep a perpetual sleep, and not wake, saith the LORD.

40 **I will bring them down like lambs to the slaughter, like rams** with he goats.

41 **How is Sheshach** [*another name for Babylon*] **taken** [*how quickly it falls*]! and **how** is the praise of the whole earth **surprised!** how is Babylon become **an astonishment among the nations!**

The imagery in verse 42, next, takes advantage of the fact that Babylon is built in a desert. Just as it would seem impossible to believe that a tidal wave would destroy Babylon, so also it seems impossible to many that such a large kingdom as that of the devil could be destroyed suddenly. It is not impossible for the Lord. Babylon was destroyed. Satan's kingdom will be destroyed.

42 **The sea is come up upon Babylon: she is covered with the multitude of the waves thereof.**

43 **Her cities are a desolation**, a dry land, and a wilderness, **a land wherein no man dwelleth**, neither doth *any* son of man pass thereby.

44 And **I will punish Bel** [*the main false god of Babylon*] **in Babylon**, and I will bring forth out of his mouth that which he hath swallowed up: and the nations shall not flow together any more unto him [*people will no longer gather to Babylon to participate in wickedness*]: yea, **the wall of Babylon shall fall**.

45 **My people** [*Those who wish to be part of righteous Israel*], **go ye out of the midst of her, and deliver ye every man his soul** [*save your souls*] from the fierce anger of the LORD.

After reading Revelation 18:9–10, quoted next, verses 46–49 of Jeremiah, which follow, appear to include the fall of spiritual Babylon in the last days.

Revelation 18:9–10

9 And the kings [*powerful, wicked leaders*] of the earth, who have committed fornication [*who have been extremely wicked*] and lived deliciously [*riotously*] with her [*the "whore," Satan's kingdom, Babylon*], shall bewail her [*mourn losing her*], and lament for her [*instead of repenting*], when they shall see the smoke of her burning [*the wicked will be devastated by the destruction of their lifestyle*],

10 Standing afar off for the fear of her torment, saying, Alas, alas, that great city Babylon, that mighty city! for in one hour is thy judgment come [*the Second Coming will change things quickly; they can't believe how fast she was destroyed!*].

46 And [*flee from Babylon—verse 45, above*] **lest your heart faint** [*lest you be sorry when Babylon falls*], **and ye fear for the rumour** [*the news that Babylon has fallen*] that shall be heard in the land; a rumour shall both come *one* year, and after that in *another* year *shall come* a rumour, and violence in the land, ruler against ruler.

47 **Therefore, behold, the days come, that I will do judgment upon the graven images of Babylon:** and **her whole land shall be confounded** [*in confusion; startled; perplexed*], and all her slain shall

fall in the midst of her.

48 **Then the heaven and the earth, and all that** *is* **therein, shall sing for Babylon** [*will rejoice because Babylon is gone*]: for the spoilers shall come unto her from the north, saith the LORD.

49 As Babylon *hath caused* the slain of Israel to fall, so at **Babylon shall fall** the slain of all the earth [*the wicked of the earth*].

50 **Ye that have escaped the sword** [*you who still have the opportunity to repent*], go away, stand not still: **remember the LORD** afar off, **and let Jerusalem come into your mind**.

51 **We** [*Israel*] **are confounded, because** we have heard reproach: shame hath covered our faces: for **strangers are come into the sanctuaries of the LORD's house** [*because of our wickedness, our temple has been defiled*].

Now, back to the destruction of Babylon.

52 Wherefore, behold, **the days come, saith the LORD, that I will do judgment upon her graven images**: and through all her land the wounded shall groan.

No matter how strong and powerful Satan's kingdom seems to get, the Lord can and will destroy it. Jeremiah continues using prophetic repetition to emphasize the details of this prophecy against Babylon.

53 Though [*even if*] **Babylon should mount up to heaven** [*as was attempted by the builders of the Tower of Babel*], **and though she should fortify the height of her strength,** *yet* **from me shall spoilers come unto her**, saith the LORD.

54 A sound of **a cry** *cometh* **from Babylon**, and great destruction from the land of the Chaldeans:

55 **Because the LORD hath spoiled** [*ruined, destroyed*] **Babylon**, and destroyed out of her the great voice; when her waves do roar like great waters, a noise of their voice is uttered:

56 Because the spoiler is come upon her, *even* upon Babylon, and **her mighty men are taken, every one of their bows is broken: for the LORD God of recompences shall surely requite** [*repay in full, in other words, the law of the harvest*].

Since we know that the Lord does not make people wicked, we need to interpret verse 57, next, as saying that He will allow them their agency to choose wickedness. The idea is that Babylon is filled with people who are through and through wicked.

57 And I will make drunk her princes, and her wise *men,* her captains, and her rulers, and her mighty men: and **they shall sleep a perpetual sleep, and not wake** [*they will be destroyed*], saith the King, whose name *is* the LORD of hosts.

58 Thus saith the LORD of hosts; **The broad walls of Babylon shall be utterly broken, and her high gates shall be burned with fire** [*perhaps symbolic of the burning of the wicked at the time of the Second Coming*]; and the people shall labour in vain, and the folk in the fire, and they shall be weary.

Verses 59–64, next, provide a historical note informing us that Jeremiah wrote down the prophecy contained in chapters 50–51 and sent them to Babylon with Seraiah, who accompanied King Zedekiah, king of Judah, when he traveled to Babylon on political business about 594 B.C. Seraiah was instructed to read the prophecy after he arrived in Babylon and then to tie a rock to the scroll and throw it into the Euphrates River. You will see the purpose behind this act as you read verse 64.

59 ¶ **The word which Jeremiah** the prophet **commanded Seraiah** the son of Neriah, the son of Maaseiah, **when he went with Zedekiah** the king of Judah **into Babylon** in the fourth year of his reign [*he reigned for eleven years—see Jeremiah 52:1*]. And *this* Seraiah *was* a quiet prince [*German Bible: Seraiah was*

the officer in charge of all details for the trip].

60 So **Jeremiah wrote** in a book [*on a scroll*] **all the evil that should come upon Babylon,** *even* **all these words** [*chapters 50–51*] **that are written against Babylon**.

61 And **Jeremiah said to Seraiah, When thou comest to Babylon,** and shalt see, and shalt **read all these words**;

62 **Then shalt thou say,** O LORD, thou hast spoken against this place [*Babylon*], to cut it off, that none shall remain in it, neither man nor beast, but that it shall be desolate for ever.

63 **And** it shall be, **when thou hast made an end of reading this book** [*this scroll*], *that* thou shalt **bind a stone to it, and cast it into the midst of Euphrates** [*the Euphrates River*]:

64 **And** thou shalt **say, Thus shall Babylon sink, and shall not rise** from the evil that I [*the Lord*] will bring upon her: and they shall be weary. **Thus far** *are* **the words of Jeremiah** [*NIV The words of Jeremiah end here*].

We see similar action by an angel in the vision of John as described in Revelation. It, too, depicts the final destruction of Babylon.

Revelation 18:21
21 And a mighty angel took up a stone like a great millstone, and cast *it* into the sea, saying, **Thus with violence shall that great city Babylon be thrown down, and shall be found no more at all.**

JEREMIAH 52

Background
Bible scholars don't really know who added this chapter on to the end of Jeremiah's writings, which end with the last verse of chapter 51 (see note at the end of 51:64 in this study guide). Jeremiah 52 is pretty much a repeat of the material in 2 Kings 24:18 through 25:21. It is also quite similar to parts of Jeremiah 39.

In this chapter, we are given a summary of events at the time Jerusalem fell to the Babylonian army of King Nebuchadnezzar. The prophecies given by Jeremiah concerning the fall of Jerusalem were fulfilled at this time. As stated previously, Jeremiah is one of the few prophets who have seen many of their prophecies fulfilled in their own lifetime. It begins with a brief history of King Zedekiah of Judah, who is mentioned by Nephi in 1 Nephi 1:4. As you will see, he was twenty-one years old when he became king.

1 **ZEDEKIAH** *was* **one and twenty years old when he began to reign** [*in about 598 B.C.*]**, and he reigned eleven years in Jerusalem**. And his mother's name *was* Hamutal the daughter of Jeremiah of Libnah.

2 **And he did** *that which was* **evil in the eyes of the LORD**, according to all that Jehoiakim had done [*he was wicked just like the king who preceded him*].

3 For through the anger of the LORD it came to pass in Jerusalem and Judah, till he had cast them out from his presence, that **Zedekiah rebelled against the king of Babylon** [*not a wise political move*].

4 ¶ And it came to pass **in the ninth year of his** [*Zedekiah's*] **reign, in the tenth month, in the tenth** *day* **of the month**, *that* **Nebuchadrezzar king of Babylon came**, he and all his army, **against Jerusalem**, and pitched against it [*and laid siege to it*], and built forts against it round about.

5 So the city was besieged unto the eleventh year of king Zedekiah.

By the time we get to verse 6, the Babylonian armies have had Jerusalem under siege for about eighteen months. Consequently, the Jews there are suffering from severe lack of food.

6 And in the fourth month, in the ninth *day* of the month, **the famine was sore** [*severe*] in the city, so that there was no bread for the people of the land.

7 **Then the city was broken up** [*the Babylonian soldiers broke into Jerusalem*], and all **the men** of war **fled** [*including Zedekiah*], and went forth out of the city **by night** by the way of the gate between the two walls, which *was* by the king's garden; (now the Chaldeans *were* by the city round about:) and they went by the way of the plain.

8 ¶ **But the army of the Chaldeans pursued after the king, and overtook Zedekiah in the plains of Jericho**; and all his army was scattered from him.

9 **Then they took the king, and carried him up unto the king of Babylon** to Riblah [*about two hundred miles north of Jerusalem*] in the land of Hamath [*in Syria*]; **where he gave judgment upon him** [*where he sentenced Zedekiah*].

10 **And the king of Babylon slew the sons of Zedekiah before his eyes**: he slew also all the princes of Judah in Riblah.

We know that one of the sons of Zedekiah was not killed. We know from the Book of Mormon that his son, Mulek, escaped, and was brought by the Lord to America. We will include two references from the Book of Mormon here:

Helaman 6:10

10 Now the land south was called Lehi and the land north was called Mulek, which was after the son of Zedekiah; for **the Lord did bring Mulek into the land north**, and Lehi into the land south.

Helaman 8:21

21 And now will you dispute that Jerusalem was destroyed? **Will ye say that the sons of Zedekiah were not slain, all except it were Mulek?** Yea, and do ye not behold that the seed of Zedekiah are with us, and they were driven out of the land of Jerusalem? But behold, this is not all—

11 **Then he put out the eyes of Zedekiah**; and the king of Babylon **bound him in chains, and carried him to Babylon, and put him in prison till the day of his death**.

12 ¶ **Now in the fifth month, in the tenth** *day* **of the month** [*about a month after the fall of Jerusalem*], which *was* the nineteenth year of Nebuchadrezzar king of Babylon, **came Nebuzar-adan, captain of the guard,** *which* **served the king of Babylon, into Jerusalem,**

13 **And burned the house of the LORD** [*the temple in Jerusalem*], **and the king's house** [*the palace*]; **and all the houses of Jerusalem, and all the houses of the great** *men,* **burned he with fire**:

14 **And** all the army of the Chaldeans [*Babylonians*], that *were* with the captain of the guard, **brake down all the walls of Jerusalem** round about [*symbolizing that they had completely conquered the city*].

15 **Then Nebuzar-adan** the captain of the guard [*one of King Nebuchadnezzar's chief military officers*] **carried away captive** *certain* **of the poor of the people**, and the residue of the people that remained in the city, and those that fell away, that fell to the king of Babylon, and the rest of the multitude.

16 **But Nebuzar-adan** the captain of the guard **left** *certain* **of the poor of the land for vinedressers and for husbandmen** [*to farm the area around Jerusalem*].

Next, in verses 17–23, the Babylonians gather up the things of value from the temple in Jerusalem and take them to Babylon.

17 Also **the pillars of brass** that *were* in the house of the LORD, and the bases, and the **brasen sea** that *was* in the house of the LORD, the Chaldeans brake, **and carried all the brass of them to Babylon**.

18 The **caldrons** also, and the **shovels**, and the **snuffers**, and the **bowls**, and the **spoons**, and all the **vessels of brass** wherewith they ministered, took they away.

19 And the **basons**, and the **firepans**, and the **bowls**, and the **caldrons**, and the **candlesticks**, and the **spoons**, and the **cups**; *that* which *was* of **gold** *in* gold [*NIV made of pure gold*], and *that* which *was* of **silver** *in* silver, took the captain of the guard away.

20 The **two pillars**, **one sea** [*large font*], and **twelve brasen bulls** that *were* under the bases, which king Solomon had made in the house of the LORD: the brass of all these vessels was without weight [*too much to weigh*].

21 And *concerning* the pillars, the height of one pillar *was* eighteen cubits [*about twenty-seven feet*]; and a fillet of twelve cubits did compass it; and the thickness thereof *was* four fingers: *it was* hollow.

22 And a chapiter of brass *was* upon it; and the height of one chapiter *was* five cubits, with network and pomegranates [*decorations made of brass*] upon the chapiters round about, all *of* brass. The second pillar also and the pomegranates *were* like unto these.

23 And there were ninety and six pomegranates [*made of brass*] on a side; *and* all the pomegranates upon the network *were* an hundred round about.

Next, in verses 24–27, King Nebuchadnezzar's chief military officer in Judah rounds up several dignitaries of the Jews who had been close associates of King Zedekiah and takes them about two hundred miles north to Riblah, where Nebuchadnezzar executes them.

24 ¶ And **the captain of the guard took Seraiah** [*apparently not the same person as in Jeremiah 51:59*]

the chief priest, and **Zephaniah** the second priest, and **the three keepers of the door**:

25 He took also out of the city **an eunuch** [*an officer—see footnote 25a in your Bible*], which had the charge of the men of war; and **seven men of them that were near the king's person** [*who had been close associates and advisors of King Zedekiah*], which were found in the city; and **the principal scribe** of the host, who mustered the people [*drafted people for military duty*] of the land; **and threescore** [*sixty*] **men** of the people of the land, **that were found in the midst of the city.**

26 **So Nebuzar-adan the captain of the guard took them, and brought them to the king of Babylon** to Riblah.

27 **And the king of Babylon smote them, and put them to death** in Riblah in the land of Hamath. **Thus Judah was carried away captive out of his own land** [*as prophesied*].

Verses 28–30, next, inform us that Nebuchadnezzar (often spelled "Nebuchadrezzar," as seen in verse 28) carried a total of forty-six hundred Jews into captivity (see verse 30) over the next several years. He had already taken many others, including Daniel and Ezekiel, in earlier waves of conquest against the Jews in Jerusalem and Judah.

28 **This** *is* **the people whom Nebuchadrezzar carried away captive**: in the seventh year **three thousand Jews and three and twenty**:

29 In the eighteenth year of Nebuchadrezzar he carried away captive from Jerusalem **eight hundred thirty and two persons**:

30 In the three and twentieth year of Nebuchadrezzar Nebuzar-adan the captain of the guard carried away captive of the Jews **seven hundred forty and five** persons: **all the persons** *were* **four thousand and six hundred**.

Verses 31–34, next, are a sort of appendix, containing a very brief history of Jehoiachin, who had been king of Judah for just a few months (about 598 B.C.) before he and his court were taken into exile to Babylon and imprisoned. King Zedekiah followed him as king. When Nebuchadnezzar died, his successor, Evil-merodach, freed Jehoiachin after thirty-seven years in prison and gave him good treatment in Babylon for the rest of his life.

31 ¶ And it came to pass **in the seven and thirtieth year of the captivity of Jehoiachin king of Judah**, in the twelfth month, in the five and twentieth *day* of the month, *that* **Evil-merodach king of Babylon** in the *first* year of his reign lifted up the head of Jehoiachin king of Judah [*released him from prison*], and **brought him forth out of prison**,

32 **And spake kindly unto him**, and set his throne [*gave him a status*] above the throne of the kings that *were* with him in Babylon [*other kings, probably from other nations that had also been conquered by Babylon*],

33 **And changed his prison garments: and he did continually eat bread before him** [*he ate at the king's table*] **all the days of his life**.

34 **And** *for* **his diet, there was a continual diet given him of the king of Babylon, every day a portion until the day of his death**, all the days of his life.

SOURCES

Answers to Gospel Questions. Compiled by Joseph Fielding Smith. 5 vols. Salt Lake City: Deseret Book, 1957–66.

Clarke, Adam. *The Holy Bible Containing the Old and New Testaments, With a Commentary and Critical Notes.* 6 vols. New York: Abingdon-Cokesbury, 1940, 1966.

Hymns of The Church of Jesus Christ of Latter-day Saints. Salt Lake City: The Church of Jesus Christ of Latter-day Saints, 1985.

International Bible Society. *The Holy Bible: New International Version (NIV).* Grand Rapids, Mich.: Zondervan, 1984.

Josephus, Flavius. *Antiquities of the Jews.* Philadelphia: John C. Winston Co., n.d.

Kiel, C. F., and F. Delitzsch. *Commentary on the Old Testament.* 10 vols. Grand Rapids, Mich.: William B. Eerdmans Publishing, 1991.

Old Testament Student Manual, I Kings–Malachi (Religion 302). Salt Lake City: The Church of Jesus Christ of Latter-day Saints, 1981.

Richards, LeGrand. *Israel! Do You Know?* Salt Lake City: Deseret Book, 1954.

Smith, Joseph. *Joseph Smith's "New Translation" of the Bible.* Independence, Missouri: Herald Publishing House, 1970.

Smith, Joseph Fielding. *Doctrines of Salvation.* 3 vols. Edited by Bruce R. McConkie. Salt Lake City: Bookcraft, 1954–56.

Sperry, Sidney B. *The Voice of Israel's Prophets.* Salt Lake City: Deseret Book, 1952.

Teachings of the Prophet Joseph Smith. Selected by Joseph Fielding Smith. Salt Lake City: Deseret Book, 1976.

The Holy Bible. Authorized King James Version. Salt Lake City: The Church of Jesus Christ of Latter-day Saints, 1979.

The Old Testament with the Joseph Smith Translation. Compiled by Steven J. Hite and Julie M. Hite. Orem, Utah: The Veritas Group, 2001.

About the Author

David J. Ridges taught for the Church Educational System for thirty-five years and has taught for several years at BYU Campus Education Week. He taught adult religion classes and Know Your Religion classes for BYU Continuing Education for many years. He has also served as a curriculum writer for Sunday School, seminary, and institute of religion manuals.

He has served in many callings in the Church, including Gospel Doctrine teacher, bishop, stake president, and patriarch. He and Sister Ridges served a full-time eighteen-month mission, training senior CES missionaries and helping coordinate their assignments throughout the world.

Brother Ridges and his wife, Janette, are the parents of six children and make their home in Springville, Utah.